Spanish Spaces of Crisis

Contemporary Hispanic and Lusophone Cultures

This series aims to provide a forum for new research on modern and contemporary hispanic and lusophone cultures and writing. The volumes published in Contemporary Hispanic and Lusophone Cultures reflect a wide variety of critical practices and theoretical approaches, in harmony with the intellectual, cultural and social developments that have taken place over the past few decades. All manifestations of contemporary hispanic and lusophone culture and expression are considered, including literature, cinema, popular culture, theory. The volumes in the series will participate in the wider debate on key aspects of contemporary culture.

23 Esther Gimeno Ugalde, Marta Pacheco Pinto and Ângela Fernandes, eds, *Iberian and Translation Studies: Literary Contact Zones*

24 Ben Bollig, *Moving Voices: Poetry on Screen in Argentine Cinema*

25 Daniel F. Silva, *Empire Found: Racial Identities and Coloniality in Twenty-First-Century Portuguese Popular Cultures*

26 Dean Allbritton, *Feeling Sick: The Early Years of AIDS in Spain*

27 Ana Fernandez-Cebrian, *Fables of Development: Capitalism and Social Imaginaries in Spain (1950-1967)*

28 María Chouza-Calo, Esther Fernández and Jonathan Thacker, eds, *Daring Adaptations, Creative Failures and Experimental Performances in Iberian Theatre*

29 Anna Tybinko, Lamonte Aidoo and Daniel F. Silva, eds, *Migrant Frontiers: Race and Mobility in the Luso-Hispanic World*

30 Robert Bayliss, *The Currency of Cultural Patrimony: The Spanish Golden Age*

31 Ailsa Peate, *Subverting Sex, Gender, and Genre in Cuban and Mexican Detective Fiction*

32 Tess C. Rankin, *Feeling Strangely in Mid-Century Spanish and Latin American Women's Fiction: Gender and the Scientific Imaginary*

33 Maria Reyes Baztán, *Anticolonialism, Race and Violence in Basque Radical Nationalism (1892–1936)*

34 Carlos Garrido Castellano, *Chorus: Sonic Politics of the Carnivalesque in Tragic Times*

35 Ricki O'Rawe and Eamon McCarthy, eds, *Women, Religion and Culture in Spain and Latin America, 1900–2000*

Spanish Spaces of Crisis

Cultural Responses to the Global 2008 Financial Crisis in Spain (2007–2017)

MAITE USOZ DE LA FUENTE

LIVERPOOL UNIVERSITY PRESS

First published 2026 by
Liverpool University Press
4 Cambridge Street
Liverpool
L69 7ZU

The manufacturer's authorised representative in the EU for product safety is: Easy Access System Europe, Mustamäe tee 50, 10621 Tallinn, Estonia https://easproject.com (gpsr.requests@easproject.com)

British Library Cataloguing-in-Publication data
A British Library CIP record is available

ISBN 978-1-80596-541-1
eISBN 978-1-80596-547-3
ePub ISBN 978-1-80596-552-7

Typeset in Borges by
Carnegie Book Production, Lancaster
Printed and bound by CPI Group (UK) Ltd, Croydon CR0 4YY

Contents

Acknowledgements

This book has taken far longer to write than I originally expected or intended – in part because of my decision to engage with a fairly diverse theoretical corpus, but mostly due to other, more prosaic, paratextual matters. For one, and despite multiple attempts, I was unable to secure any grant funding to facilitate additional, focussed writing periods. These repeated rejections notwithstanding, I remained committed to the project, whose interest was not just obvious to me, but also endorsed – from a very early stage – by Chloe Johnson (now Chloe Johnson-Walsh – yes, that is how long this has taken) and others at Liverpool University Press. Without their unwavering support (and patience!) this book would not exist.

The Covid pandemic also had an impact on this project – not only was my time eaten up by caring responsibilities, but my ability to conduct research (or, indeed, to think or write clearly) was also considerably constrained by lockdown restrictions. Through the height of the pandemic and beyond, interactions with colleagues in ALCESXXI at the annual 2020 conference (planned for Oviedo, but held online) and at the later, in-person 2024 edition in Santiago de Compostela afforded me the opportunity to discuss ideas and concerns central to this text. Particular thanks go to Álvaro L. Pajares, who coordinated our working group in 2020, and to Ana Fernández-Cebrián and Miguel Caballero, seminar leads in 2024. Without their insights and encouragement, as well as that of other group participants, I would not have been able to see this through. Helena Miguélez-Carballeira, with whom I collaborated on a separate project during the course of writing this monograph, has also been an incredibly generous mentor; as have other scholars and friends (or scholars who are also friends) such as Daniela Omlor, Alicia Kent, Mercedes Carbayo-Abengózar, Tom Whittaker, Leticia Blanco, Carmina Gustrán, Stuart Davis, Deirdre Kelly, Santi Pérez-Isasi, Hannie Lawlor, Lesley Wylie, Rabah Aissaoui, Martin Halliwell, Zalfa Feghali, Sheldon Penn, Clara Garavelli and Emma Staniland.

Finally, and closer to home – in a very literal sense – I want to thank my family. My parents and my brother, who share – and therefore understand and encourage – the type of stubbornness (or persistence, if one is feeling generous) that has allowed me to complete the writing of this text. And, of course, my partner, who has witnessed, endured and survived the ups and downs that come with this type of project, and has helped me stay sane and grounded. Last but not least, my three daughters: Hannah, Emmie and Alice – for their tolerance towards their often-absent-minded and self-absorbed mother, and for all the cuddles.

Introduction

Crisis and Space: The Cultural Field in Post-Austerity Spain

My decision to embark on a study of the cultural reflections of the global 2008 crisis and its effects in Spain started with a hunch: that the newly fashionable umbrella term *literatura de la crisis* did little to account for the diversity of approaches – and their, at times, conflicting ideological underpinnings – to be found in contemporary Spanish texts focussing on the economic downturn and its consequences on a thematic level. Rather than a methodologically useful descriptor for a new narrative subgenre, *literatura de la crisis* appeared as an opportunistic marketing device to publicise and boost sales of new releases. I was not alone in my scepticism in relation to the newly minted term: David Becerra suggested a useful distinction between a 'novela de oposición' (2015: 15) which questions the social, economic and symbolic frameworks which we inhabit, and the crisis-driven proliferation of 'relatos desde la pérdida' (21–22), which merely mourn the loss of status of large sections of the Spanish middle class; Pablo Valdivia proposed the alternative 'literatura desheredada' (2016), which allowed him to draw a genealogy between certain post-2008 texts and the Spanish exile literary tradition; while Anne-Laure Bonvalot preferred 'literatura indignada' (2019) as a term that enabled her to connect certain literary texts to the broader *indignados* movement, and to draw a distinction between socially committed and simply topically opportunistic crisis texts. My own contribution to the terminological debate came in the form of a 'literature in crisis' (2020), which meta-discursively problematises its own enunciation and whose origins, I argued elsewhere, antedated the global financial crisis of 2007–8.

The question of terminology is not trivial or anecdotal, for it testifies to a simultaneous – if implicit – disavowal of the dominant label *literatura de la crisis*, rejected not only due to its ubiquity or its opportunistic uses, but also due to its diffuseness of definition, which problematically conflates very different texts; and to the recognition that the effects of 2008 and the ensuing austerity policies have had a tangible effect on Spain's cultural sphere – just as they have transformed the country's social and political landscapes. How, then, to account for such changes without resorting to the somewhat empty signifier of *literatura de la crisis*? Pierre Bourdieu's work on the interplay between socio-political power and cultural production in his seminal *The Rules of Art* (1996 [1992]) provides a starting point from which to make sense of the fluctuations within the cultural field in post-2008 Spain. For Bourdieu, the cultural and socio-political spheres are closely connected, and the literary work is endowed with the ability to reconstruct 'the structure of the social world in which it was produced and even the mental structures which, fashioned by these social structures, form the generative principle of the work in which these structures are revealed' (1996: 32). In other words, literary works are simultaneously shaped by a set of specific socio-historical conditionings, and have the potential to expose or render visible such constraints in a manner that, according to Bourdieu, often surpasses the capacity of 'writings with scientific pretensions' (32).

Bourdieu's work thus negates the supposed autonomy of the artistic and cultural fields, showing instead how these are partly shaped by their insertion within a broader social framework within which different discourses circulate, and a range of constraints operate. Yet his rejection of autonomy does not entail a socially deterministic view of art and culture as mere reflections of or reactions to a specific social reality or historical moment; rather, he endows cultural works with the capacity to reveal, at least partially and indirectly, the very 'rules' that articulate both them, and, more broadly, the social reality from which they originate. Such a revelation has the potential to lead to a destabilisation or displacement, both within the cultural field and beyond, since 'each artistic act which leaves its mark by introducing a new position in the field "displaces" the entire series of previous artistic acts' (1996: 160). Along similar lines, Jacques Rancière ascribes a political dimension to aesthetics, inasmuch as the arts contribute to the articulation of what he terms 'the distribution of the sensible', that is, 'the level of the sensible delimitation of what is common to the community, the forms of its visibility and its organization' (2017: 13); politics and art both 'construct "fictions", that is to say *material* rearrangements of signs and images, relationships between what is seen and what is said, between what is done and what can be done' (35). For Rancière, then, what we consider or label as 'common sense' is not an innocent or self-evident category, but one shaped by aesthetics and ideology – two realms which cannot be easily disentangled.[1] Both French thinkers, therefore, redefine the political

1 Note that in Steven Corcoran's 2010 translation into English of Rancière's essays, published under the title *Dissensus: On Politics and Aesthetics*, Corcoran renders this term as 'commonsense' rather than 'common sense', perhaps as a means to underline

dimension (or potential) of art and culture, which is seen not as resulting from the explicit alignment or adscription of an artistic movement, work or author to a specific political project, but rather to the capacity of creative works to reflect, expand, and challenge what is visible and sayable, to their potential to 'produce "disorder in the established system of classification"' (Rancière 2017: 35–36).

In Spain, the belated vindication of figures who had previously occupied relatively marginal positions within the country's cultural establishment can be read as a prime example of displacement within the country's literary field (following Bourdieu), or a modification in the distribution of the sensible (á la Rancière). Rafael Chirbes (1949–2015) is perhaps the epitome of this trend, but other similarly peripheral figures who had been publishing assiduously since the mid-1990s, such as Belén Gopegui or Marta Sanz, also gained considerable visibility in the post-2008 context.[2] Similarly illustrative of this reconfiguration is the publication of several influential works engaged in critiquing the Spanish cultural establishment, such as Martínez and colleagues' *CT o la Cultura de la Transición* (2012), David Becerra's *La novela de la no-ideología* (2013), Luis Moreno-Caballud's *Cultures of Anyone* (2015a) and Ignacio Sánchez-Cuenca's *La desfachatez intelectual* (2016). Such texts have in common their questioning of the hegemonic cultural discourses, practices and works of the pre crisis democratic period (roughly between 1978 and 2008), which, according to Martinez and colleagues (2012) and Becerra (2013), in particular, acted as an uncritical extension of the politics of *consenso* that characterised the Transition process, which it served to legitimise.[3] Moreno-Caballud reaches a similar conclusion, as he argues that

the redefinition of the term undertaken by the French philosopher. I have chosen to retain the conventional spelling, partly because it seems closer to the original French 'bon sens', and partly because Rancière is not coining a neologism that designates something new, but is rather invested in redefining an already-existing, widely used and seemingly transparent notion (i.e. common sense).

2 An illustrative example of such a marked change in the perception and status of certain authors in the post-2008 context can be found in the introductory text to an interview with Belén Gopegui by Javier Rodríguez Marcos, published in January 2015, in which the interviewer rhetorically asks: '¿Qué tiene que pasar para que el libro de una *aguafiestas* se convierta en un certero retrato social sin cambiar una coma? Una crisis, eso es lo que tiene que pasar. Podría ser el caso de algunas novelas de Belén Gopegui'. The full interview is available online at https://elpais.com/cultura/2014/12/30/babelia/1419945272_995715.html [last accessed 9 July 2024].

3 In Spain, the concept of *consenso* (consensus in English) became ubiquitous during the Transition period (1975–86) and beyond, and denoted the perceived necessity that political antagonists work together to lay the foundations of the new democratic state. More recently, however, historians and cultural studies scholars

> [e]ssentially, what was called Spanish 'democratic normalization' can be considered the apotheosis of a system for establishing and organising reality. This system is supported by the authority of experts and intellectuals who are heirs to the long tradition of cultural elites who pedagogically guide the people towards 'modern progress'. In a clear continuation of this tradition, such 'progress' has often been called 'Europe', since, as noted above, to be 'progressive' is to be 'European'. (2015a: 55)

For Moreno-Caballud, a central question is who is deemed to have the right to construct the reality of which he writes in the quote above – a question that emerged with vehemence during the 15M protests. Indeed, one of the main slogans during that wave of protests was 'No nos representan' [They do not represent us], an accusation levelled primarily against a political class – or 'caste', as Pablo Iglesias put it (Anon. 2014b: online) – regarded as out of touch with the Spanish general public and wilfully oblivious to (and neglectful towards) its struggles in the post-2008 context. However, the slogan's mobilisation of the referent-less pronoun 'they' arguably allowed for different readings and uses of the motto – for instance, as an accusation waged against a cultural elite that had failed, or refused, to engage in the symbolic representation of certain social realities, such as growing socio-economic inequality.[4] Sánchez-Cuenca, meanwhile, articulates a less radical, but more derisory critique, as he takes several Spanish 'intellectuals' to task for their lack of academic rigour, inviting readers to question their supposed expertise – and thus their authority. Such a wide-ranging questioning of established cultural practitioners and intellectuals proves that the transformation within the Spanish cultural field following the global financial crisis is far more wide-ranging than the *literatura de la crisis* label suggests, even if the emergence of a considerable number of literary texts – and other cultural works – engaging with the aftermath of 2008 can be read as one of its symptoms. As Bourdieu reminds us, however, in order to fully grasp these recent changes occurring within the cultural sphere in

have questioned both the extent of that supposed consensus (Ortiz Heras 2012), and – in some cases, influenced by the work of Rancière – its very desirability (Delgado 2014), since the French theorist vindicates dissensus as a key attribute of a true (rather than merely formal) democracy.

4 For a recent overview on inequality in Spain over the past five decades, see the report *Radiografía de medio siglo de desigualdad en España* by Luis Ayala and Olga Cantó, published by Observatorio Social La Caixa in January 2022, and available online at https://elobservatoriosocial.fundacionlacaixa.org/documents/22890/492074/T01_ID_ES_AyalaCant%C3%B3.pdf/ [last accessed 19 December 2023].

Spain, we need to turn our attention to the broader contextual, economic and socio-political transformations that have taken place in the country since 2007.

Effects of the Great Recession in Spain

Spain was one of the countries most affected by the global 2007–8 financial crisis: hailed as a Eurozone economic success story in the years leading up to 2008, with GDP growth levels only surpassed by those of Ireland (Royo 2020), the Great Recession exposed the fragility of the so-called 'Spanish miracle',[5] as the country's economic (over)reliance on the construction and tourism sectors made it particularly vulnerable to the downturn. The bursting of the real estate bubble – land prices increased 500% in Spain between 1997 and 2007, the largest increase among the OECD countries (Royo 2020), with house prices rising by almost 200% in the same period (Rodríguez López 2007) – led the country's financial institutions to the brink of collapse in 2012, and required the implementation of an emergency EU rescue plan in the summer of that year to avert a collapse of the Spanish banking sector. Real GDP per capita contracted by 9% in the period 2007–13, a figure only comparable to the falls experienced in Ireland, Portugal and Greece – the three European countries which, with Spain, came to be grouped together under the infamous – and damaging – acronym PIGS (Brazys and Hardiman 2015).

But the effects of the 2007–8 crisis in Spain undoubtedly had repercussions beyond the economic sphere, as Sebastián Royo argued as early as 2013. The Spanish state's inability to protect its citizens from the consequences of the crisis – unemployment, in particular, became a serious and widespread social problem, and led in some cases, as we shall see in the second chapter, to eviction and eviction-related suicides – led to a questioning of the country's political framework.[6] This questioning took several forms: arguably

5 The phrase 'Spanish miracle' is often deployed in relation to the country's economic growth in the period between the mid-1950s and the late 1960s, as General Franco's regime abandoned post-war autarkic policies in favour of an opening up of the country's economy to foreign investment (*aperturismo*). Pavlović (2011) and Fernández-Cebrián (2023) offer detailed studies of that period, and of the cultural effects of that economic shift. Interestingly, the same term was redeployed in the late 1990s and early 2000s to refer to Spain's impressive growth in the years leading up to the Global Recession in both the domestic and the international press (cf. Rojo 2007; Faiola 2008; Rachman 2008). It is in this latter sense that I use the term here.

6 According to data from the World Bank, unemployment surpassed 26% at its peak in 2013, while youth unemployment exceeded 50% in the period

the most obvious example is the 15M movement, in which thousands of ordinary citizens took to the streets in cities across Spain in May 2011 in a large-scale public outpouring of political discontent that lasted months. Political scientist Juan Carlos Monedero reads the 15M as the result of a crisis of political legitimacy: as Spain's (and Europe's) middle classes became *proletarianised* due to the implementation of neoliberal policies – a phenomenon which antedates the global economic crisis of 2007–8, but which gathered significant pace in its wake, as austerity measures were implemented to bring sovereign debt under control – the lack of an alternative political model or discourse led to a disenchantment with formal party and parliamentary politics that eventually manifested itself in street protests (2019: 21–63). While the effects of the 2007–8 crisis were felt worldwide, and although there were similar grassroots protests in other countries – the Arab Spring, Occupy Wall Street – each movement responded to a geographically, culturally and historically specific set of circumstances, and was thus articulated differently.

Many of the movements that emerged globally in the wake of the crisis denounced a (neoliberal) capitalist model, as the recession laid bare its human cost. The slogan 'Gente sin casas / casas sin gente', for instance, drew attention to the paradox of Spain's stubbornly unaffordable housing market, in spite of an (over)abundance of vacant housing stock and the crash in prices that resulted from the economic downturn. The denunciation of the crippling effect of austerity policies on an already-threadbare welfare system became another vector of protest in several Western countries – in Spain, through the so-called *mareas*, that is, specific 'tidal' protest movements conceived to highlight the precarity of different state-funded sectors, such as healthcare and education.[7] But whereas the general critique of late-stage, neoliberal, globalised capitalism was common to many of the protest movements that emerged around the world after 2007, in Spain attention turned also to some of the questions which had been deemed intractable – or non-negotiable – during the country's Transition process in the late 1970s. The role and legitimacy of the monarchy were thrown into question in the wake of a series of corruption scandals that culminated with the abdication of King Juan Carlos I in June 2014. Data from Spain's Centro de Investigaciones Sociológicas (CIS) shows how the institution's rating plummeted from a mark of about 7 over 10 at the turn of the millennium,

2012–14. For further details, see https://data.worldbank.org/indicator/SL.UEM.TOTL.NE.ZS?locations=ES and https://data.worldbank.org/indicator/SL.UEM.1524.ZS?locations=ES.

7 For more on the *mareas* phenomenon, see Romanos and Sádaba 2022.

to less than 4 over 10 in the period 2011–13. While the monarchy's approval levels recovered slightly in the wake of Felipe VI's accession to the throne in 2014, CIS has not conducted any polls on the subject since 2015, so more recent surveys conducted by media outlets tend to be heavily skewed depending on their readership.[8] It seems clear, however, that the hardships experienced by many in Spain in the wake of the 2007–8 recession, coupled with the corruption scandals involving members of the royal family that came to light during the crisis, have significantly undermined support for the monarchy.

Spain's 'territorial question' – that is, the contested issue of its articulation as a plurinational state within which different languages, cultural traditions, and national or place-based identities coexist – also re-emerged in the wake of 2007–8, most notably in the Catalan referendum, and subsequent unilateral declaration of independence, of 2017. It would be reductive to point to the consequences of the Great Recession as the sole or main factor that boosted the Catalan pro-independence movement which culminated in the events of 2017; yet the role of the crisis cannot be overlooked, either, as argued by Guzmán Ramírez and Quiroga Riviere (2013) and Colomer (2018), among others. The mobilisation of the motto 'Espanya ens roba' [Spain steals from us] by secessionist parties is perhaps the most obvious sign of how the social discontent resulting from the crisis and from post-2008 austerity policies was instrumentalised in order to increase popular support for Catalan independence (Dowling 2014). Although the movement for Catalan independence appears to have lost momentum since 2017, the political polarisation that both led to and was exacerbated by that territorial and institutional crisis remains unresolved. And, while it was the emergence of new political parties in the wake of 15M – most notably Podemos and Ciudadanos – that initially appeared as the main threat to Spain's bipartisan system, more recently the rise of the far-right party Vox, as well as the consolidation of a distinctive and plural electoral landscape in the country's historical regions, constitutes the main challenge to lasting political stability – as illustrated by the three general elections held in the four-year period 2019–23. It seems beyond doubt, then, that the 2007–8 economic crisis had a transformative impact across the social, political and

8 For instance, a poll commissioned by the progressive online news outlet eldiario.es in November 2023 gives Republicans a slim lead (44.7%) over monarchists (43.5%) in a hypothetical referendum (Herrera and Oliveres 2023: online). Yet in a similar poll conducted by the conservative *La Razón* a few weeks earlier, 65% of respondents expressed their support for the monarchy (Lorente Ferrer 2023: online).

cultural fields, in Spain and, arguably, beyond – with effects which continue to be felt today.

(Dis)Placing *literatura de la crisis*

As I intimated in the opening lines of this Introduction, the label *literatura de la crisis* became something of a fad in the aftermath of the 2007–8 recession. The sudden *boom* in (neo-)social realist and socially critical writing also attracted considerable scholarly attention.[9] The most comprehensive English-language study to date is Olga Bezhanova's 2017 *Literature of Crisis: Spain's Engagement with Liquid Capital*, in which the US-based academic provides an incisive analysis of a selection of essays, novels and poems published in the aftermath of the Great Recession (2007–15). Bezhanova contends that the texts she analyses

> serve as a space where private experiences and public concerns meet in a way that disrupts acquiescence with the narratives that serve the interests of the increasingly liquid capital. Despite the ideological, generational, and stylistic differences between the writers who have contributed to the literature of the crisis, their work relies on shared imagery, concepts, and concerns. This allows one to posit the existence of a genre of crisis literature, as opposed to isolated works of art that discuss the crisis. (2017: xxxiv)

9 I sketch some of what I consider to be the key trends in scholarship on both *literatura de la crisis* and, more broadly, the changes that occurred in the Spanish cultural landscape in the aftermath of the Great Recession in this section; however, I have chosen to discuss a select number of representative examples in detail, rather than attempt an in-any-case-impossible exhaustive literature review. However, it is worth citing, at least in a footnote, some valuable contributions which I have not included in my discussion above, such as Justyna Ziarkowska's '"Poderoso caballero es don dinero." Las metáforas del simulacro y desengaño en auxilio de los actuales discursos españoles de la crisis' (2018), in which she traces Golden Age and Baroque motifs in crisis literature; Bécquer Seguín's 'Environmental Apocalypse and the Spanish Crisis Novel', *Hispanic Issues Online*, 24 (2019); Magda Potok's 'Mujer y economía. La "narrativa de la crisis" desde la perspectiva de género', *Studia Romanica Posnaniensia*, 47:1 (2020): 93–105; Luis Martín-Cabrera's 'Contra la suspensión de la mirada crítica: reflexiones sobre la persistencia del conflicto capital/trabajo en la cultura contemporánea española', *Arizona Journal of Hispanic Cultural Studies*, 14 (2010): 117–38; and Luis Martín Estudillo's work on what he terms 'porno-precariedad', which he defines as the 'entramado visual que explota y consume principalmente como forma de entretenimiento la exhibición de la miseria provocada por la crisis económica y biopolítica de la última década' (2017: 196).

While Bezhanova acknowledges 'the ideological, generational, and stylistic differences' between authors of crisis texts, this does not lead her to question or problematise the notion of 'crisis literature' as a diffuse and arguably (over-)capacious category. This notable elision privileges engagement with the notion of 'crisis' at a thematic level over any other (formal, ideological) concerns, without interrogating – at least at this point – whether such a limited engagement can, in fact, effect the type of disruption of 'narratives that serve the interests of liquid capital' which she establishes as the defining feature of the genre. In fairness, Bezhanova's subsequent analysis of specific crisis texts unapologetically identifies the limitations of certain approaches, such as those which suggest 'the crisis as a problem that can be addressed by isolated individuals' (31); or those that deploy 'Transition-era rhetoric to silence the discussions about the legacy of the dictatorship and its impact on today's political and economic structures of Spain' (149).[10] In other words, some of the factors whose importance is minimised in the Introduction, in an attempt to preserve a semblance of cohesion around the notion of *literatura de la crisis*, prove critical, later on, in terms of determining the effectiveness of a text in conducting the type of disruption which Bezhanova regards as the defining trait of the genre.

The tension between upholding a generic definition, which inevitably requires an elision of specificities, and the analysis of individual works identified in Bezhanova's pioneering monograph is not intended as a criticism – indeed, the evolution from the Introduction to the case studies that follow is, in my view, a testament to the author's intellectual honesty. Rather, this tension seems symptomatic of a broader trend, within critical analyses of crisis texts, that favours engagements with certain tropes at the level of enunciation (an explicit discussion of the economic downturn and its effects) or plot (the narrativisation of individual experiences of financial destitution) over other features, such as linguistic experimentation or the destabilisation of narrative or generic conventions. Sanz Villanueva alerted us to this privileging of plot, which he termed 'tematismo o contenidismo' as far back as 2016 (18), although his warning seemed directed primarily at authors and readers, rather than constituting a questioning of the critical paradigm of *literatura de la crisis* itself. In contrast, and somewhat provocatively, Pablo Gutiérrez, author of *Democracia* (2012), proposed in a 2017 essay that Spanish

10 Alison Ribeiro de Menezes also underlines the centrality of memory in engagements with the effects of the 2007–8 crisis in her article 'Memory as Disruption: Entanglements of Memory and Crisis in Contemporary Spain', *Bulletin of Hispanic Studies*, 94:8 (2017): 883–901; as do Sebastián Royo, from a different disciplinary angle, in his already-cited 2020 book and Mauro Jiménez (2016) in his work on Rafael Chirbes.

narrative fiction from the picaresque novel onwards reflects a flawed and corrupt society, and might therefore be considered also 'crisis literature'. This very radical disavowal of *literatura de la crisis* as a contemporary and new phenomenon, while understandable as a reaction towards the perceived opportunism of the term (and, perhaps also, towards the readiness with which it was accepted and adopted in some critical circles), nonetheless does little to explain the changes that occurred within the Spanish cultural field in the years after 2007–8 outlined above.

In this regard, David Becerra's *Después del acontecimiento* (2021) is illuminating as it undertakes an exploration of the changes that occurred to the Spanish literary and cultural fields in recent years, while simultaneously critiquing what he regards as the commercially opportunistic and ideologically not innocent crisis texts, in which

> se pone en funcionamiento una suerte de relato de la pérdida ante la descomposición de un horizonte de expectativas vital que, a causa de la crisis, no va a poder cumplirse. En ellas [novelas comerciales de la crisis], hay más de añoranza por un mundo perdido que una apuesta por un mundo que ganar. Cuando la crisis funciona como temática en el fondo no hace más que desactivar el componente político que pudiera tener su narración. (2021: 77)

In contrast to such crisis bestsellers, which lament the demise of the Spanish middle class, Becerra identifies other narrative texts that he defines as 'novelas del retorno de lo político'. In spite of the apparent similarities – as both types of texts engage in a narrativisation of moments or experiences of crisis – the latter group of novels does not simply chronicle the downfall; they also engage in an interrogation of 'el poder y sus dispositivos para disciplinar los cuerpos y las subjetividades' (87). This clear differentiation between novels that merely use the 2007–8 crisis as a setting or theme, on the one hand, and texts that explore the power dynamics underlying it, on the other – a questioning that often leads authors to interrogate also the form, language and role of the literary text itself – is useful and pertinent. Indeed, my own primary corpus is comprised primarily of 'novelas del retorno de lo politico', as defined by Becerra. However, there are some differences in modulation between Becerra's work and my own: for Becerra, the titular, Badiou-type of event which marks a turning point and helps explain the shift in the Spanish cultural field is the 15M, that is, the series of mobilisations that took place in Spanish towns and cities in May 2011. While he acknowledges that some 'political' novels antedate the events of 2011, and, indeed, the downturn of 2007–8, his attention is focused mostly on texts published after 2012. Of course, any attempt at periodisation entails an element of (inevitably) subjective choice; I have opted to focus my attention on the decade 2007–17 because, while I agree with Becerra that there are notable crisis texts published in Spain before the generally acknowledged start of the Great Recession, it is that event, rather than the 15M, which I regard as decisively transforming the Spanish cultural field.[11] In other words, while Becerra reads the 15M movement as the main cause of the shifts in the Spanish cultural landscape, I believe that the global financial downturn – and the ensuing austerity policies, which exacerbated its effects – had a more significant impact. A second important difference is that Becerra's analysis focuses entirely on literary texts, as traditionally defined (mostly novels, with the inclusion of a smattering of poetic or dramatic texts);[12] whereas, influenced by cultural and area studies, I combine the study of literary fiction with the exploration of visual texts and journalistic chronicles, in an effort to elucidate how these other, increasingly pervasive, cultural forms also reflect, shape or challenge the 'common sense' (in Rancièrian terms) at a given moment and in a specific place.

Further criticism of the notion of a post-2007–8 *literatura de la crisis* relates to the elisions which, some scholars claim, the term enables. Pablo Valdivia, for instance, has argued that the label mainly privileges 'literary representations of, first, urban spaces; second, the tragedy caused by the loss of certainty; and, finally, the present as a process of identitarian dispossession' (2017: 164).[13] For the Spanish critic, the term originally served

11 Becerra mentions Colectivo Todoazen's *El año que tampoco hicimos la revolución*, published in 2005, as an example of a crisis text that antedates the Great Recession. Elsewhere, I have argued that much of Belén Gopegui's literary production in the 1990s and early 2000s should also be read as crisis literature (Usoz de la Fuente 2020); and Marta Sanz, whose *Clavícula* (2017) is analysed in the closing chapter of this book, described her 2003 novel *Animales domésticos* as a crisis text, since it took notice of the inequality and the erosion of the middle class in Spain years before the 2007–8 implosion of financial markets (Vallés 2018: online).

12 In fairness to David Becerra, his approach does not entirely exclude non-literary texts: his introduction in fact mobilises the musical evolution of singer-songwriter Nacho Vegas as a metonymic example or illustration of the changes effected in the Spanish cultural field in the post-2011 context.

13 As if to confirm Valdivia's contention that the archetypical *novela de la crisis* is also an urban novel, several critics have pointed to the relationship that some of these texts establish between economic downturn and urban decay. See, for example, Carolina León Vegas' 'En busca del espacio perdido. La crisis y el espacio urbano en *La habitación oscura* de Isaac Rosa y *Animales domésticos* de Marta Sanz', *Revista de Literatura*, LXXXI:162 (2019): 549–72. My own analysis of Elvira Navarro's *La trabajadora* in the third chapter of this book connects the experience of crisis of the central character and narrator, and her experience of urban space, in a reading

commercial and opportunistic aims; yet its marketing appeal also made possible the emergence of new authorial voices who did not necessarily fit into the label as originally conceived. Valdivia thus simultaneously critiques the limitations of *literatura de la crisis* as conventionally defined, while recognising the opportunities that the literary trend offered to new or aspiring writers, or to voices normally at the margins of the publishing industry. This study undertakes a similar double gesture, challenging, on the one hand, the generally accepted definition of *literatura de la crisis* as a label that applies solely to literary texts engaging in an explicit depiction of the effects of the Global Recession – and that applies to all of those texts, regardless of their formal, discursive and ideological underpinning – while also acknowledging that the transformations that took place within the Spanish cultural field after 2007 (of which the emergence of a so-called *literatura de la crisis* is one of the most visible examples) have had wide-ranging ramifications. Among them, we can think of the rural turn in contemporary Spanish culture, as argued by Ibarretxe and Delgado (2022) and Usoz de la Fuente and Miguelez-Carballeira (2024); as well as the emergence of ecocritical readings of contemporary Spanish narrative fiction (Prádanos 2018; Vidal Pérez 2019; Seguín 2019; O'Dwyer 2022).

The approaches that have most contributed to shape my own thinking and work are those that, like Becerra and Valdivia, simultaneously mobilise and query the notion of *literatura de la crisis* – and, in some cases, the very concept of crisis.[14] This often involves transcending the purely thematic, as, for instance, Christian Claesson does in the collective work he coordinated (2019). As Claesson explains in the Introduction, the volume proposes readings of post-2008 texts which focus on their role in producing and shaping subjectivities. This emphasis on the role of cultural texts in articulating subjectivities allows for a broader thematic range, not limiting the understanding or definition of *narrativas precarias* (used in the title of Claesson's edited volume, instead of the more ubiquitous *literatura de la crisis*) to accounts of economic hardship or destitution in the wake of 2008, but rather including contributions by different scholars which analyse contemporary narratives on issues including the Basque conflict, mental ill health, activism and dystopian fiction. Rather than an engagement at the thematic level with the 2007–8 downturn and its effects, what binds

that is indebted to the work of María-José Furió Sancho (2015), Noelia Suárez García (2016) and Francisco Javier Dueñas (2018), among others.

14 For several authors, the downturn of 2007–8 is not a cyclical or isolated crisis, but the culmination or acceleration of a process of precarisation that starts in the 1970s, if not before, and gathers pace throughout the 1980s and 1990s. See, for example, Lorey (2010); Palley (2013); and Bauman and Bordoni (2014), among others.

these articles together is an implicit conception of culture as a discursive praxis that plays a central role in the shaping of individual subjectivities, in the first instance, and which thus has the potential to shape collective practices, too – rather than merely reflecting them. So, while the thematic scope of the works analysed in this edited volume is broadened, the focus on cultural texts that seek to question or destabilise dominant or hegemonic subjectivities means that titles which engage with the present in seemingly 'neutral', 'objective' or 'unideological' ways are not given much attention, even if they depict some of the effects of the crisis.[15] The collective volume *La imaginación hipotecada* (2016), coordinated by Palmar Álvarez Blanco and Antonio Gómez López-Quiñones, enacts a similar double gesture of simultaneously exploring and questioning notions of precariousness and precarity, and their cultural articulations. A distinctive feature of this text is its centring on theoretical issues, rather than on cultural texts, and its extension of the analytical focus beyond Spain in some cases, such as Isabell Lorey's contribution, which discusses precarisation policies across the European Union, for instance.

If my work is indebted to the aforementioned collective volumes in its privileging of cultural texts that question hegemonic discourses on the 2007–8 crisis and its effects, my decision to include titles which blur the boundaries between fiction and non-fiction – such as Cristina Fallarás' autobiographical *A la puta calle* and the collection of journalistic chronicles *Mediterráneo descapotable*, as well as visual works, particularly photography – is indebted to works such as the collective *Cultura, literatura e imaginación política* (2018), edited by Jaume Peris Blanes, which includes contributions on film, music, dance and gastronomy, among others. Not only does this volume broaden the scope of analysis beyond the literary; it also explores the role of the imagination and of collective cultural practices in terms of shaping how we think about our past, present and possible futures – a task meta-discursively undertaken also by many of the cultural works studied in the volume, and one which implicitly challenges the commonly held perception of culture as separate and autonomous from other discursive and social realms. The work of Germán Labrador has also been a recurring

15 As David Becerra argued in his influential *La novela de la no-ideología* (2013), seemingly unideological narrative fiction of the type which dominated the Spanish cultural landscape throughout the 1980s and 1990s in fact serves a distinctly ideological function, namely, to naturalise the status quo and discourage public debate about the established political and economic order – thus contributing to its perpetuation. Christian Claesson makes a similarly powerful case for the ideological role (and thus emancipatory potential) of cultural texts in the introduction to the aforementioned 2019 edited volume.

influence, both in terms of the mobilisation of a corpus of texts that transcends the purely literary to include also forms of popular culture, such as reality TV shows (2012; 2014); and in his impressive mobilisation of a broad and varied range of theoretical approaches. Indeed, his 2013 critical survey of the spatial turn in Peninsular cultural studies partly inspired me to think of the Great Recession not just as a temporality of crisis (Labrador 2014: 242), but also as a phenomenon that manifests itself and unfolds spatially.

Rather than simply contributing to the scholarship on *literatura de la crisis*, then, this monograph seeks to explore how a selection of recent Spanish cultural texts that engage with the aftermath of 2007–8 can also be read as anticipating pressing questions about the sustainability – environmental, communal, individual – of an extractive, growth-oriented capitalist model; questions which have only become more pressing in the wake of the Covid-19 pandemic and the unfolding climate emergency. In that regard, Christian Claesson's contention that it is possible to identify crisis novels which antedate the downturn of 2007–8, and thus show that the Great Recession was not an isolated event, but rather a process with deeper roots which reached a turning point at that specific moment (2007–8) (2019: 14), can also be projected onto the future. Western economies may have seemingly stabilised in the closing years of the 2010s, but the root causes of the Great Recession – such as the limits of debt-fuelled economic growth, or the sustainability of an economic system predicated on environmentally harmful practices – remain unresolved; and its consequences, such as growing inequality and worsening living conditions for the majority of the world's population, continue to be felt today.

From Global Financial Crisis to Planetary Poly-Crisis[16]

From the vantage point of the mid-2020s, following the experience of the Covid-19 pandemic and relative to the unfolding climate emergency, the global recession of 2007–8 might seem like a distant memory, and as a comparatively small-scale event. Yet historian Adam Tooze in fact points to the Great Recession as a turning point, marking the start of what he terms 'the world of polycrisis'; that is, a global context marked by shocks that 'are disparate, but they interact so that the whole is even more overwhelming than the sum of the parts' (2022: online). One example of how such seemingly

16 I am deliberate in my choice of terminology here, contrasting the more ubiquitous (and thus seemingly transparent) notion of the 'global' with the concept of the 'planetary', which Neil Brenner (2013) defines in distinctly spatial-geographical terms.

distinct problems are intertwined can be found in the already-cited Covid-19 pandemic, as the ability of healthcare systems to respond to the emergency in some countries, including Spain, was hampered due to the underfunding of such services that resulted from the implementation of austerity policies in the post-2008 context (Otero-García et al. 2023). The rise of far-right political parties and movements across much of the Western world – including Spain, where Vox became the third-most-voted-for party in November 2019 – offers a further example. This phenomenon has been linked to post-2008 austerity (Bieling 2021), as well as to the rise in migration resulting from globalisation and conflict (Davis and Deole 2017). But it is perhaps the currently unfolding planetary climate crisis that offers the best illustration of the complexity and scope of the challenges we face – and of what is at stake. Defining the economic meltdown of 2007–8 as a turning point, however, is not the same as designating it as the sole or main cause or origin of our contemporary woes. As Zygmunt Bauman and Carlo Bordoni contend (2014), the roots of the 2007–8 crisis can be traced back to at least the 1970s, and to the progressive reduction of the role of the state within a globalised economic order. Robinson (2012) echoes this diagnosis, pointing to the 'disjuncture between a globalizing economy and [a] nation-state based system of political authority' (171). It would be a problematic simplification, therefore, to conceptualise 2007–8 as the beginning of a still-ongoing unravelling; rather, the near collapse of the financial system at that point in time merely accelerated – and therefore rendered more visible – the 'slow violence' inherent to neoliberalism (Nixon 2011). One of the central aims of this book is to explore how a selection of recent cultural texts from Spain reflect and respond to the increased visibility – and to the more palpably destructive effects – of that violence.

While this monograph does not chart the evolution from Great Recession to planetary poly-crisis put forward by Tooze, the literary texts selected as a primary corpus, and their classification into three thematic areas of concern – impact on the landscape and the environment; the experience of home loss; and the bodily effects of both pre-recession neoliberalism and post-downturn austerity – implicitly suggest that the 2007–8 crisis and the economic boom that preceded it had wide-ranging and pervasive effects that continue to be felt in the present. Environmental degradation, job insecurity, access to affordable housing and the impact of worsening living conditions on physical and mental health are all themes featured in the texts analysed in this monograph as resulting from an economic framework that the events of 2007–8 proved unsustainable. Yet almost two decades on from the near collapse of the global financial system, progress on addressing these challenges – or, indeed, on devising a more sustainable and equitable framework – remains limited. While such a failure is, first and foremost, political in nature, it can also be seen as symptomatic of a broader shortcoming of our ability to conceive of alternatives to late-stage capitalism – as per the famous quote, alternately attributed to Fredric Jameson and Slavoj Žižek, that it is easier to imagine the end of the world than it is to envisage the end of capitalism.[17] Although the texts analysed in this monograph do not offer up such an alternative, they do, in different ways and to varying degrees, challenge the official narrative which posited the 2007–8 downturn as the product of unrestrained human *foibles* (greed, hubris), and thus fixable through technocratic means. Instead, the works featured question the sustainability and desirability of an economic and political system – neoliberalism – by exposing its nefarious effects on the environment and on individuals. But, unlike certain other exemplars of *literatura de la crisis*, which chronicle some of the effects of the 2007–8 crisis without considering their own role and positioning in relation to the hegemonic ideology, the texts selected for this study acknowledge the pervasiveness and seductiveness of certain neoliberal tropes (meritocracy, individualism), and are alert to their own internalisation of, or complicity with, such narratives. Indeed, as my analysis in the following pages will demonstrate, the varying forms and degrees of linguistic and formal experimentation in which these titles engage ought to be read as a deliberate effort to transcend the purely testimonial, opting instead for a broad-ranging and radical questioning of the usually invisible, as naturalised, norms and parameters that shape both contemporary common sense (in Rancière's definition) and the articulation, circulation and role of cultural texts at a specific time and in a specific place. In other words, the texts analysed do not simply engage in a critical representation of contemporary Spanish society; they also question their own role in contributing to the shaping of that society, acknowledging their limited potential for social intervention, while seeking to maximise it.

17 Jameson notes that '[s]omeone once said that it is easier to imagine the end of the world than to imagine the end of capitalism' in a 2003 article about Rem Koolhaas' *Project on the City*, published in *New Left Review* in May/June 2003. The full text is available at https://newleftreview.org/issues/ii21/articles/fredric-jameson-future-city [last accessed 19 August 2024]. Žižek attributes the idea to Jameson – even if the latter claims the idea originally came from someone else – as he writes 'as Fredric Jameson perspicaciously remarked, nobody seriously considers possible alternatives to capitalism any longer, whereas popular imagination is persecuted by the visions of the forthcoming "breakdown of nature", of the stoppage of all life on earth – it seems easier to imagine the "end of the world" than a far more modest change in the mode of production' (2003: 1) in the opening lines of his introduction to the collective volume *Mapping Ideology*, also from 2003.

Crisis and Space

As my discussion of the evolving concept of crisis in the preceding lines illustrates, space is at the heart of several interrelated contemporary crises: the difficulty in responding to global challenges – whether the financial crash of 2007–8, the Covid pandemic of 2020–22 or climate change – is, at least in part, the result of the 'disjuncture' identified by Robinson between political frameworks that operate primarily at a national level, and a globalised economy that produces planetary problems that nation-states are unable to solve or address individually. This disagreement in scale has, in turn, further spatial effects: in the form of the movement or displacement of populations in response to shifting economic flows, or due to armed conflicts or environmental disasters. Further examples of the spatial dimension of such crises include the relocation of industries (and thus jobs) to lower-cost countries, which often leads to environmental destruction in recipient countries, and to the simultaneous dismantling of manufacturing centres and the degradation of adjacent urban areas in (formerly) industrialised regions; or, conversely, through the flow of global capitals – in the form of foreign investment and tourism – into inner-city areas that drives processes of urban gentrification, which often result in the out-pricing of local residents. An exploration and understanding of how these different scales are interconnected – how a global phenomenon such as industrial relocation can be felt at a local level, negatively impacting crime levels and life expectancy in post-industrial areas, for instance – is key in any attempt to conceive of or formulate an alternative imaginary, as geographer David Harvey contends in his seminal *Spaces of Hope* (2000). In that text, Harvey sketches 'a way in which "globalization" and "the body" might be more closely integrated with each other and explore[s] the political-intellectual consequences of making such a connexion' (15), in an attempt to link 'two discourses that typically remain segregated, to the detriment of both' (16). The aim of such an endeavour is not purely theoretical, but is rather intended as a first step towards the mapping of spaces and forms of political imagination and contestation, a task that seems even more urgent from the vantage point of the 2020s than it did at the time of the book's original publication.

Harvey's work provides a key theoretical underpinning to my own research, as it deftly interconnects global phenomena to local problems and responses, using the latter as case studies that can help inform (re)actions elsewhere, without either ceding to universalising impulses or allowing particularism to obfuscate his clear-sighted identification of global trends. His reading of the spatial effects of globalised capitalism is particularly relevant to the first chapter of this book, which focusses on contemporary cultural representations of the rapid and often destructive changes to the Spanish landscape – especially along the Mediterranean coast – which took place in the early twenty-first century, and which fuelled the country's economic boom, before the meltdown of 2007–8. More generally, this monograph proposes a reading of the selected contemporary Spanish cultural texts as 'spaces of hope'; that is, as spaces that can help readers bridge the gap between seemingly distant or abstract global phenomena and individual embodied experience – a necessary, if insufficient, first step towards the construction of alternative collective imaginaries which, for Constantino Bértolo (2015), constitutes the most challenging task of a truly revolutionary political project.

Influenced by the French urban theorist Henri Lefebvre, Harvey recognises the importance – indeed, the centrality – of both practice and imagination in the ongoing 'struggle over how the production of and access to public space and public goods is to be regulated, by whom, and in whose interests' (2012: 73). As a geographer, however, his case studies tend to focus on spatial practices, on examples of grassroots activism and initiatives that contest the commodification of urban space; yet his words about the struggle over public goods and public space can also be applied – via Rancière – to language and the cultural sphere, respectively. In fact, the so-called *indignados* or 15M movement in Spain provides a vivid illustration of precisely such an intersection between spatial praxis – the reclaiming of public space through encampments – and cultural activity – through improvised workshops and assemblies that sought languages, ideas and imaginaries capable of articulating a challenge to the status quo. Rather than adding to the already-gargantuan bibliography on 15M, however, this monograph is concerned with exploring how a selection of contemporaneous texts articulate their critique of global neoliberalism spatially, as its effects are experienced as gradually encroaching upon individuals – first destroying the landscapes they inhabit; then claiming their homes, as rent or mortgage payments become unaffordable; and, ultimately, threatening their mental and physical integrity. If, as Lefebvre contends, the ways in which we conceive of and imagine physical spaces affect our interactions with those spaces, thus contributing to their (re)articulation (1991: 31), then the texts included in this study, which share a concern with the destructive effects of late-stage capitalism on spaces at varying scales – the landscape, the home, the body – invite readers to question the feasibility and desirability of an economic growth paradigm dependent on the exploitation of the environment and the precarisation of human lives (Lorey 2015). As I will be arguing in the chapters that follow, their success – that is, their ability to impact readers' subjectivity – is not merely due to the deftness with which they portray increasingly untenable living conditions, but also due to their destabilisation of literary and genre conventions, which prevent them from constituting mere denunciations or – worse – comforting stories in which adversity is ultimately overcome (as is the case with some of the bestselling titles of the so-called *literatura de la crisis*). Instead, the works selected probe, to varying degrees, the norms and assumptions underlying their own enunciations, thus indirectly encouraging their readers to undertake a similar self-reflexive questioning.

Chapter Outline

As briefly sketched earlier, this book is divided into three main chapters, each with a distinct focus. The opening chapter, subtitled 'Ruin(ed) landscapes in Rafael Chirbes' *Crematorio* (2007) and *En la orilla* (2013), Íñigo Domínguez's *Mediterráneo descapotable* (2008/2015) and NoPhoto Collective's *This Is Spain* (2015)', is concerned with the transformations occurring in Spanish landscapes, both in the years immediately before the Great Recession and in its aftermath. Taking Rafael Chirbes' crisis diptych as its starting point, and drawing on David Harvey's work on geographical spaces as traversed and shaped by global capital flows, this chapter explores how Chirbes' foregrounding of the fictional coastal town of Misent in *Crematorio* – and his juxtaposition of its different iterations from the 1940s and on to the mid-2000s – might be read metonymically as a critique of Spain's capitalist development, in both its *desarrollista* and neoliberal phases. However, the text is not merely a lament for a lost landscape or past; rather, it underlines the centrality of place as a mnemonic anchor, in a manner analogous to language and, particularly, to literary discourse. While *Crematorio* highlights how over-development has dramatically changed the landscapes of localities along the Spanish coast, *En la orilla* turns its attention to the Mediterranean's backyard: the marshlands which, although environmentally degraded by nearby urban development, have not (yet) been fully co-opted by capital. The persistence of such heterotopic spaces is indicative of their potential: both offering shelter to the disenfranchised, and as sites in which alternative memories, narratives and practices can survive. The remainder of the chapter is concerned with two non-fictional texts: the collection of journalistic chronicles *Mediterráneo descapotable*, analysed through the prism of kitsch; and the photo-book *This Is Spain: An Incomplete Travel Guide*, considered through its mobilisation of the trope of the ruin in its depiction of post-2008 Spain. These two texts, while more firmly anchored in a time close(r) to the present, also draw links between Spain's situation in and after 2008 and the *desarrollista* period. And, as with Chirbes' novels, their critical portrayal of the country transcends the mere lament for a lost prosperity characteristic of what David Becerra terms 'relatos de la pérdida' (2021: 77), as they engage in a self-reflexive questioning of the narratives, aspirations and fantasies that paved the way for large-scale financial and environmental havoc.

In the second chapter, my attention turns to the narrativisation of the experience of home loss, as I analyse four texts – a novel, an autobiographical account, a photography project and a graphic novel – that chronicle experiences of eviction in the wake of the Great Recession. Cristina Fallarás' *A la puta calle. Crónica de un desahucio* (2013) and Doménico Chiappe's *Tiempo de encierro* (2013) offer fictionalised accounts of home loss resulting from an inability to meet mortgage repayments, although the former is based on Fallarás' own eviction process, which culminated in 2012; and Chiappe's text is inspired by a true story reported in the press. As well as charting the practical and psychological impact of the threat of home loss upon the novels' protagonists, both texts question the language of crisis, drawing readers' attention to the insurmountable gulf between the technocratic rhetoric of economists and politicians and the actual consequences of the downturn as experienced by those most acutely affected by it. In so doing, Chiappe and Fallarás emphasise the role of language, representation and mediation in terms of shaping collective understandings and reactions to the Great Recession and to its consequences, thus also implicitly (re)claiming the potential of their own enunciations to challenge the apparent post-2008 consensus that there was no alternative but to implement austerity policies that worsened the effects of the crisis for the majority of the population. Carlos Luján's photo-reportage *Desahucios. Los escenarios del horror* (2013) confronts viewers with one of the most shocking aspects resulting from home evictions in Spain, namely, eviction-related suicides. In contrast with the somewhat sensationalist title, Luján's images are striking precisely because of their understated, anodyne visual style. This approach not only avoids spectacularising these events; it also demands an interpretative effort from readers, thus encouraging a reflective, as well as an affective response. This section closes with an analysis of the graphic novel *Aquí vivió. Historia de un desahucio* (2016), a collaboration between the writer Isaac Rosa and the illustrator Cristina Bueno. This coming-of-age story follows the political awakening of teenage Alicia, who discovers that the flat into which she has recently moved with her mother, following her parents' separation, had been repossessed by a bank after the eviction of its previous occupants. This discovery leads Alicia to become involved in the activities of the anti-eviction Plataforma de Afectados por la Hipoteca (PAH), learning, in the process, about the historical roots of the contemporary eviction crisis. Like Chirbes' novels, then, this text historicises the post-2008 phenomenon of home evictions by connecting contemporary attitudes towards home ownership with policies dating as far back as the 1950s; as well as by establishing parallels between the suffering resulting from the Great Recession and the violence derived from armed conflicts such as the Spanish Civil War and the Second World War. Further, and in spite of its apparent narrative simplicity, this novel, like the other texts analysed in the chapter, engages in a self-reflexive exploration of how discourse and form (visual, as well as verbal) mediate our understanding of the relationships between past and present, and between fantasy (or fiction) and reality.

Finally, the closing chapter in this monograph focuses on the somatisation of the experience of crisis; that is, on the physical and psychic (ill) effects derived not just from the Great Recession itself, but, more broadly, from a social, political and economic order that imposes increasingly precarious – or, rather, following Judith Butler's distinction (2004), precarised – living conditions on individuals. Pablo Gutiérrez's *Democracia* (2012) is a polyphonic, fragmented and exuberant account of the breakdown experienced by the novel's protagonist, Marco, after he loses his job on 15 September 2008, the exact day on which Lehman Brothers collapsed. Marco can be read as a metonymy for the Spanish aspirational middle class, which had to significantly recalibrate its expectations in the post-2008 context. His transformation from model citizen to urban graffiti artist, to radical agitator, to homicidal outcast functions as a stark warning about what can happen when governments wilfully ignore the human cost of an unsustainable and unfair economic order. But this text also explores how events and discourses in seemingly distant places and at seemingly different scales (public policy speeches, poetry, popular culture motifs) ricochet in various contexts, to unexpected effect. If *Democracia* is concerned with the nervous breakdown resulting from the experience of unemployment, Belén Gopegui's *El comité de la noche* (2014) hones in on the vampiric nature of late-stage capitalism. The real, 2012 proposal by a pharmaceutical multinational to pay a weekly wage of 70 euro to the unemployed in exchange for blood 'donations' serves as an inspiration and as the point of departure for a medical thriller set between Spain and Slovakia (in acknowledgement, perhaps, of the globalised nature of contemporary processes of privatisation). The novel's focus on healthcare – specifically, on a corporate conspiracy to achieve the privatisation of blood banks – renders visible the way in which capitalism conditions individual lives, and how crises facilitate increasing encroachment of such control. In Gopegui's novel, capital no longer merely influences individuals' life chances or likelihood of success; it can determine who lives and who dies. Elvira Navarro's *La trabajadora* (2014) shares with *Democracia* its preoccupation with the mental health effects of unemployment, as well as an interest in the potential of urban space as a site for (symbolic) acts of resistance. While Navarro's text is less radically experimental than Gutiérrez's novel, both authors simultaneously vindicate the disruptive potential of creative work, while also acknowledging its limits, and the difficulty of pursuing such labour in the absence of sustainable material conditions. The last work analysed in this chapter, Marta Sanz's autobiographical *Clavícula* (2017), undertakes a similarly ambivalent gesture: its narrator, Marta Sanz, is ravaged by unexplained pain in her collarbone area, and turns to writing in an attempt to document and hopefully understand this mysterious ailment and its causes. While the writing process helps the narrator understand that her malady is the result of the over-work and the (self)exploitation to which she has been driven in the wake of her husband's loss of his job, rather than a symptom of a specific and treatable medical condition, her realisation cannot cure her, as it is not enough, in and of itself, to improve her living conditions. Creative work may not significantly improve the narrator's situation, but it successfully reframes physical pain, positing it as a collectively experienced problem resulting from an exploitative economic order, rather than as an individual issue to be resolved by medical-pharmaceutical means.

As these chapter summaries evidence, all the cultural works included in this study reclaim their socially critical – counter-hegemonic, even – potential, while simultaneously acknowledging their limited sphere of effect. In so doing, they implicitly align with Rancière's definition of critical art as 'not so much a type of art that reveals the forms and contradictions of domination as it is an art that questions its own limits and powers, that refuses to anticipate its own effects' (2010: 149). Rather than adopting a programmatic or moralising approach, then, these seemingly disparate literary, journalistic and visual texts make for disquieting reading, as they *both* subtly question or mock some of the ideological foundations of neoliberal capitalism – such as its democratic nature and legitimacy, or its compatibility with both human and non-human forms of life – *and* their own status, complicity and mode of articulation within that framework. In so doing, they point to the urgent task of imagining and building alternative frameworks of production and reproduction – a collective endeavour that requires (as a necessary, if insufficient, condition) a new imaginary. The titles featured in this monograph might be read as contributions to that effort, which is always, of necessity, a work in progress.

CHAPTER ONE

Landscape

Ruin(ed) Landscapes in Rafael Chirbes' Crematorio *(2007) and* En la orilla *(2013), Íñigo Domínguez's* Mediterráneo descapotable *(2008/2015) and NoPhoto Collective's* This Is Spain *(2015)*

This chapter is concerned with how four recent cultural texts depict the dramatic changes to the Spanish landscape over the past few decades. While the time span, geographical and thematic focus, and genre of the selected texts varies, all four share two key features that justify their grouping together, and which will be explored in detail in what follows. First, all four texts analysed exceed the testimonial and denunciatory – as the texts do not merely articulate an environmental lament that could be seen as analogous to Becerra's notion of the 'relatos desde la pérdida' (2015: 21–22), and favour instead an exploration of the commonly held beliefs, values and aspirations that have led to the environmental degradation portrayed in the texts. Second, all of the works featured undertake an implicit or explicit interrogation of their own internalisation of, or complicity with, the hegemonic 'common sense' that has led to the present situation – a questioning which, as I will show, is undertaken in different ways (narratively, meta-discursively, formally) in each text. In order to contextualise my analysis of these texts, I start by offering an overview of the key socio-historical developments behind Spain's most recent (at the time of writing) construction boom at the turn of the millennium. I then engage with recent contributions to the field of Iberian environmental studies, as well as with more canonical critiques of urbanisation processes, as these works have influenced my own analysis of the selected texts – which is then presented individually, but brought together in the concluding paragraphs of the chapter.

The decade 1996–2006 saw what the late Ramón Fernández Durán termed a building 'tsunami' in Spain, with around 800,000 homes built in 2005 – more than the sum of those built in France, Germany and the UK in the same year (Fernández Durán 2006: 24). As the Spanish author and environmentalist explains, however, this phenomenon did not affect all areas of the country evenly, but was largely concentrated in its main urban centres and surroundings (particularly Madrid) and in coastal areas. The boom of the construction sector was due to several factors, chief among them the liberalisation of building regulations enacted through the so-called Ley del Suelo of 1998.[1] This legislation ostensibly sought to simplify matters surrounding urban planning and construction; in practice, as Tudela and Delgado (2018) document, it decreed that all areas could be developed, unless explicitly protected, and left planning decisions in the hands of corrupt (or corruptible) regional and local administrations. Moreover, and contrary to the basic law of supply and demand, this increase in housing stock did not make homes more affordable – at least not in the short and medium term. Instead, and thanks to the availability of cheap credit and to demand from European buyers looking for a second (or third) residence – their 'place in the sun' – as well as from foreign and domestic investors, a real estate bubble emerged, with housing prices rising by almost 200% in the period 1989–2007 (Rodríguez López 2007: 11).

The consequences of the real estate and construction bubbles in Spain were multiple. Perhaps the most obvious and visible one was its impact upon the landscape, particularly along the Mediterranean coast, which saw dramatic and, in some cases, devastating transformation as a result from unbridled, un- or under-regulated and speculative building practices. Luis Iñaki Prádanos (2018) points to 'the cultural logic of a socially and environmentally unsustainable growth imaginary' (38) as the underlying cause of the global 2007–8 crisis; in the Spanish case, the economy's (over)reliance on the construction and real estate sectors arguably made that unsustainability more obvious, as the territory susceptible to be developed is finite, and the impact or effect of uncontrolled development is plainly visible. More recently, Begoña Méndez (2023) has explored the ecocide in La Manga del Mar Menor (Murcia), establishing interesting analogies between mass tourism and other extractive and unsustainable practices such as intensive farming or mining. Méndez and Prádanos, like Fernández Durán (2006), and David Harvey (2003; 2012), among others, demonstrate that processes of spatial reconfiguration and environmental degradation have both causes and effects which transcend the spatial, and touch on the economic, social, cultural and political. Harvey's work is pioneering in its theorisation of the global trend towards urban development and gentrification in the West as partly resulting from capital over-accumulation, that is, of (over)accumulated capital seeking – indeed, requiring – a new

1 The law's official name is Ley 6/1998, de 13 de abril, sobre régimen del suelo y valoraciones, and the full text can be accessed here: https://www.boe.es/buscar/doc.php?id=BOE-A-1998-8788.

outlet for investment, and finding a suitable venture in real estate – not just through the construction and sale of property, but also through the financialisation of the sector via the creation of investment products such as mortgage-backed securities. However, these processes both rely on and exacerbate what Harvey terms 'accumulation by dispossession' in order to be profitable. That is, they rely on divesting individuals or communities of either ownership or use of land or property in order to develop it for profit. Gentrification of inner-city neighbourhoods, with the attendant displacement of their original inhabitants, is frequently cited as an example of accumulation by dispossession. In the Spanish context, the figure of the 'agente urbanizador' offers an even more vivid illustration of such a practice. As Tudela and Delgado explain,

> La Ley Reguladora de la Actividad Urbanística Valenciana (LRAU) [...], permitía a un promotor particular presentar un proyecto para urbanizar un terreno aunque no fuese suya ni una maceta y adjudicarse el proceso si el gobierno municipal de turno le daba el visto bueno. [...] Hacerse rico gracias al suelo sin tener suelo. Los contactos como única materia prima. (2018: 437)

In Spain's Valencia region, then, it was possible for an 'urban developer' to obtain approval to build on land they did not own, and set the terms to expropriate the legal owners, as long as their plan was approved by local authorities. Accumulation by dispossession in its starkest form. Rubén Bertomeu, the central character of Rafael Chirbes' *Crematorio* (2007), the first text analysed in this chapter, is one such 'agente urbanizador'. As the extensive epilogue to Íñigo Domínguez's journalistic chronicle *Mediterráneo descapotable* (2015), the third text considered, lays bare, many Spanish local authorities were all too ready to overlook all manner of irregularities, local concerns and plain injustices in exchange for payments or other services rendered by unscrupulous property developers.

David Harvey (2003; 2012) and Ramón Fernández Durán (2006) conceptualise the spatial transformations taking place in the West and in Spain, respectively, at the end of the twentieth and the beginning of the twenty-first centuries as more than visual, cosmetic or surface phenomena. For both authors, these changes in fact reflect a neoliberal political–economic rationale which places individual interest over collective rights, and profits over principles. The result of these processes is not simply a modification of the landscape and the destruction of ecosystems, but, as Fernández Durán argues, it entails also 'un verdadero borrado cultural de las señas de identidad de la cultura mediterránea' (2006: 60), as local communities are torn apart and/or displaced to pave the way for new, large-scale real estate projects. Along similar lines, Prádanos states, following Michel Serres, that '[g]lobal capitalism destroys not only biodiversity but epistemological diversity as well' (2018: 50). Writing specifically on the Iberian context, Ann Davies makes a convincing case for the centrality of landscape 'as a surface which points to a national or regional entity lying behind it' (2012: 2). Germán Labrador, meanwhile, warns of the risk that 'con el canto a la plasticidad ubicua de los espacios, perdemos de vista que del relato histórico han desparecido las comunidades que mantuvieron con esos espacios una relación de identificación' (2013: 227), and remarks on the need for spatial approaches to incorporate geopolitical, ecocritical and historical concerns to avoid the erasure of local, socio-historically determined specificities.

In this respect, the work of David Harvey, with its emphasis on the dynamic, evolving and often paradoxical relationship between place, space and landscape and notions of culture, identity and belonging, is useful in dispelling any totalising, universalising or ahistorical temptations. For Harvey, places with 'claims to uniqueness, authenticity, particularity, and specialty underlie the ability to capture monopoly rents' (2012: 104); that is, places are valued for their singularity, a symbolic or cultural capital, in Bourdieu's terminology, which can be monetised. Yet radical difference precludes marketability; and success in accruing a significant degree of symbolic capital can lead to a loss of singularity – the so-called 'Disneyfication' of historical European cities constitutes a prime example. As Harvey explains, 'the more Europe becomes Disneyfied, the less unique and special it is. The bland homogeneity that goes with pure commodification erases monopoly advantages; cultural products become no different from commodities in general' (2012: 92–93). In short, for Harvey space is suffused and traversed by a global flow of capitals, in processes that are place-specific (the intensity and form of transformation varies depending on local conditions), yet simultaneously contribute to erase (or, at least, erode) local specificities.

This chapter is not primarily concerned with tracing such spatial commodification processes in Spain – even though, as we shall see, these are featured prominently in both *Crematorio* and *Mediterráneo descapotable*. Rather, it is concerned with the discursive dimension or apparatus which accompanies such processes, which Harvey also foregrounds (2012: 89–112). If landscapes simultaneously mirror socio-economic practices and cultural identities, and contribute to their shaping and articulation, as the aforementioned critics argue, following Harvey (2012) – who, in turn, is following Henri Lefebvre (1991) – then we might ask ourselves to what extent and in which ways spatial practices (how we use, engage with, think about and represent spaces) might also, dialectically, affect processes of spatial transformation. For reasons of scope, this chapter cannot consider space-based forms of activism, although the centrality of urban space to the 15M movement is well-documented.[2] Instead, I focus my attention on four texts which seek to expose, question or disrupt hegemonic spatial practices focussed on a notion of development defined exclusively in terms of economic profit. As Luis Iñaki Prádanos contends, following Lawrence Buell, 'the environmental crisis involves a crisis of imagination, for it becomes almost impossible to imagine a postcarbon, postgrowth, post-capitalist, post-neoliberal, post-patriarchal, decolonial society that is desirable and viable' (2018: 25). While the texts featured in this chapter may not (yet) delineate such an alternative, they certainly succeed in undermining the economic growth imaginary ubiquitous in pre-2008 Spain.

The first two novels analysed in this chapter, both by the late Rafael Chirbes, have come to be regarded as canonical crisis texts in Spain. In *Crematorio* (2007), Rubén Bertomeu's success as an architect and property developer is framed within a context of corruption – defined not just in political terms, but also as physical decay and moral degeneracy. Death is present from the very title, which alludes to the cremation of the recently deceased Matías, Rubén's younger brother. The later *En la orilla* (2013) also has decay and degeneracy at its heart, but whereas in *Crematorio* the arch-capitalist Rubén Bertomeu shows a remarkable capacity for self-justification, reinvention and regeneration – the novel closes with the revelation that he has fathered a child in his mid-seventies – in spite of the destructiveness of his actions, in *En la orilla* the necropolitical is all-pervasive, and is metaphorically represented by the swamp alluded to metonymically in the title. The mobilisation of the swamp as a spatial symbol of systemic decrepitude is no coincidence, and can be read as an ecocritical denunciation of the excesses of globalised capitalism (Vidal Pérez 2019). Simultaneously, however, the swamp also functions as a memory site, as readers are made aware of its different uses over time – as a communal hunting ground, as a hiding place for Republicans in the early post-war period and as a 'reward' offered up to collaborators with the Francoist regime. The depiction of the *pantano* as a changing space – in terms of its appearance, but also in the practices it fosters and thus in its use and exchange values – resonates with Germán Labrador's aforementioned injunction to not lose sight of the social and historically specific vectors that traverse (and transform) spaces.

2 See, for example, Diz 2013; Sevilla Buitrago 2014 and 2015; Díaz Parra and Candón-Mena 2014; Medina 2015; Nin and Shmite 2015.

Íñigo Domínguez's *Mediterráneo descapotable* (2008/2015) is a compilation of newspaper articles first published in serialised form during the summer of 2008 in the regional newspaper *El Correo*. Those texts, written before the extent of the global financial crisis was properly understood (or, indeed, felt by the general population), are complemented by an epilogue written closer to the time of publication of the book (2015). Domínguez's work thus offers an insight into two distinct moments: the cusp of the crisis (2008), and its painful and extended aftermath (2015). While the first part of Domínguez's text offers a humorous take on the kitsch aesthetic of the (over)developed Spanish coastline, the second part is sober and, at times, melancholic in tone – a combination reminiscent of some theorisations of kitsch which underline its affinity with death and destruction (Friedländer 2015; Friedlander 1997; Veld 2019). The final text analysed in this chapter is concerned with the aftermath of the crisis. The photography project *This Is Spain: An Incomplete Travel Guide* (2015) charts an eerie landscape of ruins – abandoned or unfinished housing developments – and fragments (sections of road or motorway, of buildings, of billboards). Kathy Korcheck's work (2015) on what she terms 'speculative ruins' and on crisis photography in Spain, as well as classical theorisations on the notion of ruin, will inform my reading of that text.

Crematorio (2007)

Rafael Chirbes' diptych *Crematorio* (2007) and *En la orilla* (2013) have been hailed as 'among the earliest and most profound mediations on the apparent enigmas of Spain's most recent economic and political crisis' (Van Tongeren 2022: 121). *Crematorio* in particular has been described by some as prophetic – its stark depiction of the millionaire property developer Rubén Bertomeu, whose business emporium has been built on greed, violence and destruction – both of the landscape and of those who stand in his way – laying bare the environmentally unsustainable and morally bankrupt nature of the economic, social and political order that led to the global financial crisis, before the 2008 collapse of Lehman Brothers and its worldwide and lasting effects popularised such a view.[3] *Crematorio* is structured in 13 fragments which convey the reactions of several interrelated characters to the death of Matías Bertomeu, the younger brother of millionaire property tycoon

3 In an interview with Ángel Ferrero, Chirbes remarks that, while some reviewers have described his novel as prophetic, he does not agree with that reading; instead, he considers himself simply a witness of the times: '[m]e limité a contar lo que estaba a la vista' (Ferrero 2012: 8).

Rubén. It is significant that death and destruction are central to the text, and are referenced in the title, which alludes to the crematorium where Matías' body will be incinerated, but which has also been read as a symbol for 'una sociedad terminal y decrépita, materialista y envilecida, que ha perdido el norte moral y la esperanza en la capacidad de regenerarse' (Calvo Carilla 2011: 140).

The narrative is fragmentary, combining Rubén's first-person accounts with segments of free indirect speech from the point of view of other characters. The most extensive three fragments, strategically placed at the start, middle and closing of the text, correspond to first-person narration by Rubén, who, upon his brother's death, is compelled to look back at his own life, and reflect upon his trajectory and choices – of which, we learn, his brother, childhood friends and daughter disapproved. The remaining ten fragments, in free indirect speech (with one exception) from the point of view of characters connected to Rubén, feature his daughter Silvia and her husband Juan, who despise Rubén's activities, but are happy to enjoy the privileges derived from them; Mónica, Rubén's youthful second wife, who, we learn at the end of the novel, is expecting a baby; Collado, a former business associate of Rubén, recovering in hospital from a brutal attack seemingly orchestrated by Rubén; Federico Brouard, a novelist and former childhood friend of Rubén's, whom he featured in barely disguised form as the villain in one of his earlier works; and Yuri, a Russian immigrant who works for Russian mafia boss Traian, and whose shady activities occasionally overlap with Rubén's. The result of this juxtaposition of voices is a polyphonic narrative in which, however, all of the characters – including the deceased and therefore absent Matías – appear as profoundly flawed. Chirbes' structural conceit enables readers to contrast each individual's views and self-perception with those of their (supposedly) nearest and dearest, thus undermining the self-justificatory narrative spun by each of them.

Although the narrating time is condensed – the reflections of all characters occur over the morning following Matías' death – the narrated time spans more than five decades, going as far back as Rubén's and Matías' childhood in the early post-war period, as the characters look back at the past they shared with the deceased. This collapsing of narrative time frames not only allows readers to track the evolution of the main characters over time; it also responds to a Benjaminian conception of history as layered, rather than linear. For both Benjamin and Chirbes, the present cannot be entirely dissociated or disentangled from the past, as the past remains latent in the present. Walter Benjamin's influence over Chirbes was acknowledged by Chirbes himself in his essay collection *El novelista perplejo* (2002), and it has proved a productive avenue of enquiry for critics such as López Bernasocchi and López de Abiada (2004), Alonso (2006), Geeroms (2017), Villamía Vidal (2017) and Van Tongeren (2022). However, most readings of Chirbes' work undertaken through the prism of Benjamin focus on the Spanish novelist's treatment of history (Geeroms 2017) and memory (Villamía Vidal 2017); or on the melancholia that permeates his later work (Van Tongeren 2022).

My analysis of *Crematorio* (2007) interrogates the spatial dimension of the novel, focusing on how space, place and landscape interact with memory to produce an unflatteringly accurate portrayal of pre-crisis Spain. My privileging of space in the reading of Chirbes' crisis novels thus follows the work of critics such as Aina Vidal Pérez (2018; 2019), but while Vidal Pérez reads *Crematorio* as primarily a denunciation of 'cómo se arrebató a los lugares de sus significados históricos, afectivos, identificatorios' (2018: 87), I am interested in how the juxtaposition of contemporary and remembered iterations of the same place or landscape (and the gulf or contrast between them) suggests that, even when a landscape is transformed beyond recognition, its past iterations continue to exist in – and haunt – the memory of its inhabitants. Manus O'Dwyer (2022) also proposes a reading of *Crematorio* focusing on space in order to defend the text's status as world-ecological text. His work convincingly argues that Chirbes' novel exploration of 'the complex relationships between the personal and the systematic' (18) justifies its inclusion within an international canon of ecocritical texts. While the work of both critics informs my own, my emphasis is on how space in Chirbes' work is mobilised for its hauntingly evocative qualities – qualities which endure even when (or perhaps precisely because) it has been radically altered.

In the opening pages of the text, for instance, Rubén glimpses one of the beaches of Misent – the fictional coastal town in which all the characters live, which serves as an emblem for any over-developed town on the Valencian coast – and remarks:

> Entre los edificios que se levantan a mi derecha puedo ver las palmeras, el azul del mar, e incluso una delgada línea amarillenta, la playa del Nido. La frecuenté de niño, de adolescente, pero ahora no se me ocurriría poner los pies en ese sitio de aguas dudosamente limpias y siempre atestado de bañistas. Hace muchos años que mi lugar de veraneo es el interior de mi coche, mi playa del Nido particular, no un nido de ave, cálido; más bien, un nido fresco y húmedo, de reptil que hiberna entre las rocas. (Chirbes 2007: 15)

In the lines above, the contemplation of the beach at the time of Matías' death – situated close to the publication of the text in 2007 – leads Rubén to compare this contemporary landscape with that of his childhood, and to implicitly mourn its transformation, even though he is, as we learn in the course of the novel, one of its main architects. The beach of Rubén's childhood is no more, yet it does live on in Rubén's memory, a memory which leads him also to muse, along Lefebvrian lines, on how the changes to the landscape have provoked a modification of his habits, favouring the private, enclosed space of his luxury car over the communal, open space of the beach. The death of Matías invites Rubén to reminisce about their shared childhood and adolescence, and, in so doing, Rubén cannot help but evoke the very different environment in which they grew up: 'nosotros dos ocultos por el laberinto vegetal, oyendo el sordo fragor del viento [...], un mundo que ahora es sólo mío, de nadie más' (2007: 17). Rubén's childhood world is now only his, as the one other person able to remember it, his brother Matías, has died; but it is also only his because the spaces both brothers inhabited have been transformed in a manner that precludes the survival of the types of experiences they had – and therefore, of the types of memories they were able to forge. Playa del Nido, where the young Rubén used to swim, and the childhood home and garden where he played with his brother, no longer exist – at least in their remembered form – and that lack or erasure endows them with a haunting quality – a haunting intensified, in Rubén's case, by his awareness of his own role in their destruction.

While Rubén is undoubtedly the central character of the novel, and personifies the ruthlessly successful capitalist and arch-patriarch, he can also be read along generational lines, as a representative of those who came of age during the Spanish Transition. Olga Bezhanova (2017), for instance, grounds her reading of both Rubén and his brother Matías via the notion of the 'generación bífida' (Haro Tecglen 1988; Labrador Méndez 2017). According to that trope, the *generación de la Transición* that had engaged in anti-Francoist militancy during the regime split into two groups during and after the Transition: those willing to abandon their youthful revolutionary ideals in order to accommodate to the new, institutionally democratic but economically neoliberal order; and those who refused to compromise. Following that interpretative paradigm, Bezhanova suggests that 'Matías's death symbolizes the expiration of an alternative political project that could at least attempt to challenge the consumerist ideology of late capitalism' (2017: 45); whereas the surviving Rubén is an embodiment of the former revolutionary turned cynical free-marketeer – or indeed of the *realpolitik* of a Spanish Socialist Party only too willing to renounce Marxism to get into government.[4] Some of the brothers' peers – particularly the embittered, alcoholic writer Brouard, as well as the prematurely deceased Montoliou, who took his own life – could, like Matías, be seen as representatives of those who refused to renounce their ideals to prosper in the new times, and paid a considerable price for their resistance. Yet such a reading entails a reductive simplification of Chirbes' fictional and moral universe, for neither group is portrayed sympathetically in the text. If Rubén has brought destruction to his native Misent, his antagonists are shown to have put up a pusillanimous, ineffectual struggle – and one that, it is implied in the text, may have amounted more to posturing than to a genuine and principled commitment. For all his interest in ecology, for instance, it is hard to see in Matías the embodiment of 'an alternative political project', as Bezhanova contends, given his earlier political flirtations with the governing Socialist Party (Chirbes 2007: 228), or the fact that he eventually approaches Rubén in order to sell the family's land for development (392). Similarly, any empathy or even admiration the reader may feel towards the ageing Federico Brouard, Rubén's erstwhile friend, is tempered by the unforgiving manner in which his mistreatment of his partner, Javier, is portrayed in the text.

As Marta Sanz (2007) perceptively noted in an early review of the text, by affording Rubén the privilege of first-person narration (his son-in-law, Juan Mullor, does receive the same treatment, but in far more limited form), Chirbes in fact 'coloca al lector del lado del personaje del que nunca querría estar' (online). Sanz also notes that Rubén is the novel's most coherent and vital character – a vitality which Brouard, elsewhere in the text, defines as predicated on predation: 'la salud es el fruto de una cadena de actos de depredación. Eres sano, porque tus antepasados se han comido felizmente a otros' (2007: 306). Once Rubén abandons his youthful ideals, he is able to move on unsentimentally and unapologetically, unlike those who surround him. Germán Labrador similarly remarks on the complexity of Rubén's character, which is greater than that afforded to any of the other figures, when he remarks that

> [s]obre el mismo paisaje de grúas no ven lo mismo los ojos de la memoria, de la tradición literaria, los ojos de Walter Benjamin y los

4 For more on the context of the Transition, see Gregorio Morán's *El precio de la Transición* (1991) or Juan Antonio Andrade Blanco's and Josep Fontana's more recent *El PCE y el PSOE en (la) transición: la evolución ideológica de la izquierda durante el proceso de cambio político* (2012).

> de un constructor sin escrúpulos. La complejidad moral de la novela consiste en que [Rubén] Bertomeu tiene puestos muchos tipos de ojos a la vez. (Labrador 2016: 189)

Chirbes' masterful construction of a character as rich as Rubén – simultaneously the most corrupt and the most lucid figure in *Crematorio* – can be read as an attempt to alert his readers to their own investment in and complicity with neoliberal narratives, as stated in his essay 'La estrategia del boomerang' (2010). Indeed, in an interview with Alfonso Armada, Chirbes admitted that in both *Crematorio* and *En la orilla* 'el lector se enfrenta a cosas que no le hacen ninguna gracia, y que le hablan de sí mismo de un modo no muy gratificante' (2013: online), as both texts present readers with recognisable discursive tropes and familiar attitudes which are unmasked as self-serving, hollow alibis used by the characters to justify or conceal their ideological and existential contradictions. It is thus perhaps not surprising that Rubén's complexity as a character is partly articulated through language and rhetoric – as Bezhanova notes, '[c]ontrasted with Rubén's self-assured use of the first-person narrative, the free, indirect discourse of these [other] characters sounds tentative and shaky' (2017: 48). His engagement with, understanding of and attachment to space, as hinted in Labrador's words above, is the other vector through which Rubén's ambivalence is displayed. Indeed, Rubén's youthful idealism is partly expressed through his choice of career as an architect, and in his initial intention to build social housing, 'la Karl-Marx-Hof mediterránea, con palmeras, buganvillas y galán de noche en el patio; aunque en Misent apenas hubiera obreros, no faltaban los pobres ni las viviendas insalubres' (2007: 224). The title of his abandoned youth project, *Formas para un paisaje de nadie*, on which he embarked with his then friends Brouard and Montoliu, also points to how space – specifically, the local Mediterranean landscape – was perceived by Rubén and his friends as a privileged means through which to explore the surrounding natural environment and the historical past inscribed in it for their latent aesthetic and political possibilities. While the septuagenarian Rubén dismisses that youthful attempt as 'ingenuo' (374), he nonetheless recognises the transformative potential of architecture, in contrast to his scepticism in relation to liberal democracy ('la democracia acaba con la política', 226). And, although Rubén seems oblivious to it – he claims that the 'de nadie' of the project's title was 'un homenaje a nuestra propia angustia existencial' (374) – there is a sharp contrast and obvious irony between the project's name (and aims) and Rubén's professional trajectory: whereas the title proclaimed the local landscape had no owner, Rubén has gone on to purchase most of the region; and he has 'developed' and thus modified – arguably, destroying – the very same territory that had served as anchor and inspiration for his youthful idealism.

This view of the transformative effect of construction echoes Chirbes' diagnosis in relation to his generation, expressed in a 2007 interview with William Nichols:

> ¿quién ha sido el único alfarero del mundo? Es decir, esa generación [de la Transición] que quiso transformar el mundo. De esa gente [ahora] mayor, el único que ha cambiado [el mundo] es el especulador inmobiliario que, precisamente, ha cambiado todo esto mientras que los demás han fracasado; el escritor, el pintor, el político, que acaba siendo un cínico. (Nichols 2008: 224)

Chirbes' words above are echoed in the novel by the ageing novelist Brouard, as he contends that Rubén 'ha sido el único gran alfarero entre nosotros' since he 'ha cambiado el mundo en el que vive, aunque nosotros pensemos que es para peor' (2007: 320). This characterisation of the real estate developer as the only figure with agency to transform the world echoes Lefebvre's contention (2003) that, in late-capitalism, the transformation of physical spaces by the flows of often transnational, liquid capital – to use Bauman's term (2000) – offers privileged insights into the workings and contradictions of capitalism, a view echoed by David Harvey (2000; 2012). Construction and real estate would thus constitute the one area in which real (if also destructive) transformations can and do occur within contemporary Western societies – and those very visible and tangible changes have consequences beyond the spatial, as both urban theorists have demonstrated. Rubén himself remarks on the parallels between building work and capitalism, as he reflects that construction is 'quizás la mejor metáfora del capitalismo. Crecer supone destruir, y de eso no tengo yo la culpa: crecer es no parar de crecer y construir es no parar de destruir' (2007: 409). This insight also explains why Chirbes argued that the novel should not be read as merely a critique of the real estate sector:

> *Crematorio* no quiere ser una denuncia de la corrupción urbanística, eso de la corrupción es solo uno de los temas que circulan por detrás. Lo que se quiere contar aquí es cómo nuestra modernidad, lo que se suponía que íbamos a traer detrás del franquismo, ha dado como fruto esta especie de planta venenosa que nos asfixia. (Hermoso 2011: online)

The novel's denunciation of the political and moral corruption that accompanied Spain's real estate *boom*, and of the resulting environmental degradation, should therefore be read as a broader critique of how late, neoliberal, global capitalism has (mis)shaped contemporary Spanish society.

Vidal Pérez underlines the generational dimension of Chirbes' critique, implicit also in Chirbes' words above, when she states that the novel articulates 'una crítica al capitalismo a través de la metáfora de la construcción pero, sobre todo, una crítica a aquellos con quienes había compartido ideales: al fracaso de una generación' (2018: 15). Other critics have also alluded to the 'culpa generacional' (Sanz 2015: 221), a recurring motif in Chirbes' work.[5] However, the generational dimension seems less clear-cut here than in earlier novels by the same author. Rubén and Matías roughly belong to the same generational cohort as Chirbes – namely, those who came of age during the *Transición*. The next generation, raised in a democratic Spain, and represented by Rubén's daughter Silvia and her husband Juan, are, if anything, portrayed even more negatively than their elders. Juan's diagnosis in this respect is as clear as it is damning, when he states, addressing Federico, a further representative of the older, Transition generation: '[v]osotros equivocasteis el camino. Nosotros no hemos tenido intención de ir a ninguna parte' (2007: 314). Their elders may have abandoned their ideals, or failed to realise them, but Juan and his peers have reached middle age apathetically, lacking the principles and courage to attempt any form of change.

Silvia, Rubén's only daughter, despises her father's activities, and mourns their effects on contemporary Misent, which she describes, in terms reminiscent of Harvey's allusion to the Disneyfication of historical European cities, as '[u]na especie de inocuo parque temático, un estúpido lugar de vacación' (2007: 90), in contrast with

> el Misent de su infancia, el de las playas casi desiertas en las que el mar dejaba conchas, estrellas de mar, hipocampos, esponjas secas, y que olía a hierbas marinas que se pudrían, a algas que se secaban al sol, a pescado en putrefacción; olor de yodo, de salitre; texturas languidecientes entre lo sólido y lo líquido [...]: ese Misent ya no existe; lo han sustituido todas esas casas en construcción, las plumas de las grúas cruzando el aire, las calles a medio asfaltar. (2007: 91–92)

Silvia's reminiscences of the Misent of her childhood echo Rubén's own memories in content and in tone. Both characters mourn the loss of 'una forma de vida que teníamos' (91) – a form of life connected to a specific place and landscape (the Spanish Mediterranean coast), but also to a specific time (their childhoods in the 1940s and 1970s, respectively). Both characters'

5 Guilt is a central trope to Chirbes' narrative, and it is often framed in both generational and trans- or inter-generational terms. For example, two earlier novels by Chirbes, *La buena letra* (1992) and *Los disparos del cazador* (1994), were re-released together under the eloquent title *Pecados originales* (2013).

melancholic memories of the lost landscape are evocative of the notion of solastalgia, defined by Glenn Albrecht as 'the pain and desolation that human beings suffer as they contemplate the degradation of the natural landscape with which they identify and which they consider part of their identity and life' (Albrecht 2005: 44). Albrecht's work seeks to bring to light the damaging mental health effects derived from environmental degradation, in contexts in which those affected are local populations with no direct agency or decision-making power over the transformations occurring in their areas. In contrast, Rubén is the literal architect of many of the changes which have transformed Misent, something which he acknowledges, and appears to accept as the prize for his wealth. Silvia, however, feigns innocence and is a vocal and, at times, fierce critic of Rubén – at one point comparing his role in erasing the specificity of Misent to that of Nazi architect Albert Speer (2007: 181). Yet she is not in the least conflicted by the privileges afforded to her by her father's vast fortune, which take the form of regular cheques and lavish gifts (2007: 21) that allow her to live well beyond her means. In their readiness to claim such advantages as practically a birth right, while hypocritically clinging to an illusory moral high ground, Silvia and Juan in fact emerge as more despicable than the ruthless Rubén. Chirbes himself stated that

> [s]iempre me cae mejor el cazador que el que se come la caza y denuncia al cazador, que son los hijos de los disparos del cazador. [...] Siempre me cae mejor Torquemada con sus contradicciones, sus trampas y sus barullos, que no toda la familia del Águila, impoluta, pero que vive a espaldas y a costa suya, y encima se avergüenza de él. Me parece eso bastante más deleznable y repulsivo. (Armada 2013: online)

In the quote above, Chirbes mobilises the metaphor of the hunter, in an allusion to his earlier novel *Los disparos del cazador* (1994), and refers to Galdós' Torquemada as a referent for both the patriarch of that novel and for Rubén Bertomeu, thus making his judgement extensive to the characters of *Crematorio*.[6] It is therefore by no means obvious that Chirbes' critique is limited to the shortcomings of his own generation; rather, given the already-discussed hypocrisy and pusillanimity of their children's generation,

6 Chirbes repeatedly pointed to Galdós' *Torquemada* novels, whose eponymous protagonist is an exploitative money lender despised by his contemporaries, as an inspiration in his construction of the character of Rubén (cf. Hermoso 2011; Barjau and Parellada 2013). La Celestina, with her ability to deftly use both the codes of the aristocracy and those of the lower classes for her own benefit, constitutes a further referent, discussed at length in Llamas Martínez 2021.

and the quasi-nihilistically voracious hedonism of their grandchildren's, epitomised by Silvia's teenage, materialistic, cocaine-consuming daughter Miriam, the text reads rather like a powerful indictment against contemporary Spanish society as a whole.

Vidal Pérez proposes that 'el gran protagonista de la novela es Misent, que funciona como prototipo de ciudad turística valenciana' (2018: 4), although she goes on to concede that the town functions 'como una suerte de proyección metonímica de Rubén, y se podrá constatar cómo la evolución del personaje correrá paralela a la del paisaje costero' (5). Taking this interpretation one step further, it is possible to read both Misent's transformation from sleepy, pre-modern Mediterranean village to global, postmodern Disneyfied holiday park and Rubén's trajectory from left-leaning idealist to arch-capitalist as symbolic of Spain's evolution over the second half of the twentieth century and into the inaugural years of the twenty-first.[7] Given the degradation of place (Misent) and character (Rubén) over time portrayed in the novel, *Crematorio* has been read as offering 'una visión desengañada de la realidad, teñida de senequismo y nihilismo' (Calvo Carilla 2011: 144), and thus risking 'desagradar a los lectores que creen que todavía quedan motivos para la esperanza y para la lucha, y también a aquéllos que se niegan a ver la podredumbre que diariamente desfila por delante de sus ojos' (Sanz 2007: online). Carlos Van Tongeren ponders whether the melancholia that permeates the text might 'lead to a state of reassuring stasis that makes it harder to imagine the insecure times lying ahead' (2022: 134). In other words, the seemingly hopeless pessimism of the novel could induce a state of demoralised and somewhat self-complacent passivity or resignation in readers, discouraging protest and contestation.

Other critics have offered more positive readings of Chirbes' work: Olga Bezhanova, for instance, suggests that in both *Crematorio* and *En la orilla*,

7 It would be tempting to set the point of inflection here at the end of General Franco's dictatorship and the start of the Transition process, given those events feature prominently in Chirbes' literary oeuvre as a whole, and since Franco's death in 1975 has often been used as a point of departure in historiographical accounts as marking both the start of the Transition and a new era in Spain. However, work by authors such as Pavlović (2011), Moreno-Caballud (2015b) and Fernández-Cebrián (2023) shows that the changes to Spain's socio-economic model – which would decisively condition the scope for transformation that could be enacted during the Transition process – occurred earlier, with the adoption by the Franco regime of a *desarrollista* (i.e. decisively capitalist and consumerist) and *aperturista* (i.e. global) framework. Given the insights of these critics, and since the narrated time in *Crematorio* goes as far back as the 1950s, it seems justified to establish my point of departure then, rather than during the Transition – even if the latter enabled an acceleration of the processes set in motion during the dictatorship.

Chirbes 'attempts to indicate if not a path out of the current predicament, then, at least, a possibility that such a path will one day be found' (2017: 43), and goes on to argue that in *Crematorio*, specifically, through the figure of Rubén's son-in-law Juan, a professor of literature, literary criticism emerges as 'a space for quiet reflection from which a vision of an alternative may one day arise' (51). While the very gesture of writing and publishing *Crematorio* contradicts Calvo Carilla's argument that in the text 'ni existe ya un potencial código motriz que justifique el impulso de iluminar el mundo, ni siquiera una realidad social digna de ser considerada como materia novelable' (2011: 144), it is no less true that the view of literature and culture mediated by the text is ambivalent at best. Juan Mullor, for instance, is less optimistic about his own work than Bezhanova, describing literary critics as

> un capricho que se pagan las sociedades ricas y que a las pobres ni siquiera se les ocurre plantearse. Somos putas, flores de loto que se abren sobre la charca maloliente de la opulencia; brindamos un entretenimiento un poco más refinado que el que ofrecen las chicas al borde de la carretera (también menos intenso). (2007: 110)

The fact that the closest the novel comes to a vindication of the role of culture is undertaken by Rubén – for him, '[c]ultura es lo que levanta del suelo la mirada del hombre y lo lleva a descubrir el horizonte' (286) – is significant, as it reaffirms Juan's diagnosis that the primary role of culture in contemporary societies is to inspire, please and appease those who occupy positions of power, rather than to attempt or enact any form of social transformation. Yet Chirbes has elsewhere expressed his own conviction in the transformative power of certain forms of literature – specifically, of those texts which engage with history and offer alternative viewpoints to official narratives – even if such a change happens only at the individual level of the reader, who is prompted or forced by the text to change his or her point of view (Armada 2013: online). Juan's self-deprecatory description of his role as critic, and of the role of culture more broadly, thus contrasts with Chirbes' own views and praxis – a contrast that can be understood as an ironic move on Chirbes' part to 'de-sacralise' literature. As he explains, in his work

> hay también una ironía sobre los códigos. Por qué hemos decidido que los escritores son la cultura, que hemos decidido que es estupenda, y ser un fontanero es una mierda. Pues no, mire, usted, sin *El Quijote* puede usted vivir, pero sin un fontanero que le arregle la casa cuando se le escape la tubería, no. [...] Uno de los temas de mi novela es el respeto al trabajo. (Armada 2013: online)

Germán Labrador similarly remarks on the centrality of manual labour in Chirbes' fiction – a category to which writing would also belong, but which, in *Crematorio*, takes the form of a vindication of brickwork: 'qué belleza es el ladrillo bien trabajado [...], lleva las huellas de las manos que lo colocaron' (405). For Labrador, such forms of manual labour can be read as representative of 'una lógica económica que no es la de la acumulación y sus violencias' (2015: 233). His conclusion expands Bezhanova's, explaining, in the process, the irony with which literary criticism is treated in *Crematorio*. His words also remark on how Chirbes' valorisation of artisanal, manual work – whether plumbing, bricklaying or writing – is predicated upon a belief that human creativity and effort can transform raw matter, allowing it to transcend (or, at least, outlast) human existence. And, what is perhaps more important for a self-proclaimed materialist such as Chirbes, certain forms of manual labour can and do continue to exist beyond circuits of capitalist production, and thus manage to elude or resist the seemingly all-pervasive logic of the market.

Following from that interpretation, then, in the case of *Crematorio*, Chirbes uses language as a raw material to successfully construct different characters; to place us, as readers, in their shoes (Navarro 2008: 158). But language does not only serve the purposes of characterisation: it also (re) creates a familiar landscape – the Mediterranean coastline – which has been radically transformed in recent decades. While Rubén and Silvia mourn the demise of the Misent of their respective childhoods, even though they have personally profited from its transformation, Brouard, a vocal critic of Rubén's work, nevertheless lucidly notes how '[a]hora se machaca sobre todo el paisaje, entonces se machacaba la vida humana, los estómagos, las pieles, los cerebros' (2007: 318). His observation not only counters Silvia's and Rubén's self-complacent nostalgia for a lost landscape, as it brings to light the misery that existed within it; it also points to the continuity between the exploitation of humans in the post-war period and during the dictatorship, and the contemporary exploitation of the land through real estate development. Again, in a manner reminiscent of the work of Lefebvre and Harvey, physical space is identified as the 'last bastion' to be conquered and abused for profit by late-stage capitalism.

However, the rapid transformation of Misent has not entirely erased its previous incarnation(s), which live on in the memory of the characters. Indeed, the radical modifications to the landscape seem to have endowed it with a haunting or spectral quality, as they incite Rubén and Silvia to remember – or, rather, to mentally (re)create and mourn – their surroundings as they were at different moments in their lives. Vidal Pérez argues that in *Crematorio*, 'pérdida de la historia y pérdida del espacio caminan de la mano'

(2018: 14); yet, while it is inarguable that the novel presents a depressing and damning socio-political and environmental portrayal of contemporary Spain, the text's deft interlinking of space, memory and history through language offers a glimmer of hope. The destruction of the landscape does not entail the erasure of Rubén's and Silvia's memories; rather, it makes them more persistent. And while individual memories are, by definition, partial and finite, Chirbes' work testifies to the capacity of writing to explore and uncover the different temporal layers, the sediment, underlying the narrative spaces inhabited by his characters, thus affirming the potential of writing to resist the destructive drive inherent to a capitalist model of economic growth based on unbridled urban development. Writing may be powerless to stop the wild, uncontrolled speculation portrayed in *Crematorio*, and which took place in Spain in the years before 2008. Yet the final scene in the text, entitled 'Estampa invernal de Misent', prefigures the disaster about to befell the country, bearing witness to the potential of Chirbes' literary realism to not only portray, but also to lucidly diagnose – ahead of mainstream economists and politicians – social ills and the threats they pose. In that closing scene, a detached, unnamed observer describes the bleak, deserted beach of Misent on a winter's night. The observations here present the landscape in quasi-pathological terms, with the sand dunes likened to tumour-like 'manchas blanquecinas sobre un fondo de radiografía' (414) and the sea compared to a 'mancha espesa, como de brea' (415). The almost deadly stillness of the scene is suggestive of the calm that precedes a storm – and from that stillness, which Van Tongeren, following Benjamin, reads as melancholic deceleration (2022), emerges the smell of old carrion, pointing to the death drive inherent to contemporary capitalist societies – and to individuals caught in the elusive pursuit of fulfilment within a framework that places ever increasing demands (in terms of both productivity and consumption) on them. The motif of carrion recurs in the opening of the second title in Chirbes' crisis diptych, *En la orilla*, where, as we will see, it occupies a more prominent place.[8]

8 The motif of carrion is one of the features that has led several critics to characterise *Crematorio* as a Baroque, or at least Baroque-inspired, work. Germán Labrador describes the text as a 'monumento funeral al eros neobarroco' (2015: 27), Marta Sanz refers to it as a 'bodegón barroco' (2014: 220), while Van Tongeren suggests the novel could be read as a Baroque emblem book (2022: 127).

En la orilla (2013)

Completed in the summer of 2012, whilst Spain was being bailed out by its Eurozone partners, Chirbes' second crisis novel presents a markedly different mood and landscape to that of *Crematorio*. While in the earlier novel death and decay are recurring themes – the death of Matías is the catalyst that invites the characters' reminiscences, and the destruction of the local landscape of Misent is repeatedly alluded to – in *En la orilla* these motifs become all-pervasive. The difference in emphasis is reflected in the change in setting: *Crematorio* takes place in the fictional coastal town of Misent and its surrounding areas; whereas *En la orilla* is set in the equally fictional Olba, situated a few kilometres inland from Misent, and, significantly, located next to marshland. The contrast between Olba's swamp and the nearby sea in Misent is articulated explicitly early on in *En la orilla*, as Esteban, the protagonist, notes how '[e]l mar limpia, oxigena, el pantano pudre. Como la guerra, la comisaría y la cárcel' (2013: 42). From the outset, then, the swamp is associated with decay and corruption through the use of the verb 'pudre', and with violence, repression and confinement via its association with war and imprisonment. While the move from *Crematorio*'s seaside to the inland marsh of *En la orilla* is indicative of a change in tone, as the later text presents the reader with an even more desolate panorama, throughout this novel there is also an undermining, or at least a questioning, of the distinction between sea and swamp. In spite of Esteban's initial diagnosis, which identifies the sea with cleanliness and renewal and the swamp with decay and corruption, in his final reflections, he notes how the distinction between the two is perhaps illusory, as the sea in fact feeds the marsh ('el mar se adentraba [en el pantano] formando un arco', 421). As well as attesting to Chirbes' awareness of the interlinked and interdependent relationship existing between seemingly distinct ecosystems, the problematisation of the binary sea–swamp can also be read allegorically, as a recognition that the apparently prosperous façade of capitalist development, represented here by the sea and the town of Misent, simultaneously relies on and feeds the wasteland of the swamp at Olba. Chirbes himself commented on the importance and centrality of the marsh, explaining that

> [l]o único que tuve claro es que tenía que empezar en un pantano. Toda la trasera del Mediterráneo ha sido un pantano que se ha ido desecando y en algunos sitios ha permanecido. Me parece que era la otra cara frente al desarrollismo. Por una parte la permanencia y por otra la degradación. (Corominas i Julián 2013: online)

If the swamp of *En la orilla* serves as the obverse to the sea in *Crematorio*, then Esteban, the central character in the second novel, can be read as a photographic negative to *Crematorio*'s Rubén Bertomeu: both men belong to the same generation, but while Rubén succeeds as a businessman thanks to his ruthless ambition, Esteban apathetically resigns himself to working as a carpenter in the small, family-run business; while Rubén becomes a towering patriarch – father to middle-aged Silvia, a father-like figure to his associate Collado and about to welcome a son into the world – Esteban remains beholden to his frail, elderly father and never marries or has children – his one opportunity for procreation scuppered by his lover Leonor, who chooses to terminate the pregnancy. Rubén is wealthy and financially secure (we can assume this remains the case even in the post-2008 context, given the extent of his affluence), whereas Esteban's one belated attempt to improve his financial situation ends in ruin. Significantly, Rubén is the descendant of those who won the Spanish Civil War, whereas Esteban's father is a defeated (and, according to Esteban at least, embittered) Republican. A similar contrast emerges in *En la orilla* between Esteban and his childhood friend Francisco Marsal, the son of a Falangist who profited financially from his participation in the violent reprisals meted out against Republicans during the dictatorship – and from the impunity the *Transición* conferred upon him and his successors. While Esteban has lost everything due to an ill-timed investment decision, Francisco enjoys a leisurely retirement in his yacht and mansion-like home.

As in *Crematorio*, the narrating time is fairly condensed, with events unfolding between 14 and 26 December 2010, yet the narrated time is expansive, as the different narrative instances reflect on their respective pasts. A further similarity with the earlier novel lies in the changes in narrative voice or point of view, although these are far less frequent in *En la orilla* – an authorial choice which results in a slowing down of the narrative pace, probably intended to reflect the deceleration provoked by the 2008 crisis. The novel is divided into three chapters: a brief opening, 'El hallazgo', a third-person narration focalised in the figure of Ahmed Ouallahi, an immigrant formerly employed by Esteban; a main middle section, 'Localización de exteriores', comprising more than 400 pages, and delivered largely as first-person narration by Esteban, although complemented by other voices; and a short closing segment entitled 'Éxodo' consisting of first-person narration from the point of view of Tomás Pedrós, the property developer who has caused Esteban's ruin. The first chapter, dated 26 December 2010, stands as a prolepsis to the novel's central section, as Ahmed makes the gruesome discovery of a human arm, and other suspected human remains, in the swamp; the middle section, which opens on 14 December of the same year, is concerned with Esteban's preparations for his own death, and the death of his nonagenarian father and pet dog, in the wake of their financial ruin; and the final scene sees Pedrós at an airport, about to flee the country – and his creditors. While the longest, central chapter is mostly first-person narration from Esteban, detailing his plans to end his life and those of the members of his household at the swamp, and exposing the circumstances that have led him to take this decision, his enunciation is interrupted by fragments of first-person narration from characters who have been affected by his bankruptcy, such as his former employees Julio and Joaquín, the wife of ex-foreman Álvaro, and Liliana, the Colombian immigrant who Esteban employed to help care for his elderly father.

Esteban's father, who, as Geeroms notes, remains nameless (2017: 755) and seems incapable of speaking, is nonetheless given a voice through the transcription, in the middle section of the novel, of a series of annotations made by him, decades earlier, on the back of a calendar for the year 1960.[9] The inscriptions, introduced by a third-person narrator who explains that no-one, not even Esteban, has read them (2013: 342), undermine Esteban's own characterisation of his father as a distant, bitter man responsible for his son's failures. According to Esteban, in other calendar notes written by his father which he has read, the lack of references to family members or significant events (births, deaths) is symptomatic of his father's haughty stance towards his wife and children: 'Somos lo privado, que es deplorable, que te ata y te pone a ras de tierra [...]' (2013: 164). Yet in the inscriptions featured in the novel, the father does write about his family – even if he acknowledges his feelings of estrangement towards them, as they have been able to adapt to the post-war context of dictatorship, whereas he has not. More importantly, perhaps, the annotations provide us, as readers, with glimpses of a subjectivity shaped by pessimism, in line with his son's descriptions, but also traversed by a tenderness and a thoughtfulness which Esteban does not acknowledge.

As was the case in *Crematorio*, *En la orilla* lacks a plot in the conventional sense of the term. In the earlier novel, we are presented with the thoughts, memories and reflections of a cast of characters in the aftermath of the death of a loved one. There was no conflict or challenge to be overcome by the protagonists, no mystery to be resolved, no lesson to be learned, no denouement in the usual sense of the term. Similarly, in *En la orilla*, the reader is made aware, from early on in the second chapter, that the human

9 Maarten Geeroms sees in this choice of the calendar – an everyday, popular culture element – as the space for the father's annotations a nod to Walter Benjamin's appreciation of such objects (2017: 758).

remains found by Ahmed correspond to Esteban, his father and their dog. Chirbes thus eschews suspense; as he himself explained, the novel

> [e]s un libro que no tiene trama, porque cada vez me interesa menos la trama. La trama es una dictadura, lo decía Benet... En esta novela hay voces, luego un río central, que es el personaje, y yo quise desde el principio que fuera como un concertante, donde las distintas voces tuvieran el mismo tono y formaran un coro que contara lo único que me interesa contar, que es lo que está pasando. (Berasategui 2013: online)

Interestingly, the character of Esteban is likened by Chirbes, in yet another water-based metaphor, to a river, inasmuch as it is through him that the different narrative instances are connected, and flow cohesively. The comparison also highlights the centrality of character, place and memory to the novel as the axes used by Chirbes in order to construct a narrative that is simultaneously an *estampa* – imprint or emblem – of crisis Spain and an elucidation of the historical roots of the downturn, which also help explain its uneven effects on the different figures in the text.

The reference to carrion in the closing lines of *Crematorio* and its recurrence in the opening fragment of *En la orilla* seamlessly links both texts, as Van Tongeren points out (2022: 127); and it is also indicative of an intensification of the degradation connoted by the term, as the carrion is merely smelt in the first novel, yet appears in plain sight before Ahmed in the second. A further connection between the two texts can be found in the description of the landscape: in *Crematorio*, the nocturnal sea is described as 'resplandeciente con un fulgor de colada de acero' (2007: 414), while the pool of the swamp at the outset of *En la orilla* 'parecía una colada de acero blanco' (2013: 26). In both instances, the water is associated with a process of industrial production (steel casting) in a manner that dispels any illusion as to the 'naturalness' of the landscape, and which is also suggestive of the ways in which our gazes are shaped by an industrialised/productivist imaginary. This problematisation of the very notion of an original, pristine, 'untouched' natural environment finds echo elsewhere in the novel, as Esteban, for instance, remarks how '[l]lamamos naturaleza a formas de artificio que precedieron a las nuestras, no nos paramos a distinguir que los paisajes no son eternos, han estado y están – como nosotros – condenados a dejar de ser, no siempre más despacio que nosotros mismos.' (101). Esteban's views, which Sanz sees, at least in part, as a projection of Chirbes' own (2015: 215), throw into question, or at least nuance, some of the ecocritical readings (O'Dwyer 2022; Vidal Pérez 2019) that Chirbes' work has invited. For, while both of his crisis novels critically portray the environmental degradation resulting from the pre-2008 real estate boom in Spain, and from the subsequent bust, Chirbes' work is rooted in a materialist and humanist, rather than a post-humanist, tradition. Indeed, Esteban refers dismissively to TV nature programmes which 'muestran con beatería los paisajes que supuestamente el hombre aún no ha destruido' in an effort 'por convertir en poco menos que un paraíso o en un precioso parque natural lo que conocí' (2013: 72). His own memory of his environment in the years before the construction boom starkly contrasts with the idealised view projected by such television shows, as he recalls the insalubrity and poverty that afflicted the area. Through such utterances – we may think also of Brouard's reference, in *Crematorio*, to the exploitation of human bodies that preceded the exploitation of the landscape – Chirbes avoids the risk of utopian retro-projection latent in some environmental discourses: the striving for an illusory prior state of ecological 'purity'. Through Esteban's scepticism towards seemingly progressive environmentalist discourses which privilege the protection of the natural world over human concerns, as he muses on how 'ahora [...] el animal humano es el menos protegido de la creación' (43), and how '[l]os pecados de los pistoleros [...] los absolvió la Transición, al parecer eran pecados veniales, mientras que los pecados contra el medio ambiente no prescriben' (44), Chirbes alerts us to the naïvely nostalgic and dangerously reactionary implications of the longing for a utopian past that never was.

In fact, the *pantano* is valued by Esteban precisely for its impurity: 'la insalubridad, la fetidez, lo ayudan a mantenerse intacto, preservan su inocencia, o lo redimen, y constituyen su peculiar forma de pureza' (375). Whereas Esteban's perception of the sea nearby has changed over time – a change that he believes may be linked to a diminishing of his sensorial abilities due to age, but which the reader will associate with the large-scale developments that have taken place along the coast, the swamp 'continúa idéntico a sí mismo en su degradación, yo lo veo idéntico, el que tengo ante los ojos, como el que recuerdo; lo huelo como entonces' (415). The despoiled marsh landscape is prized by Esteban on at least two levels: as a repository of counter-hegemonic memories, as, during the post-war period, the area was populated by *maquis*; and as a reminder of human ignominy, as it became the hunting grounds for regime sympathisers who hounded out the Republicans hidden in the area. That process, described as 'una mezcla de estrategia militar, venganza política y rapiña económica' (98), as the 'hunters' were rewarded for their services with land plots around the marsh, which they proceeded to drain and cultivate, illustrates the connections between political repression and violence and economic prosperity established after the Spanish Civil War, and which would remain unchallenged during and after the Transition. In an interview published shortly after the publication of *En la orilla*, Chirbes insisted on this idea, rhetorically asking '¿Tras la guerra civil hay alguna fortuna legítima? Ninguna. Porque las que las han mantenido ha sido por connivencia y los que se han enriquecido a la primera ha sido por expropiaciones, por contratas, por subcontratas. No hay riqueza inocente' (Armada 2013: online).

The association of the swamp with basic human (and animal) drives – hunger, violence, greed, sex – is further reinforced by its contemporary role as a site for the sex trade, as a dumping ground for toxic waste and weapons, and through its continued use, over centuries, as a fishing and hunting ground, whether for the purposes of mere survival or for sport. Following Labrador, the marsh can be read as a physical manifestation of 'aquello que se necesita que permanezca invisible para que pueda seguir sosteniendo lo visible' (2015: 32), that is, of the structural violence underpinning the capitalist order. Labrador's characterisation echoes Michel Foucault's definition of heterotopia as a space which has

> the curious property of being in relation with all the other sites, but in such a way as to suspect, neutralize, or invert the set of relations that they happen to designate, mirror, or reflect. These spaces, as it were, which are linked with all the others, which however contradict all the other sites [...]. (1986: 24)

It should be noted that Foucault ascribes these qualities to both utopias and heterotopias. However, utopias are not physical spaces, but projections; whereas heterotopias do have a material existence. Within Foucault's categorisation, the swamp constitutes a heterotopia of deviation, that is, a space 'in which individuals whose behaviour is deviant in relation to the required mean or norm are placed' (1986: 25).[10] In the case of the marsh, it was inhabited by the ideologically non-conforming (Republicans) during the post-war period; and it now shelters the economically deviant (the unemployed, such as Ahmed, or those working in the informal economy, such as sex workers). In terms of its function in relation to other spaces, the swamp acts as a heterotopia of illusion, as it 'exposes every real space [...]

10 Foucault divided heterotopias into different categories. As well as heterotopias of deviation (which, he writes, are the most common type in our societies), he acknowledges also the existence of heterotopias of crisis, which, however, he notes are becoming rarer. Heterotopias of crisis are spaces where those undergoing a moment of existential transition or change would be placed – for instance, specially designated places for teenage initiation rites, for menstruating or pregnant women, or for the elderly.

as still more illusory' (1986: 27). In rendering visible the social exclusion of undocumented migrants, the exploitation of the poor and vulnerable, and the environmental degradation on which wealth accumulation is predicated within globalised capitalist systems, the *pantano* forces us to confront the less savoury, normally concealed aspects of our society, pointing to the illusory nature of notions such as 'prosperity', 'development' and 'welfare'. This reading of the swamp as a heterotopia of illusion, coupled with its radical otherness – a feature which, following Harvey (2012), precludes its gentrification and marketisation – allows a more hopeful reading of the marsh. While far from a hospitable place – indeed, it is precisely its degraded and inhospitable nature that have allowed it to resist commodification – the swamp's role in collecting and preserving discarded materials (and individuals) testifies to the fault lines in hegemonic narratives of the past and the present, to the stubborn resilience to assimilation of certain (admittedly peripheral or marginalised) by-products of capitalism, and to the possibility of retrieving memories and practices that had been side-lined or forgotten.

If the swamp symbolises the stubborn persistence of objects, persons and memories discarded by the hegemonic order, the function of words as memory repositories is also explicitly alluded to by Esteban in the text:

> En Misent, sin ir más lejos, hay urbanizaciones junto a la playa que se llaman La Laguna, Las Balsas, Saladar o El Marjal, y cuyos vecinos se quejan de que se les inundan las casas cada vez que llega la gota fría de otoño. Pero a quién se le ocurre comprarse un bungalow en un sitio que se llama así. Los nombres de los lugares guardan la memoria de lo que fueron. Barrizales. Charcas. Fangales. Balsas para la explotación de la sal. (2013: 43)

The earlier incarnations of the landscape of Misent are shown in this quote to live on in language, in the names chosen for some of the new real estate developments, which reference their previous form. Indeed, Esteban's words point to the mnemonic insistence or persistence of both the names given to the new developments, and of the places themselves, which display a proclivity to regress to their earlier incarnations as flooded bogs or mudflats, in spite of developers' efforts to transform these spaces. A parallelism is therefore drawn between words (or language, more broadly) and physical space: in both instances, in spite of (or perhaps because of?) their apparent plasticity, territories that had been ostensibly drained, treated and 'gained' for development – and words which had been co-opted and re-signified – are shown to contain a potential kernel of resistance that can lead to the resurfacing of seemingly erased qualities under certain (climatic, historical) conditions.

This connection between the marsh and language is elaborated further in the text through the metaphor of nourishment. Germán Labrador (2015) reads *En la orilla* primarily through the tropes of proteins and cannibalism: the swamp reveals that the proteins humans require – given that, in Esteban's words, '[l]a vida humana es el mayor derroche económico de la naturaleza' (2013: 30) – have to be procured through violent acts: the hunting and killing of animals and the cannibalistic exploitation of fellow humans. This conviction, voiced through Brouard in *Crematorio*, that human survival and wellbeing rely on acts of predation, does not, however, lead to moral relativism or nihilism, but can instead be read as an ethical injunction. In this regard, we might think of Esteban's uncle's statement that 'un pescador, un cazador, tienen que convertirse ellos mismos en la pieza que capturan, pensar como ellas. Por eso el verdadero cazador, el pescador de verdad, se enamora de su víctima: se está cazando a sí mismo' (51). The acknowledgement of the depletion of natural resources required to sustain human lives and communities is thus accompanied by a call for radical empathy with both human and non-human beings. (Self-)awareness and empathy thus emerge as two key vectors that can help temper human covetousness – and thus human destructiveness. Yet the role of the swamp is not just symbolic or pedagogical: it is also a place that directly contributes to fulfil the dietary needs of characters over time – from the post-war Republicans who hid within its confines, to their disenfranchised families, to contemporary figures such as the unemployed Ahmed. The marshland therefore nourishes those at the margins literally as well as symbolically. Language, meanwhile, is also described in the text as having an analogous nourishing function, as Esteban muses on its role in relation to his father: '[l]o alimentaban nuestras palabras. Ahora ya sé que las palabras nutren' (98). In this quote, Esteban is referring to the nourishing effect on his father of the accounts by his wife and children of the violence and repression meted out by those on the winning side of the Civil War on dissidents. The information procured by those around him fed the father's resentment, ensuring he remained firm in his Republican convictions, in a manner that evokes Chirbes' contention that 'Walter Benjamin sabía que la legitimidad está en la permanencia del rencor por una injusticia que se cometió en el pasado y que la lucha por la legitimidad es la lucha por apropiarse de la injusticia del pasado' (2002: 29). Chirbes thus vindicates, via Benjamin and in his construction of the figure of Esteban's father in *En la orilla*, the legitimacy of resentment in the face of injustice. Such 'permanencia del recor' is guaranteed in the novel by the inalterability of the swamp and through the power of language to articulate counter-narratives, or reframe hegemonic ones.

This legitimate resentment in the face of injustice is not only vindicated through the setting and through language; it is also embodied in the figure of the father, who represents the historical injustice towards those on the losing side of the Civil War; and in other working-class figures, who are shown to be far more vulnerable to the effects of the 2008 crisis and the ensuing austerity policies than those who most benefitted from the boom years, such as Esteban's friend Francisco Marsal or the fugitive real estate developer Tomás Pedrós. Readers are granted an insight into the plight of regular workers through the incorporation of first-person narrative segments from two of Esteban's erstwhile employees, Julio and Joaquín, now struggling to make ends meet. The wives of both Joaquín and Álvaro are also granted first-person narrative segments but, significantly, Álvaro – Esteban's longest-standing employee, considered by the father a part of the family – is not given a voice. As Carlos Van Tongeren writes in relation to the silence of Esteban's father, the absence of Álvaro's voice suggests 'that there may be complex political and personal reasons for which some voices may be working towards their own destruction, while those of other characters are clamorous and rightly available' (2022: 133). Readers can therefore only know of Álvaro's reaction to the news of his sacking through Esteban's account, which underlines Álvaro's stupor and rage (Chirbes 2013: 230–44), leading Esteban to reflect:

> Descubro la persistencia de lo que Francisco y yo hubiéramos llamado en otros momentos la lucha de clases. Pero no puede ser: la lucha de clases se difuminó, se disolvió, la democracia ha sido un disolvente social [...]. [...] Pero, de repente, desde hace un par de años, parece que se palpa la reconstrucción de un orden más explícito, menos insidioso. Es visible el nuevo orden, arriba y abajo claros [...].' (246)

Interestingly, the notion of persistence – in this case, of the class struggle – is invoked once again in Esteban's words above. For him, the 2008 crisis and its effects have done away with the illusion, promoted during the years of Francoist *desarrollismo* and reinforced during the democratic period, of Spain as a prosperously classless (or, at least, mesocratic) society. While Esteban's employees respond differently to their new situation of unemployment, thus undermining the notion of class-based collective struggle and solidarity, Esteban's awareness of the insurmountable gulf that separates them from those at the top has the potential to feed the legitimate resentment of the increasing number of people disenfranchised as a result of the 2008 crisis.

The ability to weather the 2008 downturn is connected, within the novel, to the characters' prior trajectory, which is linked, in turn, to the outcome of the Spanish Civil War: Esteban and Álvaro are both children of the defeated and now face financial hardship (or absolute ruin, in Esteban's case), whereas Francisco Marsal, the Falangist's son, remains unaffected. Chirbes, however, does not propose a deterministic framework: not all characters on the losing side of the war are shown to fail; and the inclusion of younger and migrant characters, with no direct memory of the war or the dictatorship, adds nuance and complexity – and, of course, realism – to the novel's universe. However, the passive, silent and thus arguably somewhat spectral presence of Esteban's father, as well as Esteban's own reflections about Olba's past, serve to historicise Spain's recent past and present. This allows Chirbes to implicitly question the Transition consensus, which enabled the survival of continuities between dictatorship and democracy while ensuring such continuities remained hidden from public view, through the so-called 'pacto del olvido'. The 2008 crisis was, of course, a global phenomenon, but Chirbes demonstrates, through his two crisis novels, how its distinctive local features – among them, the extent and severity of its effects on the general population – can only be understood through an engagement with the country's recent history.

The closing segment of the novel, barely ten pages long, is entitled 'Éxodo', in an ironical nod to the eponymous biblical text, and it insists on the centrality of appearance and discourse in shaping perception, albeit from a different point of view. In first-person narration, Tomás Pedrós, the real estate developer who has defrauded Esteban, reminisces on the good times of Spain's construction boom while waiting to board a plane that will take him to an undisclosed foreign country. While the fragment, unlike the two preceding chapters, is not dated, we can assume it takes places synchronously, in or around December 2010, and that Pedrós is in fact leaving Spain to avoid prosecution, as his flight is mentioned in the central chapter of the novel. In this closing section, a further connection is established with *Crematorio*, as Pedrós recalls a meeting, in the years before the crisis, with an unnamed developer who readers of the earlier novel will nonetheless be able to identify as Ramón Collado, Rubén Bertomeu's former associate. The fragment opens with an extensive enumeration of the delicacies on offer at an event attended by both Pedrós and Collado during the times of prosperity, which functions as one of several signifiers of excessive consumption (luxury brand items, cocaine and paid-for sexual services complete the picture) mobilised in the chapter to characterise the mood in the country during the years of the so-called 'Spanish Economic Miracle' (Etxezarreta et al. 2011: 14). The description of the bountifulness of the early noughties can also be read, however, as an ironic mobilisation of the trope of the garden of Eden, as Pedrós refers to that era as 'aquellos tiempos de inocencia' (433) in which money arrived, Manna-like, 'caído del cielo' (433). Indeed, the text closes with an even clearer Biblical allusion, as Pedrós reflects on the enduring value of commodities such as gold and gems, noting how these items 'siguen conservando el valor que tenían el octavo día de la creación del mundo, cuando Eva vio una serpiente y le echo la mano creyéndose que era un collar de esmeraldas' (436–37). Noticeably, in Pedrós' retelling, the fall from grace is not the result of Eve's thirst for knowledge, but of her materialism and greed; yet this central lesson is obscured by his own fixation on the monetary worth attached to – and the related fetishist attraction exerted by – certain commodities.

In spite of his own unrepentant materialism, Pedrós also notes a change in mood as a result of the crisis: '[e]n el ambiente se palpan nuevos valores, virtudes franciscanas [...] ...me atrevería incluso a decir que está de moda ser pobre y que te embarguen la casa y el coche [...]' (435). In these new, post-2008 times of austerity, Pedrós adds, 'está mal visto que te pillen los de la tele local en un cinco estrellas jugando al golf' (435–36). The contrast, however, between Pedrós' diagnosis and his own attitude – nostalgically longing for the good old times of the boom – and actions – fleeing the country to elude any responsibility for his actions – seem indicative of the superficiality and limited scope of the new, crisis-induced atmosphere. Further, the juxtaposition of Pedrós' fate (a comfortable escape and lavish retirement in some exotic locale) with that of Esteban and his family (murder-suicide at the swamp) further reinforces the impression that the post-2008 transformations will effect only illusory modifications – with the more vulnerable bearing the brunt of the crisis, and those at the top preserving their privileges and eluding their responsibility for the financial meltdown. Yet this pessimistic prognosis should not be read as a disavowal, on Chirbes' part, of the role of narrative and language in shaping how we view (and thus exist in) the world. Elsewhere, the author argued that '[l]a novela es el cambio, la transformación. Que empiezas a leer acerca de un personaje y cuando terminas es otro, lo miras desde otro punto de vista. Transforma al lector, y transforma al escritor también. No te consuela' (Armada 2013: online). In another interview, Chirbes explained that his novels operate

> como una trituradora, como un espejo poliédrico que te hace enfrentarte con tu imagen parcela a parcela y que te descubre que toda esa sucesión de figuritas que aparecen en el poliedro no se corresponden con lo que tú creías. Te obligan a mirarte, irónicamente te facilitan la tarea de demolición a ti, que decías que querías saber tu verdad. (Navarro 2008: 156)

Chirbes' well-documented pessimism (de Arana 2010; Larraz 2016) should thus be interpreted not as a disempowered or disempowering lament, but rather as an attempt to shake his readers, to dismantle their certainties and force them to look at themselves – and the world surrounding them – anew. While Chirbes acknowledges such an exercise is not comforting ('no consuela'), it is nonetheless important, as an ethical exercise in self-knowledge that can set alight, or keep alive in readers, their legitimate portion of Benjaminian resentment in the face of injustice.

Mediterráneo descapotable (2008/2015)

Íñigo Domínguez's *Mediterráneo descapotable* was first published as a series of journalistic chronicles during the summer of 2008 in the regional newspaper *El Correo*. Like Chirbes' *Crematorio*, Domínguez's articles pre-date the collapse of Lehman Brothers in September 2008, regarded by many as a decisive turning point – if not the inaugural event – of the global 2008 recession.[11] However, the collection of articles was republished seven years later in book form, with the accompanying subtitle 'Viaje ridículo por aquel país tan feliz' – a phrase that points to how the events unfolding in Spain after 2008 led Domínguez to a re-evaluation, or at least a reframing, of his original project. The chronicles consist of 18 articles which detail the author's journey along the Spanish Mediterranean coast, from Colliure in France and Portbou on the other side of the border in 'Etapa 0', to Gibraltar in the closing instalment of the series. My analysis will focus on the book, which, as well as the original chronicles, includes an introductory note and an extensive appendix which portrays the aftermath of the crisis and explores the connections between the pre-crisis real estate boom, political corruption and an apathetic or duped citizenry, seduced by the promise of imminent wealth (Domínguez 2015: 191).

The opening 'Nota previa' incorporated in the book version points to a connection between the degradation of the physical landscape and a more profound, moral corruption which echoes Chirbes' diagnosis in his crisis novels:

> En aquel entonces yo llevaba siete años fuera de España. Cuando iba y venía en vacaciones tenía una sensación creciente de que todo el

11 See, for instance, Baba and Packer 2009. Domínguez himself points to the collapse of Lehman Brothers as a significant moment: 'A las dos semanas de la publicación del último capítulo, quebró Lehman Brothers, el 15 de septiembre de 2008, y quedó oficialmente inaugurada la crisis, con mayúscula' (2015: 8).

> mundo se estaba volviendo loco y mi país cada vez me gustaba menos. La degeneración del paisaje visual, el explícito, me parecía a mí, era resultado de un concreto paisaje moral, oculto, o no tanto. (2015: 8)

Domínguez's status as a foreign correspondent – based in Rome for almost 15 years – provides him with a distinct viewpoint on pre-crisis Spain, as the changes to the country appear both more obvious and less comprehensible (as well as less palatable) to him now that he occupies the position of a semi-outsider. Of course, the 'Nota previa' is written with the benefit of hindsight, at a time close to the publication of the book (2015), yet the sense that the changes occurring in Spain in the early twenty-first century are both profound and not unequivocally positive finds echo in the very first chronicle, originally published in July 2008 and reproduced in the book in unmodified form: 'España [...] ha cambiado mucho. A mejor en algunas cosas y a peor en más de las que parece [...]' (15).

While Domínguez's work falls within the genre of journalistic reportage, and is therefore a non-fiction text, the style is often literary, with nods to the gonzo tradition.[12] The subjective point of view of the traveller – as the narrator refers to himself, often in the third person – is privileged throughout, with frequent recourse to hyperbole and humour. Ostensibly, the focus is on the present, that is, on the Spanish Mediterranean coast as traversed by the author during the summer of 2008, yet the past is referenced frequently – as a point of contrast, or in an attempt to explain what the traveller encounters. Significantly, we learn in 'Etapa 0' – the first chronicle – that the plan had originally been to undertake the journey along the Mediterranean coast in 'un Seiscientos o un Dos Caballos, por el efecto cómico-nostálgico' (16). Although that idea is ditched due to concerns as to the viability of conducting such a long journey – involving, in many cases, little-used secondary roads – in a vintage car, the reference seems nonetheless important, and not merely for the nostalgic-comical reasons acknowledged by the narrator. As Tatjana Pavlović explains, the SEAT Seiscientos in particular became an emblem of the Spanish economic miracle of the 1960s and 'the popular cultural icon par excellence' of that era (2011: 186). While perhaps unconsciously, through his original choice of vehicle, Domínguez establishes a link between the Francoist *desarrollista* period and the Spain of the pre-crisis real estate boom – two moments of unprecedented economic growth achieved through large-scale infrastructure and real estate

12 In fact, one of the early reviews of Domínguez's book, by Carlos Prieto (2015) bore the title 'Miedo y asco en Marina d'Or', in reference to Hunter S. Thompson's *Fear and Loathing in Las Vegas*, considered one of the paradigmatic examples of gonzo.

development, an economic rationale which ultimately proved unsustainable, both in environmental and in economic terms.

Further connections with a (relatively) recent past are made in this first fragment as the traveller visits Colliure, in France, the final resting place of Spanish poet Antonio Machado, who died in the town shortly after crossing the border to flee from Spain in 1939, in the wake of the Nationalist victory. With somewhat sinister symmetry, the first town across the border in Spain, Portbou, is the place where Walter Benjamin took his own life in 1940, although there is no grave to visit here as, the traveller notes, 'no se sabe dónde terminó su cuerpo' (19). A further reference to a more distant past is also made in relation to Colliure and the expulsion, in 1493, of the last 39 Jews of the region of Rousillon, which is commemorated by a plaque at the town's harbour. All three events – the deaths of Machado and Benjamin in foreign lands and the banning of the Jewish population from their native soil – serve a dual purpose. On the one hand, they invite the traveller to muse about notions of belonging and displacement. While the historical episodes recounted are, of course, far more extreme, violent and traumatic, the narrator's own condition as an expatriate who struggles to reconnect with his country of origin means that these notions nonetheless resonate with him. On the other hand, the focus on past episodes of violence and exclusion serves to undermine the pleasant, harmonious, modern façade of these localities, suggesting that their current prosperity is not an inherent, natural or permanent state, but a temporary and potentially precarious one.

The references to the past throughout the text can be divided into two, often overlapping categories: the personal memories of the narrator, mostly dating back to the 1980s and 1990s, and the allusions to a past which, while often relatively recent, the traveller has not experienced directly. One example of how both strands are interwoven in the chronicles can be found in the fourth instalment, which corresponds to the stretch of coast between Blanes and Sitges. During this journey, the narrator passes the town of Arenys, birthplace of a Spanish exile who he met while in Venezuela. The memory leads the narrator to reflect on the erasure of Republicanism and exiles from the collective Spanish imaginary, as he notes how '[c]ientos de miles de personas se acuerdan de España todos los días y, en cambio, nadie los recuerda a ellos' (55). As in Chirbes' crisis novels, in Domínguez's text the suppression or repression in contemporary Spain of certain figures (those on the losing side of the Civil War) and the ideas and ideologies for which they stood is implicitly connected to the concrete fever ravaging the Spanish coastline – the rapid and radical transformation of the physical landscape arguably reflecting the efforts to forget or rewrite the past. This link is established more directly in the sixth leg of the itinerary, between Salou and Vandellós, as we are told how

> el viajero se entristece definitivamente por un país enfermo de ladrillo que sepulta la casa de Miró para hacer una autovía que encima no hace falta. [...] El viajero se asusta como un ingenuo al pensar que, si no se preservan los símbolos, los reductos de la memoria cultural, cómo puede esperar la gente corriente reencontrar la plaza donde jugaba, la ribera donde iba a bañarse o el rincón del primer beso. (2015: 75)

While Joan Miró's family *masía*, which the artist immortalised in several paintings, still stands in the village of Montroig, its tower is now crowned by a busy motorway, a development which the narrator sees as symptomatic of Spain's pathological fixation with construction ('un país enfermo de ladrillo'). The obvious disregard for the local landscape and for the heritage value of this specific building leads the traveller to wonder about the effects on the general population of such contempt for shared spaces and cultural symbols – which, as well as the explicitly articulated erasure of personal memories, also risks eroding their sense of a shared, collective identity, and thus their sense of belonging to a community.

Local specificities, the narrator notes from the outset, are being replaced by non-places (Augé 1992), such as the roadside service areas, which, we are told, 'no cambian aunque uno haga quinientos kilómetros. Pertenecen a una misma cadena y parece que los ha diseñado todos una misma persona' (17). This obliteration of particularities is also noted in relation to the seaside towns (or, increasingly, holiday resorts – the line between both becoming blurred at times) visited by the traveller, as he reflects that '[c]ualquier pueblo mediterráneo español ya es igual a cualquier sitio. No tienen nada. Croacia, Turquía, Túnez y hasta Libia trabajan a destajo en arrasar su litoral para equipararse al canon' (122). The melancholy underlying such observations, however, is tempered in the text by humour and by an ironic distancing – noticeable in the already-mentioned tendency by the narrator to refer to himself in the third person – which enables the traveller to mock some of the 'horrores urbanísticos' (23) he encounters along the way. Indeed, hyperbole becomes a recurring motif in the text, a red thread of sorts, as the narrator establishes early on in his quest that 'la costa mediterránea es una sucesión de superlativos. Cada día se topará con uno, y no siempre bueno' (28), and proceeds to identify several examples: El Bulli, at the time of writing heralded as the world's best restaurant (34); Port Aventura, Spain's largest amusement park (61); the then (relatively) new holiday resort of Marina d'Or, described as 'el clímax de un frenesí ibérico de la última década', and which hosts 'el balneario [...] más grande de Europa de agua marina' (92); Benidorm, the town with the highest number of skyscrapers per capita in the world (112); and Escombreras, the ugliest place in Spain, according to the narrator (134).

The focus on excess serves not only the purpose of comic relief – it also underlines the kitsch aesthetic that, for the traveller, has taken over much of the Spanish Mediterranean coast. Nowhere is this more evident than in the Marina D'Or complex, visited at the halfway point of the narrator's trip. Ironically renamed 'tierras de Mord'Or' (91), in reference to Tolkien, and El reslpand'Or (94), in a nod to the Spanish title of Stanley Kubrick's film *The Shining* (1980), the narrator proceeds to detail the garish décor of the resort, consisting of copies of Michelangelo's Sistine Chapel frescoes; fake Classical statues; as well as the projected construction of reproductions of well-known landmarks, including Venice's St Mark's Square and the Eiffel Tower. Domínguez does not merely object to the resort on the grounds of its questionable taste, but seems to have deeper reservations, as he notes how 'este sitio es uno de esos lugares donde uno piensa que el mundo va mal' (91). The malaise that Marina d'Or induces in the narrator thus seems something other than mere snobbery – snobbery, after all, can be reassuring, inducing a sense of superiority over others in the beholder. Instead, Domínguez's observation that many of Marina d'Or's customers are regarded with suspicion and disdain by the complex owners, as they are considered 'la plebe, que también quiere hacer las cosas de los ricos' (92), echoes Gary Tedman's insight of kitsch as an aesthetic 'which attempts to sublimate their alienation [i.e. the alienation of members of the working class] and which offers them the illusion of being a part of the ruling class' (2010: 66). In Marina d'Or, the class tourism discussed by Tedman overlaps or coincides with mass tourism through kitsch, as theorised also by Ludwig Giesz (1969).

Tedman concludes that kitsch is reactionary because its function is compensatory: it creates the illusion among the working classes that they can enjoy the same pleasures (and thus the same privileges) as the wealthy. In Domínguez's text, however, the rejection of kitsch is not so explicitly predicated on that function, but also on other, ostensibly less ideological effects: the traveller refers for instance to the acute 'soledad existencial' (2015: 94) that he experiences amidst the crowds that populate the resort. This loneliness can be explained through Byung-Chul Han's distinction between feelings and affect or emotions (2021). For Han, feelings are intersubjective, they open up a (sociable) space and cannot be consumed (or, therefore, commodified). In contrast, emotions or affect are experienced individually, 'can be something very anti-social, something that separates or is separated' (2021: 109) and can become consumable. For Han, there is a direct correlation between what he terms the 'crisis of feeling' (109) and the rise of affect in contemporary societies. While Han does not specifically discuss kitsch as the aesthetic mode of affect or emotions – he uses the adjacent concepts of 'smoothness' or 'smooth' (79–84) – his contention that the contemporary fixation with affect precludes the emergence of feeling is reminiscent of Susan Sontag's contention that kitsch 'is stultifying. It closes off possibilities. It unfits people from having certain kinds of attention spans and an appetite for complexity' (Friedländer et al. 2015: 323).[13]

For the traveller in *Mediterráneo descapotable*, his rejection of kitsch seems linked to the implicit identification of kitsch as an aesthetic of affect, and not of feeling. This is exemplified in his remark that 'Marina d'Or es una ciudad de vacaciones. [...] Es una fila de edificios ante la playa, con una segunda hilera detrás, con hoteles, pistas deportivas, restaurantes y alguna tienda. No hay cines, ni correos, ni iglesia, claro, esto es el neopaganismo turístico' (2015: 93). His words simultaneously touch on the fact that pleasure and enjoyment at the resort are predicated on consumption (of food or purchasable items), and that such an assumption precludes the emergence or existence, within the complex, of communal spaces of non-consumerist sociability, such as the cinema, the post office or the church. In Domínguez's words, the reference to sports facilities ('pistas deportivas') could be read as suggestive of the preservation of at least some communal spaces of non-consumerist sociability within Marina d'Or, yet the narrator dispels any such illusion as he notes how in the resort '[l]a salud es la última frontera del consumo' (95). That statement is not made in relation to the resort's amenities for physical exercise, but rather in connection to the offer for a free blood test as part of his holiday package. The blood test, however, is just the most obvious example of the complex's overall emphasis on health and wellbeing, which extends also to its spa, to the medical-cosmetic treatments on offer and to its fitness facilities. For the traveller, such a focus on health can be explained by the realisation that '[c]on el dinero, claro, aumenta el miedo a morirse' (95), and that such a fear can be exploited for profit. Byung-Chul Han concurs with Domínguez, as he argues that

13 I describe Han's deployment of the notion of 'smoothness' as adjacent to the concept of kitsch because Han defines the former as linked to an avoidance of depth, difficulty or harm (or 'negativity', in his parlance). As such, the notion of smoothness – which he deploys in connection with the work of Jeff Koons, a visual artist whose work has frequently been labelled as kitsch (Lichfield 2008; Rosenberg 2011; Maltby 2012) – seems to have clear resonances with kitsch as an aesthetic mode lacking substance or depth, as per Clement Greenberg's classic characterisation (1939).

> [c]apitalism is obsessed with death. The unconscious fear of death is what spurs it on. The threat of death is what stirs its compulsion of accumulation and growth. This compulsion drives us towards not only ecological but also mental catastrophe. [...] We optimize ourselves to death. The separation of life and death that is constitutive of the capitalist economy creates an undead life, death-in-life. [...] Only life that incorporates death is truly alive. (2021: 8–9)

Han's words explicitly articulate what Domínguez's traveller glimpses through his stay at Marina d'Or: that both the creation of a vacation city on such a scale (with the attendant environmental destruction) and its success in attracting visitors compelled by its faux-luxe and its promise of wellbeing paradoxically attest to a destructive drive at the heart of contemporary capitalism. For the Spanish author, as for the Korean philosopher, the frenzied building follies in Marina d'Or and elsewhere along the Mediterranean coast – Domínguez notes wryly at the outset of his journey how 'el símbolo por excelencia del Mediterráneo español, que ha dejado de ser el pino o el olivo para ser la grúa' (2015: 23) – and the compulsive consumption on which such development is dependant, and which it simultaneously incites and feeds further, appear as misdirected and futile attempts to evade death. Yet these efforts to accumulate growth, to transform (and, arguably, therefore control) the environment, to 'live life to the fullest' (or, at least, to consume life to the fullest) are not only pointless, as death cannot be avoided or eliminated: they in fact depreciate and destroy life, ruining natural environments and landscapes; restricting spaces and opportunities for sociability; and muting individuals' capacity for feeling, for critical thinking and for risk taking.

Domínguez's identification of Marina d'Or as a lifeless site which subverts 'valores como belleza, salud y tiempo libre' (97) explains the angst he feels during his stay at the resort. Yet during that time, he is also forced to recognise that 'para mucha gente, que no entra en otras consideraciones, Marina d'Or está muy bien' (94) and that 'estos sitios monstruosos [...] dan de comer a mucha gente normal' (95). This tension between the narrator's bewilderment and horror at the 'horizonte de grúas' (82) that dominates the Spanish Mediterranean coastline, and the indifference, when not enthusiasm, with which such developments are greeted by those who he encounters on his journey, further compounds the traveller's sense of alienation. Having established that even in areas that are supposed to be unspoiled, or protected due to their ecological importance, '[e]l ladrillo siempre está ganando metros' (146), in the closing chronicle the traveller recalls Dino Risi's 1962 film *La Escapada* (*Il Sorpasso* in the Italian original, *The Easy Life* in its English-language version) and its portrayal of 'un país eufórico por el progreso, fascinado por el éxito, ansioso de borrar su pasado, sumido en la banalidad y la fealdad' (186). With perhaps unintended circularity, the narrator invokes, as he did in the first chronicle, the years of *desarrollismo* – a period which coincided with the transition from a Fordist to a post-Fordist economy in the West. In so doing, he frames the pre-crisis economic boom in Spain – driven mainly by the construction and real estate sectors, as well as by debt-fuelled consumption – as the, if not logical, then perhaps inevitable, consequence of globalised capitalism. In comparing the Spain of 2008 to the Italy of the early 1960s, Domínguez is not only historicising the present; he is also pointing to the global(ised) dimension of some of the problems identified at the local level, such as the ecological unsustainability of the globally hegemonic economic model, as well as its negative impact on communities undermined by competition and individualism and homogenised to ease the flow of capitals.

Although Domínguez balances his pessimistic views on contemporary Spain by stating that these are 'solo divagaciones del viajero, que vive en el extranjero y es de dudoso criterio. Además de listillo, quizá en el fondo es un puritano' (187), the 'Apéndice' that accompanies the 2015 book edition of the text suggests that the author's 2008 diagnoses were nothing if not prescient. This section retraces the traveller's original route along the coast, from north to south, though, as Angulo Egea notes, on this occasion the route is undertaken 'mental y documentalmente' (2019: 130), that is, through a well-documented account of the corruption scandals that have emerged in each of the localities visited in 2008 in the years since. Starting with Lloret de Mar, whose former mayor, Xavier Crespo, is about to face trial on charges of bribery and corruption which connect him to a Russian mafia boss at the time at which Domínguez is writing, this section of the text is an inevitably incomplete (as many investigations were still in course at this point) attempt to catalogue the widespread corruption behind the pre-2008 real estate boom.[14]

The section dedicated to Port Aventura focusses on the figure of Enrique Bañuelos, 'uno de los paradigmas del auge especulativo y la caída libre del ladrillo mediterráneo' (199), according to Domínguez. Bañuelos, like

14 In the specific case of Xavier Crespo, he avoided jail and was instead banned from public office for nine-and-a-half years in a sentence passed in November 2015, after the publication of *Mediterráneo descapotable*. In October of the following year, the ban was reduced to two years by the Spanish Supreme Court. Further details, including the text in full of that second sentence, can be found at the website of the Spanish judiciary: https://www.poderjudicial.es/cgpj/en/Judiciary/Supreme-Court/Pressroom/Press-Archive/El-Tribunal-Supremo-condena-al-exalcalde-de-Lloret-de-Mar--Girona--por-recibir-regalos-de-un-empresario-ruso-.

the fictional Rubén Bertomeu of *Crematorio*, made his fortune as an *agente urbanizador*, identifying, purchasing, reclassifying and developing (or sometimes merely re-selling) land which had originally had a protected status. In his discussion of the Delta del Ebro region, Domínguez turns his attention from speculation and corruption to the environmental threat faced by this specific area, where the UN has estimated the sea level could rise by almost a metre by the end of the century (200). In Marina d'Or, the planned expansion which had horrified the traveller in 2008 has been abandoned, we are told, following the bankruptcy of the company that ran the complex (202). While the economic downturn seems to have saved some of the coastal areas from unbridled development, Domínguez warns readers that the companies and individuals behind such projects have not given up in their quest to build everywhere and anywhere, as they '[e]stán a la espera, no se crean' (202). The author's scepticism regarding the potential of the 2008 financial crash to encourage a change of paradigm is expressed again, and further supported, by the BCN World macro-project discussed a few pages earlier, which Domínguez notes has taken off 'ahora, cuando se supone que hemos salido escaldados de los excesos de la crisis' (198). Elsewhere, he warns readers that 'estos politicos son células durmientes que volverán a activarse para cometer nuevas barbaridades cuando el contexto sea favorable' (208), dispelling – again – the illusion that anything has changed since, or been learnt from, the 2008 debacle.

While the Mediterranean landscape and the people that inhabit or traverse it occupied the attention of the traveller in the 2008 chronicles, the dissection of the corruption scandals that have arisen since then in this final segment lays bare their reach beyond the construction sector. For example, the discussion of the region of Valencia (home to the infamous Marina d'Or) reveals that the excesses and abuses within real estate had ramifications elsewhere, as the pattern of irregular awarding of public contracts that had allowed the construction of housing and leisure developments in protected areas was reproduced in other sectors, such as sport, leading to the celebration of several heavily subsidised – and ruinous – events like the Castelló Masters golf tournament (2008–11) (206) or the Formula 1 races held in Valencia between 2008 and 2012 (247). The apparent rationale or justification for public sponsorship of these competitions lies in their role in promoting the region as a tourist and leisure destination, and thus helping support the business case for the building of further golf courses, hotels and other attendant infrastructure – projects in which local politicians often had a vested interest, either through direct participation in the companies responsible for the developments or through contributions made by those companies towards political campaign costs. As Domínguez concludes, 'el pelotazo inmobiliario habría pagado las campañas electorales del partido [PP] en esa región [Valencia]' (242) – although of course similar instances of corruption uncovered in other regions, such as Murcia (262), are also discussed in the text.

The overall effect of Domínguez's overview of crisis Spain is bleak. His attempts at a post-mortem of the 'paisaje de una resaca monumental' (191) – a characterisation that echoes Pedrós' description of the downturn as hangover in *En la orilla* (2013: 433) – closes with some sobering statistics, including, for instance, the fact that more than half of all Spaniards will have experienced a corruption case in their municipality (2015: 284). The scale of the rescue package for Spanish banks and savings societies (cajas de ahorro) is also registered as constituting 5% of the country's GDP – a sum that Spanish taxpayers are unlikely ever to be able to retrieve. While the sober enumeration of the litany of corruption scandals uncovered in Spain since the circulation of the chronicles contrasts with their ironic, incredulous, dark humour, both sections of the text share a sense of bewilderment: at the scale of the developments along the Mediterranean coast in the first part, and at the number and extent of the corruption cases brought to light in the aftermath of the crisis. Domínguez links both phenomena – real estate boom and political corruption – as he contends that an understanding of the latter helps explain and understand the former (191). However, and perhaps due to his explanatory intent, Domínguez's account does not undertake an exploration of the physical ruins left behind after 2008, in spite of his allusion to landscape in the opening lines of the Appendix. That task of documenting the ruins and fragments of post-crisis Spain – the unfinished and abandoned real estate projects, or the finished developments which have been rendered obsolete by the crisis – corresponds to the next text discussed in this chapter.

This Is Spain: An Incomplete Travel Guide (2015)

Published in the same year as *Mediterráneo descapotable*, *This Is Spain* is described by its authors as 'una guía de viajes incompleta sobre un territorio histórico en descomposición' (NoPhoto Collective 2015: 3). Throughout 2014, seven photographers from the collective NoPhoto embarked on seven different routes through different regions of Spain – Costa Sur, Euskadi, Cataluña, Camino de Santiago, Centro, Al-Ándalus and Levante – in an attempt to portray 'una época convulsa [...] en un país conmocionado social y económicamente' (3). Unlike Domínguez's text, largely written at a time in which the extent and effects of the 2008 crisis were not yet known or fully understood, this unconventional travelogue, described as part guide, part diary on NoPhoto's website, portrays a ravaged country, marked by contemporary ruins: fragments of unfinished real estate developments and abandoned infrastructure projects – or finished facilities which have, however, been rendered superfluous in the wake of 2008. For Germán Labrador, these remnants are ruins 'solo de un modo particular, porque en muchos casos están completamente nuevas', and they therefore do not attest to the passage of time, as we might expect; instead, he sees these ruins as representative of the passage from one temporal mode – that of hyperdevelopment – to another – that of crisis (2013: 232). His diagnosis echoes Andreas Huyssen's insight that contemporary catastrophes 'have mainly left rubble rather than ruins' (2006: 20), since, on the one hand, recent remnants speak not of 'the return of culture to nature' over centuries, but of concerted, accelerated and often violent forms of destruction; and, on the other hand, the corrosive effects of the passage of time are nowadays counteracted by a heritage industry invested in restoring and preserving certain historical sites. Yet Huyssen leaves open the possibility that contemporary rubble can be 'transformed, even aestheticized, into ruin' (2006: 8) by cultural products and practices.

Central to my analysis will be the question of whether *This Is Spain* enacts that type of aestheticisation theorised by Huyssen, and, if so, to what end. Kathy Korcheck, meanwhile, deploys the very suggestive, multi-layered notion of the 'speculative ruin' (2015) to refer to contemporary yet derelict sites in Spain. For Korcheck, 'speculative ruins' are simultaneously the result of market speculation, illustrative of Guy Debord's notion of the 'spectacle', and sites which can offer the opportunity to 'speculate about individual and collective failures in Spain's economic, financial and political institutions and contemplate the formation and transformation of cultural memories of the crisis now and in the future' (2015: 93). Korcheck's concept of the speculative ruin, as well as more general or classical approaches to the notion of ruin, such as those by Huyssen (2006), Boym (2011), Pensky (2011) and González-Ruibal (2014), will inform my reading of how post-crisis Spain is depicted in *This Is Spain*.

The brief note that opens the text invites us to read

> estos desplazamientos como ensayos particulares que reflexionan sobre conceptos como 'representación', 'representador', 'estereotipo', 'identidad' y 'relato'. Todo ello con la intención de explorar la conformidad, o la ausencia de conformidad, entre mapa y territorio, relato y territorio, entre la percepción que tenemos de nosotros mismos y la manera en la que somos percibidos por los demás. Esto es España pero perfectamente podría ser cualquier otro lugar. (2015: 3)

The notion of displacement invoked in this quote refers, in the first instance, to the journeys undertaken by the photographers to fulfil their briefs. Yet displacement also evokes the temporal discontinuity or disjointedness which Georg Simmel and Walter Benjamin identified as a characteristic feature of ruins (Boym 2011; Pensky 2011); and it alludes also to the destabilisation of terms such as 'stereotype' or 'identity' – flanked by quotation marks to indicate that their meaning is not taken as a given, but will be problematised throughout the text. Further, as if to dispel the spectre of essentialism, the authors close this introductory note by insisting that what they have portrayed is a Spain which 'perfectamente podría ser cualquier otro lugar' – an assertion that implies that the goal of this project is not just to portray a specific country at a critical juncture, but to reflect on the global(ised) economic and socio-cultural dynamics which have led Spain to its current predicament.

Each of the seven routes or 'chapters' in the book opens with a short text which serves to frame the images which follow – themselves generally accompanied by captions – and which also help guide viewers' interpretation of the photographs. In the first section, 'Costa Sur', Eduardo Nave, its author, notes how '[e]n algunos puntos de Andalucía, el vocerío y la alegría típicos de esta tierra parecen haber desaparecido' (NoPhoto Collective 2015: 7), giving way to 'paisajes y escenarios silenciados y cargados de nostalgia' (7). Whether that nostalgia is felt in relation to the region's heyday in the 1960s and 1970s, when, we are told, it was a glamorous tourist destination which attracted the likes of Frank Sinatra and Grace Kelly; or whether it is experienced in connection to the more recent promise of a prosperous future which has failed to materialise is not made clear in the text. The photographs, however, connect both of these temporal frames: the first two images – of a night sky with a barely visible moon (10) and of an unfinished or broken stretch of road that dramatically plunges downhill in Torrox, Málaga (11) – reference a present landscape described as 'en sombra' in one of the accompanying captions (10). The following double-spread image of the skeleton of a new housing development, 'ruinas contemporáneas que ha dejado la burbuja inmobiliaria' (12), further adds to the impression of post-2008 desolation. Yet these images are followed by others which allude to the Costa del Sol's past: the retro, dated façade of Hotel Pez Espada (14), the first five-star establishment in the region, frequented by Hollywood, as well as by actual, royalty in the past, as the caption explains. Opposite, a view of the hotel's lobby testifies to its current, somewhat tired interiors – an impression of mundanity which is reinforced by the presence of an ageing and not particularly glamorous couple (15). 'Aquí empezó todo', states the text accompanying this image – thus drawing an explicit link between the tourism boom in Costa del Sol in the 1950s and 1960s and the previously depicted twenty-first-century ruins. As in other texts discussed in this chapter, then, a direct connection is established between the *desarrollista* and *aperturista* economic policies implemented by the Francoist regime from the late 1950s onwards and the current situation of crisis.

Rather than an explicit and unequivocal condemnation of an economic model based primarily on tourism and real estate, however, this section reflects on its cultural and affective underpinnings. The final six images feature Poblado Western Leone and Mini Hollywood, two former film studios in Almería province which currently operate as theme parks. Located in the Tabernas desert, the only desert in Europe, according to one of the captions, the photographs allude, on one level, to the recent past and the cultural heritage of this area, in which iconic 1960s and 1970s Westerns were filmed. On another level, the images testify to the enduring power of fascination of certain foundational myths – in this instance, that of the 'conquest' of the American 'Wild West' by valiant cowboys. While this is an American, rather than Spanish, foundational myth, it is not difficult to see why it is so easily transposable to a Peninsular context: the so-called Spanish 'Reconquista', like the myth of the Wild West, is predicated upon a gradual gaining of territory, control of which is wrested from an Other presented as uncivilised or barbaric (Native Americans in the US, Muslims in Spain), whose displacement, expulsion or annihilation is thus justified. These parallels, while not mentioned explicitly, are at least hinted at through a double-spread panoramic view of Poblado Western Leone (24–25), which, without the accompanying contextual information, could be assumed to depict a US location. Further, the knowledge that these images portray not 'real' locations, but 'fake', reconstructed simulacra can be read as a reminder of the always already constructed and mediated nature of national foundational myths – which, as these examples illustrate, can be convincingly recreated in a completely different location, culture and era.

The second route featured takes the reader/viewer to the Basque Country, at the other geographical end of the Peninsula. If the opening section draws on the stereotype of the loudness and joyfulness of Andalusians (through the already-cited 'vocerío' and 'alegría', described as 'típicos de esta tierra', currently muted by the context of crisis), here we find a similar cliché in the description of 'miradas que se perciben esquivas en las calles de los pueblos y francas en los txocos [*sic*]' (27), which reproduces the trope of the Basque as reserved but ultimately honest and straightforward. The imagery in this section draws heavily on local folklore, including the visually impactful and little-known mythical figure of the *momotxorro* at the carnival of Alsasua (30); the re-enactment of the Passion of the Christ at Easter in the town of Balmaseda (31); and the summer solstice festivities at San Juan de Gaztelugatxe (44–45). Some of these photographs appear to unquestioningly reproduce certain stereotypes about Basque society and culture – for instance, the double-spread portrait of an elderly couple (40–41) recalls the early-twentieth-century postcards featuring drawings of 'local folk', as does the pastoral scene depicted a few pages earlier (34–35). Yet elsewhere we find a more nuanced approach: the very first photograph, for example, is a portrait of a young man wearing jeans and a striped shirt. He could be anyone, from anywhere. The accompanying text, however, explains that he is a supermarket worker from Balmaseda called Mikel Goikoetxea, and that he will play the role of Jesus in the town's famous Easter parade. The contrast between the anodyne image of an anonymous young man and the knowledge derived from the text has a distancing effect, and serves to remind us, once again, of the constructed and performative nature of cultural traditions.

The most interesting photographs in this section rely on similar contrasts: for example, a photograph of a Bilbao soup kitchen is placed opposite a portrait of a young chef staring at an egg at the nearby Michelin-starred Azurmendi restaurant (36–37). The juxtaposition speaks for itself of the deep and growing inequalities that traverse post-crisis Spain – no commentary on the subject is either made or required in this regard. Elsewhere, an image of a colourful donkey statue – placed in the gardens of a museum in homage to a local breed at risk of extinction – appears next to a photograph depicting a highway junction cutting through a mist-enclosed landscape of rolling green hills (38–39). Both photographs allude to the difficult, at times conflictive relationship of humans to their natural environments: in the first image, the donkey statue acts as stand in for the now absent and almost extinct real animal, whose survival is threatened by changes in human activity in the region. While its presence in the public setting of the museum garden is intended to raise awareness on the situation of the species, its translocation in statue form to such a space in fact paradoxically underlines precisely the societal changes – the transformation from a rural to a services economy – that have placed the species at risk, and it simultaneously advances the very real possibility that these statues will eventually entirely replace the actual animals. In the second photograph, the otherwise idyllic landscape is marred by the eyesore of the highways, yet the accompanying caption does not comment on the visual impact of the roads. Instead, the photographer, Eva Sala, tracks her itinerary from Carabanchel in Madrid to Lezama in Bizkaia along such roads, detailing the distance and cost of her journey. In so doing, Sala implicitly recognises both the convenience that these faster routes afford and her own complicity with or acquiescence towards the existence of such infrastructure, as she is one of its users. It is also unclear whether the final remark that it is possible to cross the Peninsula in a northbound direction 'sin casi tocar una comarcal' (39) should be taken as praise at the comprehensiveness of the motorway network in that part of Spain, or as a criticism at its excessive or unnecessary sprawl. The ambiguity of the caption complicates our reading of the image, suggesting that Sala is more concerned with problematising her own position as a subject of representation who is always already enmeshed or involved in the object of her representation, than in articulating a clear critique on the visual and environmental impact of the highways she depicts.

The next instalment in the guide corresponds to a route through Catalonia, and the text that introduces the photo-essay alerts us to the fact that Jonás Bel, its author, was in Barcelona during the Diada – the National Day of Catalonia – of 2014, a particularly symbolic occasion as it marked the 300th anniversary of the region's defeat in the War of the Spanish Succession in 1714 (which is what the national holiday commemorates). For Bel, the palpable vitality of Catalan nationalism (59) seems at odds with the region's reliance on tourism:

> es extraño ver que existe una gran necesidad y reivindicación de la tierra y nación catalana a la vez que Cataluña hace todo por y para el turismo, una actividad que hace desaparecer la identidad de un lugar convirtiéndolo en un icono, un parque temático masificado. (48)

Bel's reference to a theme park above echoes David Harvey's warning about the Disneyfication of old, historic European cities, such as Barcelona. The image that opens his photo-essay depicts a tourist in front of a tourist bus with the iconic Sagrada Familia in the background (49), in a visual illustration of Bel's warning that Barcelona's architectural heritage 'se disocia de la vida, creando una ciudad de cartón piedra, un espectáculo' (48). The negative effects of mass tourism on the city and the wider region are one of the thematic foci of this route (50–51, 52, 53), alongside questions of identity and of the relationship between past and present.

The depiction of Barcelona's Feria (54–55), a festivity of Andalusian origin, serves as a reminder of the wave of internal migration that saw hundreds of thousands of Spaniards move from the rural south to Catalonia in the 1950s and 1960s, leading to the emergence of hybrid identities, such as that of the *charnego* or *xarnego* – that is, Catalans born in other regions of Spain. More recent examples of migration are depicted elsewhere, in images that portray Sub-Saharan migrants who make a precarious living in Barcelona as scrap collectors (62) or street vendors of fake luxury items (63). Interspersed between these two sets of images that attest to different migratory waves, we find two images of the Diada (58–59), which is, according to the caption, 'una fiesta identitaria llena de orgullo y reivindicación, sobre todo para las nuevas generaciones de catalanes' (59). The tension between place-based identity, tourism and globalisation – in the form of its attendant migratory flows – while not directly discussed, is nonetheless alluded to through the juxtaposition of these images. The final photograph included in this section (64–65), and the most visually striking, depicts a large cruise-ship in one of Barcelona's ports at night time. Bel has extended the exposure to deliberately create a blurred image – a representational choice that can be read as a reference to speed, to the compression of time that characterises the contemporary 'era of destructive acceleration' (González-Ruibal 2014: online), as well as a nod to the erasure of definition or identity resulting from such acceleration.

Although the focus in this photo-essay is on tourism, identity and migration, ruins are nonetheless also featured: the remains of a stone bridge across the river Segre (NoPhoto Collective 2015: 60) are depicted side by side with the foundations of a building (61). The first image is accompanied by a short text which explains that the site featured was the scene of one of the longest and bloodiest battles during the Spanish Civil War – leading the reader to deduce that the bridge must have been destroyed during the conflict. The other ruin is not featured as prominently, but appears in the background of a portrait of local resident Joaquín and his dog; however, Joaquín's presence refers us back to the introductory text, in which Jonás Bel describes his encounter with the old man, as well as with 'el esqueleto de hormigón de lo que iba a ser una gran estación de esquí' (47) in one of the last unspoiled areas of the Pyrenees. While no connection is drawn between these two ruins in the accompanying captions, their placing next to each other suggests a relationship of continuity between the destruction resulting from the Civil War and the more recent ruins from the pre-2008 real estate bubble. The reader or viewer is thus invited to consider the impact of the contemporary economic conflagration as underpinned by a similar, if less visible, violence as that of the war.

The central section in the series, ostensibly devoted to the Camino de Santiago (66–85), appears as the most enigmatic, as the choice to photograph the route in black and white lends the images an austere, almost minimalist quality. This decision is not mentioned or explained in the opening text, although the photographer, Juan Millás, does clarify there that his concern is with 'lugares donde se articulan los interrogantes originarios o se instauran los mitos' (68). Such a concern with origin questions and myths can help explain the use of black-and-white photography as a nod to the medium's origins; and it also explicates the seeming detour from the Road to Santiago and onto the Sierra de Atapuerca, in Burgos, where some of the oldest human remains in Europe have been found. Indeed, the cover image for *This Is Spain* – a primate – belongs to this section of the book, and the text explains that the ape is a natural-scale reproduction from the Museo de Evolución Humana in Burgos. Yet while the explanatory text accompanying the image *inside* the book invites a straightforward reading, its transposition to the cover has an undoubtedly ironic, tongue-in-cheek effect, pointing not so much to the origins of our species as to Spain's perceived involution in the wake of the 2008 recession.

With a few exceptions, this chapter is devoted primarily to landscapes, and to how they record human interactions with, or existences within, them. The scale of such interventions varies, from the relatively unintrusive (a scarecrow in a field, 76; the crosses made from twigs and left by pilgrims of the Road to Santiago on a fence by the road, 77) to the dramatic (the view of a beach at Camariñas, where a large vessel was shipwrecked in January 2014, 82). While the latter image is particularly spectacular, with the broken hull of the ship framing the view of the sea and rocks, the preceding two photographs (80–81) attest to more devastating events. The ruins of Manfred Gnädinger's house, once an open-air museum, are a reminder of the environmental damage wrought by the oil spill resulting from the sinking of the tanker *Prestige* in November 2002 – a disaster which, according to local lore, the caption informs us, led to Gnädinger's death shortly after. The photograph featured alongside the ruins of Gnädinger's house also attests to environmental destruction, if of a different kind: Monte Pindo, described as the 'Olimpo Celta' (81) due to its prominence in local mythology, appears as a lunar landscape, still covered in ash a year on from the forest fires that ravaged it. The references to myths and stories in the captions accompanying these images suggest that Juan Millás is not simply interested in documenting the environmental damage in these areas, but rather, that he wants to underline how natural spaces underpin the stories that shape communal beliefs and values, and thus how the destruction of the natural world impacts our cultural identity – and therefore our sense of self. Further, the inclusion of ruins (in the broadest sense of the term) resulting from events that pre-date the 2008 crisis – as in the case of Gnädinger's house – or which do not seem directly related to it – Monte Pindo – implies a broader questioning of how contemporary humans inhabit, use and transform spaces.

The next photo-essay, by Juan Santos, focuses on central Spain. Santos' is a simultaneously vast and vague brief, as 'centrality' can be defined in different ways. In the opening text, however, it becomes clear that Santos' notion of centrality stands for prominence in economic and political terms (87), rather than a more geographically oriented approach to Spain's interior – the so called 'España vacía' (del Molino 2016). This explains the relatively limited scope of the section, which takes in Madrid, the nearby town of El Escorial and the adjacent Valle de los Caídos, as well as the medieval cities of Ávila and Toledo. In his quest to locate 'las arquitecturas del poder, o aquellas que en algún momento se consideraron como tales' (87), Santos establishes an analogy between Ávila's famous medieval walls – which sought to separate the 'civilised' old town from the 'barbarism' beyond – and the protective barriers being erected at the time of writing (2014) around Spain's parliament, to prevent demonstrators from gaining or blocking access to that seat of power (87). The question of which side represents 'civilisation' and which 'barbarism' – both terms are given in quotation marks in Santos' text to denote their simultaneously constructed, shifting and ideologically loaded connotations – is, however, left open to interpretation by readers. In fact, the opening photograph, a view of the giant cross that crowns the Valle de los Caídos complex with a grazing cow in the foreground, suggests a playful inversion of terms, with the oblivious ruminant appearing rather more dignified than the sinister monument behind it.

In this section we also find a contemporary ruin – in this case, however, it does not belong to a private, real estate or tourism-related development, but to an unfinished hospital in the outskirts of Toledo which, according to the caption, had been projected to become the largest in Europe (93). The site, we are told, now hosts 'ruinas, ni siquiera míticas o gloriosas, tan sólo obscenas' (93). This contrast between mythical or glorious ruins – which, we can assume, Santos identifies with ruins of a distant past perceived or reconstructed as epic and heroic – and the 'obscenity' attributed to the unfinished and abandoned hospital reminds us of the insights of Huyssen (2006) in relation to contemporary ruins in general, and of Labrador (2013) in the specific context of post-2008 Spain, as Santos opposes the grandeur and *memento mori* quality of Classical ruins to the bleakness of remains that testify only to the destructiveness latent in late-stage capitalism. The change of focus – from the unfinished or abandoned real estate and tourism developments to the incomplete and derelict hospital site – also serves to highlight the extent of the crisis and its impact not just on the landscape or on cultural identity, as discussed in relation to previous examples, but also on public services such as healthcare. The photograph that appears next to the hospital ruin (2015: 92) confirms this: it depicts a man lighting up a cigarette at the entrance to a Centro de Salud (GP surgery) in the Madrid district of Lavapiés. The word 'mercado' (market) appears in capitals over the lettering for the surgery, accompanied by the caption '[c]uando el mercado y la sanidad pública se cruzan' (92). While the intersection of public healthcare and market in the image is anecdotal, simply owing to the fact that the surgery building is adjacent to a market, the accompanying caption and its placing next to the photograph of the abandoned hospital attest to Santos' intention of highlighting the threat of the privatisation of healthcare in Spain in the aftermath of 2008.[15] Santos' engagement here with the remains of the unfinished hospital thus illustrates that although the contemporary ruin may lack the auratic properties of its Classical counterpart, it nevertheless serves an important function as a physical embodiment of 'modern paradoxes reminding us of the blunders of modern teleologies and technologies alike, and of the riddles of human freedom' (Boym 2011: online).

The remains of another unfinished hospital complex, located on the outskirts of Granada, are mentioned in the text that opens the section on Al-Ándalus (2015: 107), but they are not featured in the photo-essay itself. But the trope of the ruin nonetheless features prominently in this section's images, too: among the first images is a double-spread (110–11) of the remnants of Medinat al-Zahara, the town built by Abd al-Rahman III in the tenth century which, however, are not represented in spectacular fashion. That image contrasts with the monumental depiction, a few pages later, of a quarry in nearby Carcabuey. Carlos Luján, the author of this chapter, remarks how the quarry 'representa el proceso inverso al expolio sufrido por los monumentos de este recorrido a lo largo de la historia' (107), thus establishing a connection between the hollowing out of the mountain and the plunder of the monuments found alongside the route. While the text suggests that the quarry can be read as the obverse of the ruins of Medinat al-Zahara (as well as of more recent remains), the visual contrast between the photographs corresponding to both locations – the visually dramatic quarry having a far greater impact than the understated ruins – speaks of the gulf between the lasting and large-scale destructive effect of human activity on the landscape and environment, and the rather unimposing remains of the constructive efforts resulting from such processes of so-called creative destruction.

15 It is worth noting that *This Is Spain* was published in 2015, three years after the passing of the Real Decreto-ley 16/2012, de 20 de abril, de medidas urgentes para garantizar la sostenibilidad del Sistema Nacional de Salud, which effectively curtailed universal access to public healthcare, excluding undocumented migrants and those not registered as living in Spain. The passing of the decree, alongside other measures towards the privatisation of healthcare, led to widespread protests in Madrid, which came to be known as *mareas blancas* (white tides) and eventually spread throughout Spain. For more details on the *mareas blancas*, see Ribera-Almandoz and Clua-Losada 2021.

The image that closes this section is a double-spread that captures a dramatic rise of the river Guadalquivir (124–25), which Luján states he finds more compelling than the 'lugares muy concretos pero carentes de emoción' recommended in Richard Ford's classic 1830 travel guide to Spain (107). As with the juxtaposition of the quarry and the ruins of Madinat al-Zahara, the photograph of the river is far more vivid than the preceding images featuring the Basilica at Palmar de Troya (118), the remains of Seville's 1992 Expo (119) and the Benito Villamarín football stadium (122). Yet Luján's representations do not simply favour the 'natural' over the 'built' environment, or nature over culture; rather, his visually striking photographs of the river and the quarry depict the very graphic consequences of human activity on the environment, in a manner that problematises the very distinction between both.

The final section of *This Is Spain* is dedicated to the Levante region – the setting of Chirbes' two crisis novels, which also features prominently, if not exclusively, in Domínguez's *Mediterráneo descapotable*. Marina d'Or is described in the opening pages of Paco Gómez's photo-essay as 'una ciudad postapocalíptica que pone los pelos de punta' (128), a characterisation that simultaneously echoes and amplifies Domínguez's derisory sketch of the resort. In the post-2008 context, Marina d'Or is no longer the kitsch behemoth that horrified Domínguez, but an unsettling, zombie-like and mostly empty shell – a transformation that confirms Domínguez's original intuition regarding the complex. As elsewhere in this unusual guide, this section displays an interest in cultural traditions, such as the little-known 'pelota valenciana' (136), thought to be a legacy of the ancient Greek presence in the east of the Iberian Peninsula. Yet the approach to such traditions is not unequivocally celebratory – *pelota valenciana* is simultaneously connected to drinking, gambling and failure and to Classical Greece and its myths; while the most famous festival of the region, the *Fallas*, is critiqued for having deviated from its original purpose:

> Históricamente las fallas de Valencia eran la crítica anual que el pueblo hacía a los que manejaban sus destinos. El miedo a la pérdida de subvenciones ha hecho que, poco a poco, las fallas tiendan a representar la realidad como un cuento de hadas. (140)

The quote above points to the photographer's awareness of how cultural practices can be co-opted and re-signified, thus transforming their original function and meaning. Rather than simply documenting such practices to capture some of the 'local folklore', Gómez, like other photographers participating in the project, seems invested in exploring and reflecting on how these rituals come to be, how and why they evolve over time, and how such changes impact collective identities. Gómez's association of the loss of critical edge of the *Fallas* to their reliance on public subsidy further indicates an implicit recognition of the centrality of funding – and, more generally, the economy – in the emergence, development, shaping and survival (or disappearance) of cultural traditions and identities. His photo-essay – and, indeed, the book as a whole – can therefore be read as an exploration of the impact of the 2008 crisis not just on different Spanish regions and landscapes, but also on the place-based identities and cultural traditions sustained or articulated by and within those spaces.

The closing photograph of this final essay is perhaps the most dramatic image in the book as a whole, and is devoted to another contemporary ruin: the incomplete Valencia FC football stadium, modelled on the Roman Colosseum (144–45). The structure appears invested with an unexpected majesty or aura, not least due to certain representational choices – the building is featured in its entirety in a double-spread panoramic that gives a sense of its monumental scale, and is photographed at dusk, the soft, evening light contributing to aestheticise the ensemble. Such choices – and the resulting image – contrast with other depictions of contemporary ruins in the text, which deliberately avoid the temptation to aestheticise or romanticise the remnants portrayed (cf. 11, 12–13, 61, 93, 119). Such oscillations between naturalistic representations of what Huyssen (2006) would class as 'rubble', and aestheticising approaches that elevate rubble to the status of 'ruin' point to the complexity and ambivalence at the heart of contemporary remains. In his writing on the archaeology of the recent past, González-Ruibal remarks on how such remains can lead to anagnorisis, as

> we discover traces of the future in the past. We discover hope: the hope that things could have been different; that they could have been better [...]. This is the same utopianism, with a sense of emergency, that is present in Walter Benjamin's writings: an utopianism that mixes the traces of the past, with the dangers of the present and the hope of the future. (2014: online)

González-Ruibal is not referring to crisis ruins, however, but to his work in the excavation of Spanish Civil War trenches. His allusions to hope and utopianism above are therefore linked to a very different historical moment: the defeat of Republicanism, a broad political movement that embodied progressive (and in some cases utopian) values. It is harder to ascribe such utopianism to the dilapidated remainders of buildings and infrastructure created solely (or primarily) in pursuit of economic profit. Yet these physical remnants act as powerful and stubborn reminders of the scale and frenzied nature of the pre-2008 construction bubble in Spain, as well as of the environmental cost it entailed – thus inviting a questioning of the underlying economic model that allowed their coming into being. This does not preclude the possibility that these sites may be co-opted and thus re-signified in the near future: it is likely that many of these developments will eventually be re-purposed or finalised, their existence no longer serving as physical and visible proof of the excesses of late-stage capitalism.

As Domínguez writes in the epilogue to his *Mediterráneo descapotable*, and as Chirbes articulates through the character of Tomás Pedrós in *En la orilla*, the effects of the 2008 crisis appear to have led to a pause in real estate speculation, rather than to an eradication of that practice or even, more broadly, to a meaningful rethink of our growth- and consumption-oriented economic model. In their collective efforts to simultaneously document and query the nature of contemporary crisis ruins, the authors of *This Is Spain* strive to preserve these remainders as 'sites of ambivalence, whose collective memory requires ongoing philosophical interpretation' (Pensky 2011: 69). While the photographers have no control over the physical ruins, their photographic work nonetheless simultaneously immortalises them in their ambiguous state as rubble-ruin, thus preserving and protecting their function against their likely future transformation or disappearance; and it also points to the role of their medium – photography – and its attendant representational choices – from the selection of objects meriting attention, to composition, light, exposure and use of colour – in contributing to shape our 'ongoing philosophical interpretation' of these sites.

The four texts analysed in this chapter belong to different genres – narrative fiction, literary journalism, photographic reportage – yet they all approach recent transformations to Spanish landscapes as visible, legible signs and symptoms of the unsustainability of the dominant economic model of consumption-based growth. That system is not just rejected due to its destructive effect on the environment, but also on account of its less immediately tangible consequences, such as the erosion of local specificities, practices and knowledges – which in turn risks diluting place-based collective identities. Further, political (and often moral) corruption is presented in the texts as the logical result of a framework that privileges wealth accumulation over any other principle or value. The works do not, however, adopt a moralising tone; rather, in all four, we encounter different forms of critical and self-conscious questioning of the authors' own standpoint and of their inevitable participation in (when not complicity with) processes recognised as problematic and flawed. This awareness of the difficulty – or, indeed, impossibility – of entirely extricating oneself from structural dynamics deemed damaging seems to prevent the authors from imagining and articulating an alternative. Yet such an inability (or perhaps deliberate refusal?) to offer readers/viewers a hopeful outlook reinforces the unsettling quality and effect of these texts, which force us to confront unpalatable realities and to consider our own role in relation to them.

CHAPTER TWO

Home Loss

Representations of Eviction in Cristina Fallarás' A la puta calle *(2013), Doménico Chiappe's* Tiempo de encierro *(2013), Carlos Luján's* Desahucios *(2013) and Isaac Rosa and Cristina Bueno's* Aquí vivió *(2016)*

If the preceding chapter was concerned with how four cultural texts engaged with the dramatic changes effected upon Spanish landscapes in the run up to and in the aftermath of the Great Recession of 2007–8, this chapter considers how four contemporaneous works critically portray the experience of home eviction – and ensuing home loss. As with the examples discussed in the first chapter, these texts, while varied in genre – they include a literary non-fiction (or autofictional) chronicle, a novel, a photography series and a graphic novel – all undertake a critical exploration of the media discourses and collectively held beliefs and assumptions that made possible the eviction of tens of thousands of families in a relatively short time span. Moreover, and as happened with the texts featured in the previous chapter, all of the works analysed here question their own position and mode of enunciation, in a self-conscious effort to probe their limits or blind spots – and to alert readers to the perception and reality-altering potential of discursive and representational practices. In order to ground the analysis of the four selected texts, I start by outlining the phenomenon of post-2008 home eviction in Spain, before considering the very definition of the notion of home – and how this definition, as Kathy Korcheck (2015) has argued, mutated during the pre-2008 Spanish construction boom. This preamble is followed by a separate engagement with each of the texts included, which are considered comparatively in the conclusion to this chapter.

One of the better-publicised consequences of the 2008 global financial crisis in Spain was a marked rise in the number of evictions, as tenants and owners increasingly became unable to meet rent or mortgage payments. The present chapter considers how this experience is portrayed in three contemporary literary texts and a photography project: Cristina Fallarás' first-person account of the process leading to her eviction in *A la puta calle. Crónica de un desahucio* (2013), Doménico Chiappe's novel *Tiempo de encierro*

(2013), Carlos Luján's *Desahucios. Los escenarios del horror* (2013) and the graphic novel *Aquí vivió. Historia de un desahucio*, by Isaac Rosa and Cristina Bueno (2016). In order to better understand the context in and from which these works emerge, I will begin by offering an overview of the specificities of evictions in Spain in the wake of 2008, taking into account not only the (often inaccurate or incomplete) data available on the subject, but also the media portrayal of evictions and the social responses it elicited, as well as certain legal and economic particularities that contributed to make eviction a central question and a key issue in Spain after 2008.

While the term 'eviction' is defined in the *International Encyclopedia of Housing and Home* as the 'permanent and involuntary expulsion of occupiers from their residence' (Smith 2012: 130) and has traditionally been used mostly in relation to the expulsion of tenants from a rented property by the landlord, in the Spanish post-crisis context the term became associated with default on mortgage payments and the resulting foreclosure on homes. Illustrative of this tendency is the fact that the best-known anti-eviction grassroots activism group is the Plataforma de Afectados por la Hipoteca (PAH) [Platform of those Affected by Mortgages]. The cultural texts discussed in this chapter further reflect this trend, as they all feature individuals and spaces involved in or affected by evictions resulting from mortgage foreclosure proceedings. The number of evictions resulting from mortgage foreclosures that took place in Spain in the period 2007–18 varies depending on the source, and is particularly difficult to estimate for the years prior to 2013, as the data gathered up to and including 2012 does not specify the type of property affected, so that land and commercial premises, among others, are lumped together with residential properties. Government figures released in 2013 in response to a request by the Spanish MP Cayo Lara show that the number of property foreclosures increased more than four-fold in the period between 2006 and 2012, rising from 16,097 in 2006 to 75,375 in 2012.[1] However, as stated before, these figures do not discriminate by type of property; nor do they include property foreclosures that were still being processed by the courts in 2012 – a significant omission, as it is estimated that by the end of 2012 there were almost 200,000 foreclosure proceedings in the Spanish judicial pipeline. The total number of foreclosures for the period 2007–12, according to this source, is 270,033. It should be noted that this figure is for mortgage foreclosures and not for evictions. This is an important distinction since, while the former normally results in the

1 See http://imagenes.publico-estaticos.es/resources/archivos/2013/6/11/1370962080209datosgobiernoejecuciones.pdf.

latter, in some cases mortgage holders may have been able to negotiate debt restructuring or taken other measures allowing them to avoid eviction.

In a report compiled by PAH activists Ada Colau and Adriá Alemany in January 2013, the number of actual evictions (as opposed to mortgage foreclosures) for the period 2007–12 is estimated, through a comparison of two series of conflicting figures provided by two different judicial bodies, as totalling 362,776, a figure that does not tally with the government data cited above.[2] Spain's central bank, Banco de España, published eviction figures for 2013–15 (both years inclusive), totalling 120,525 over that three-year period.[3] From 2016 to 2018, there are figures for mortgage foreclosures affecting residential properties available through the Instituto Nacional de Estadística, but not for actual evictions. The trend over that period is of a decrease in such proceedings, with numbers going from 41,288 foreclosures in 2016 down to 25,903 in 2018.[4] An article published in Spanish financial newspaper *Cinco Días* in early 2018 contrasts the available data to conclude that the number of evictions for the period 2008–17 was around 510,000, although just under half of these would have involved the primary residence of the person(s) affected.[5]

While discrepancies in data gathering methodology make it practically impossible to accurately determine the number of Spanish families that lost their home as a result of the 2008 crisis, the figures quoted above suggest that, even if we take the most conservative estimates, over 200,000 households were affected.[6] As well as the significant number of cases, the dramatic consequences of processes of eviction (with several cases of individuals resorting to suicide at the moment in which their property was about to be repossessed) made it one of the more visible consequences

2 See https://afectadosporlahipoteca.com//wp-content/uploads/2013/02/RETROSPECTIVA-SOBRE-DESAHUCIOS-Y-EJECUCIONES-HIPOTECARIAS-EN-ESPA%C3%91A-COLAUALEMANY1.pdf. At the time of the report's publication, Ada Colau was primarily known as an activist; however, she was also mayor of Barcelona from 2015 until 2023.

3 See https://www.bde.es/f/webbde/GAP/Secciones/SalaPrensa/NotasInformativas/Briefing_notes/es/notabe200716.pdf and https://www.bde.es/f/webbde/GAP/Secciones/SalaPrensa/NotasInformativas/Briefing_notes/es/notabe300715.pdf.

4 See https://www.ine.es/jaxiT3/Tabla.htm?t=10743.

5 See https://cincodias.elpais.com/cincodias/2018/01/30/midinero/1517339842_922977.html.

6 Jochen Mecke, Ralf Junkerjürgen and Hubert Pöppel put forward a similar figure in their introduction to the collective volume *Discursos de la crisis: respuestas de la cultura española ante nuevos desafíos* (2017), in which they state that around 200,000 Spanish families lost their homes to evictions. Given that evictions continued post-2017 (albeit at a slower pace), this figure is likely to be a conservative estimate.

of the Great Recession, encouraging large-scale social mobilisation that contributed to effect legislative change in March 2012 to better protect the rights of mortgage holders.[7] Specifically, the change introduced in 2012 allowed mortgage holders, in very specific circumstances, to cancel their debt with their lender by transferring ownership of their property to their bank (a practice known as *dación en pago* in Spanish).[8]

Although this change was presented as redressing the legal balance in favour of consumers, it was deemed insufficient by the PAH, as it only allowed *dación en pago* in certain cases and it would not, in principle, apply retrospectively (that is, to the tens of thousands of mortgage foreclosure proceedings already underway).[9] Indeed, PAH members Colau and Alemany argue that this legislative change had a negative impact, at least in the short term, providing banks with 'la coartada perfecta para negar daciones que, fruto de la presión de la PAH, se estaban consiguiendo' (2012: 154). In other words, while the measure taken by the Partido Popular (PP) government in March 2012 was presented as providing a partial solution to a social issue – home evictions – that had captured the public's imagination, in practice, the Real Decreto had the effect of reducing the negotiating capacity vis-à-vis the banks of individual families and grassroots groups such as the PAH. Before the decree, and due to increasing social pressure, some banks were voluntarily offering this option, as described by Cristina Fallarás in her chronicle; after the decree was passed, banks could invoke it in order to justify their refusal to agree to a *dación en pago*.

7 The number of documented eviction-related suicides in Spain in the period 2008–18 is over 30, with some cases, such as that of Amaia Egaña in Barakaldo (Vizcaya) in 2012, attracting widespread media attention.

8 The Real Decreto-Ley 6/2012 of 9 March 2012 stipulates that in certain cases, mortgage owners will be allowed to use their mortgaged property to cancel their debt with the mortgage lender. Up until that point, Spanish mortgage holders who lost their homes due to their inability to meet mortgage repayments did not automatically have their debt cancelled once their property had been repossessed, but retained as debt the outstanding amount if the sum raised by the sale of their property at auction was lower than the money owed to the bank at the point of auction. Given that late interest rates on mortgages were typically around 20% at this time, and that average house prices fell on average by over 30% in Spain in the period 2008–12, it was not unusual for individuals to lose their property and still retain a sizeable debt with the bank.

9 Only households in which all members were unemployed, with mortgages up to 120,000 euro for countryside properties and 200,000 for urban properties, and with no solvent guarantor could access *dación en pago* under the new legislative framework. In practice, the PAH estimates this ruled out almost 90% of households affected by mortgage foreclosure proceedings.

Fallarás' experience of eviction, portrayed in one of the texts which will be discussed in this chapter, also highlights the limitations of *dación en pago*, which she does not accept because, she explains, 'no tengo dónde ir y, en mi situación económica, nadie en su sano juicio va a alquilarme un piso, ni el más cochambre. Yo tampoco lo haría' (2013: 33). While giving up her home would allow her to free herself from a debt she cannot repay, and which is rapidly ballooning due to additional delay interest, doing so would also render her and her two young children homeless. Her experience starkly illustrates the limitations of *dación en pago* in the Spanish context, where the social housing stock is the lowest in Europe (less than 1% of the total), and access to other benefits is far from straightforward.[10] Fallarás, echoing proposals formulated by the PAH, is willing to transfer ownership of her flat to the bank, as long as she is allowed to remain in the property as a tenant, paying them a rent she can afford – a proposal that her bank seems unwilling to consider.

As far back as 2012, Germán Labrador noted the political potential of the increasing circulation of *historias de vida* (life stories) in the Spanish public sphere, and, in particular, of stories concerning what he termed 'subprime lives' – that is, the narratives of bodies deemed expendable by the financial and political establishments in the wake of the 2008 crisis. His theory resonates with the experience of the PAH, whose first objective is described as establishing a safe space in which those at risk of eviction can share their stories – a first and necessary step towards empowerment (Colau and Alemany 2012: 94). But both Labrador and Colau and Alemany warn that for such narratives to resonate socially (and thus fulfil their transformative potential), they need to mobilise a framework in which 'relatos sobre las vidas comienzan a ser entendidos como parte de problemas estructurales mayores, y esto convierte en asunto político colectivo lo que, hasta entonces, era narrado como riesgo individual, vida privada' (Labrador 2012: 563). In other words, individual eviction narratives – and, more broadly, crisis stories – can only be socially useful, politically effective, if they succeed in destabilising the private/public (or individual/structural) binary. Following this insight, the home – a space traditionally characterised as private, yet reflective of collective cultural practices, values and beliefs (Bourdieu 1970) – emerges as a privileged site from which to effect precisely such an uncovering

10 For more details on the shortcomings of the Spanish welfare state, see Sara Mesa's 2019 essay *Silencio administrativo. La pobreza en el laberinto burocrático*, which lays bare the often-insurmountable bureaucratic obstacles that those at risk of social exclusion are expected to negotiate in order to gain access to basic help.

of the social, collective dimension of issues (such as eviction, unemployment and indebtedness) that are often perceived as private, individual problems.

Underlying the analysis of the texts considered in this chapter is the clear differentiation, on a theoretical level, between house (a physical structure, a property) and home (a place of dwelling that, following Gaston Bachelard (1965 [1958]), enables its inhabitants to locate and structure their memories, and thus plays a central role in identity-building processes). While a house can also be a home, it is not automatically one: as Mary Douglas notes, 'a home is not only a space, it also has some structure in time; and because it is for people who are living in that time and space, it has aesthetic and moral dimensions' (1991: 289). Because the notion of home is so closely linked to personal memory and identity, and given its role in providing both individuals and families not only with shelter but also with structure, the loss of the home is experienced in the narratives under consideration as something far more existentially threatening than the prospect – terrifying as it is – of the loss of shelter. For Kathy Korcheck there is a direct correlation between the shift in the concept of home 'from *residence* to *property*' (2015: 92, italics in the original) during the years of Spain's real estate boom (1997–2006) – thus 'utterly divorc[ing it] from its connotations of permanence, security and social life' (95) through its financialisation – and the obscuring of the fact that '[t]o not have a home or to lose one's home is to lose one's entire sense of place and belonging to a community' (95). The texts explored in this chapter seek to redefine the notion of home, challenging its consideration as a mere asset with a variable exchange value and exposing the dramatic consequences derived from its conceptualisation in such terms.

A la puta calle. Crónica de un desahucio (2013)

Cristina Fallarás' *A la puta calle* brings forward the dimension of hopelessness and existential threat resulting from the eviction experience from the very opening of her text, as she lists the multiple meanings, as given by the Real Academia Española, of the Spanish 'desahuciar', which not only means 'to evict', but also 'to admit that an ill person cannot be cured' and 'to deprive someone from any hope of achieving what they want' (2013: 9). Fallarás' text is structured chronologically, with an opening section that states the aims and scope of her enunciation, followed by four chapters, each covering a one-year period (from 2009 to 2012) and tracing the narrator's progressive transformation from middle-class liberal professional to unemployed evicted activist and squatter. This change is metaphorically depicted as a gradual if unstoppable fall, with its proportions likened to a fall down the longest staircase in the world, that climbing Mount Niesen in the Swiss Alps and totalling 11,674 stairs. The metaphor appears repeatedly within the text, acting in part as a structuring device, a chronotope, as noted by Babych (2018: 146). It is also a powerful image in that it allows the author to graphically depict the human cost and the actual bodily harm resulting from an experience such as hers, as she repeatedly remarks on the violence of the blows suffered on the way down.

There is another remarkable spatial metaphor in the text: that of a country torn into two halves, with a terrifying crevice of doom separating them (2013: 27 ff.). One half is gradually sliding towards that crevice, while the other half watches in horror and fear that they could be next. This image of an irreconcilably divided country resonates with the notion of 'the two Spains',[11] a recurring motif in nineteenth- and twentieth-century Spanish literature. While the nature of the division is presented here as primarily owing to circumstance (whether one has been severely affected by the crisis or not) rather than ideology, the impoverished, sliding half is, at least 'sentimentally' (27), identified with the left – that is, with progressive Spain, whose traditional constituents (the young, women, immigrants, liberal professionals) seem to have been disproportionately affected by the downturn.

While this is an avowedly autobiographical account, some of its features, such as its selective mobilisation of different elements of her experience, the notable omissions and the surrealist interludes – titled 'De cuando nos comíamos las patas de las sillas en ucronía (I) and (II)' – have invited readings of the text as fiction or autofiction (Babych 2018) or as close to gonzo journalism (Angulo Egea 2017: 178); while other elements, such as the dialogue established by the narrator between her personal, individual circumstances and collective social processes, place it close to Germán Labrador's aforementioned conceptualisation of the *historia de vida* (2012). As de Benito notes, Fallarás' text is the result of a deliberate hybridisation of fiction and non-fiction genres (2021: 65), and thus does not fit in any one category: it is not a straightforwardly fictional narrative because we can ascertain, through archival research, the veracity of much of the account; neither is it a conventionally autofictional text, in that self-fictionalisation strategies do not only serve the purpose of problematising the boundary between fiction and non-fiction, or between authorial and biographical

11 The trope of 'the two Spains' alludes to the fierce ideological divisions between Liberals and Conservatives in the nineteenth century, and between Republicans and Traditionalists/Nationalists in the twentieth century. According to this image, liberal, progressive, European Spain and Catholic, traditional Spain are engaged in a perpetual and seemingly irresolvable battle, not only over political control, but also over the past and future (and hence the very identity) of the country.

'I'; and inasmuch as this is a written account by a respected journalist and author, and published by a large editorial group (Planeta), it does not correspond to the *historia de vida* that, according to Labrador, is characterised by 'su carácter fundamentalmente oral, en su componente no letrado y en su asociación con sujetos y comunidades que no disponen de formas autorizadas de contar públicamente sus vidas' (2012: 564). This generic indeterminacy might be read as a sign that this work is not just a text about the crisis, but a text *in* crisis. Arguably, Fallarás' overrunning of traditional generic conventions – as well as the repeated meta-narrative comments on the importance of enunciation which I will discuss in what follows – bears witness to the difficulty of depicting the experience of eviction without melodramatic pathos or Dickensian paternalism.

Babych perceptively notes how Fallarás' initial attempt to define the book, in the segment that precedes the chronologically linear chapters, takes the form of negative dialectics: we are told what the book is not ('Este libro no es un ensayo sobre los desahucios ni sobre la crisis económica', 17), but in fact this gesture is 'a rhetorical figure that unconsciously directs the attention of the reader precisely to the objects of negation' (Babych 2018: 145). The text is later defined as

> la narración de mi desahucio, un proceso de hundimiento en la miseria que arranca el día que me despidieron de un diario, a finales de 2008, y termina aquella tarde del 13 de noviembre de 2012 en la que el tipo llamó a la puerta y me convirtió en desahuciada. (Fallarás 2013: 18)

As Babych argues, the text is not only the first-person chronicle of Fallarás' experience of eviction, as stated here: its mobilisation of unemployment figures and the multiple references to social and political developments such as general strikes or the 15M movement allow the author to frame her individual experience within a specific political and socio-historical context: post-2008, crisis Spain. In that sense, the book is *both* an individual first-person account of the experience of eviction (as the quote above states) *and* a book about the specific effects of the global financial crisis of 2008 in Spain: a radical impoverishment (to the point of destitution) of some sectors of the middle classes, who lost not only their jobs – and hence their income – but also their savings and, ultimately, their homes. The use of the initial rhetorical negation in fact serves not so much to manage readers' expectations, as to underline the inextricability between an individual experience and its enunciation, and the context in which that experience takes place. Fallarás may not have set out to write a chronicle of the effects of the 2008 crisis on a significant number of Spanish middle-class families, yet inevitably her tale acquires a social/collective dimension, as she can only make sense of the recent events in her life by considering the circumstances in which they take place. Chief amongst these circumstances is, for Fallarás, the loss of her job as deputy editor of the now defunct online news portal *ADN* in October 2008.

From the outset, Fallarás' dismissal is presented as a result of the crisis and is framed within a context of rapidly growing unemployment rates in Spain. Given the unprecedented levels of joblessness in Spain in the aftermath of 2008 (with unemployment peaking at just over 25% in 2013, the year in which *A la puta calle* was published), the economic downturn is presented as no longer affecting specific social groups or economic sectors, but as increasingly felt by all. Hence Fallarás refers to unemployment as '[e]sta lotería [que] ha empezado a tocarle con furia a los miembros de lo que llaman clase media profesional. Elija usted dónde se encuentra y mire bien sus números' (2013: 19). Her words not only highlight the ways in which the crisis is reaching sections of society which for years had imagined themselves to be financially secure, but also point to the arbitrariness of job destruction – conceptualised here as a lottery whose results cannot be determined or influenced by players.

Fallarás' status as a middle-class professional is presented, within her enunciation, as both an advantage and a disadvantage. On the one hand, as a professional journalist and writer, she is

> una desahuciada capaz de narrarlo [el desahucio] por escrito, de contarlo argumentando ante una cámara y con experiencia, algo sumamente cómodo, claro. Un testimonio directo en primera persona resulta muy cómodo e impactante. Periodismo, por lo visto, de santísima trinidad, objeto, sujeto y análisis. Una y trina. (13)

Her ability to tell her story in an articulate manner and her experience in front of a camera make her a convenient chronicler of the crisis, since, as she ironises above, she can simultaneously become the object and subject of her own analysis. Yet her very eloquence and her self-possessed manner and appearance lead some to question her credibility, with writer Fernando Sánchez-Dragó telling her 'Oí lo de tu desahucio. Imagino que no será verdad, ¿no?' (13), or an acquaintance telling Fallarás' mother that she finds it difficult to believe her story because, on TV, 'yo la vi muy mona' (39). Such reactions are revealing of prejudices around what a victim of destitution should look like, or how they should behave, which are not entirely dissimilar to the credibility issues faced by victims of sexual violence, whose behaviour and appearance are often expected to conform to certain patterns in order for their allegations to be deemed credible and legitimate. Fallarás understands this resistance on the part of others to believe her predicament, as she reflects that

> [n]o hay nada más difícil que admitir la miseria, la quiebra, de un igual. Porque es la nuestra propia. Si yo, una profesional con veinticinco años de oficio a mis espaldas, [...] puedo ser desahuciada, puedo llegar a perderlo todo, hasta el techo, y eso sin dejar de trabajar y remar y pedalear, si eso es así, significa que a quienes están en la situación en la que yo estaba, a los que quedaron allá arriba en el territorio no desplomado, les puede suceder lo mismo. (38)

For Fallarás, then, the reluctance of some to believe her story is due mainly to fear – a fear that the same could happen to them. Given the unemployment figures in Spain in the wake of the 2008 crisis, particularly over the period 2010–15, when the unemployment rate consistently remained at over 20%, that fear is not unfounded, as the eviction figures quoted at the beginning of this chapter illustrate. One of the singularities of Fallarás' chronicle (and arguably one of its key achievements) is how the eviction process is portrayed as inextricably linked to her situation of unemployment – a strategy that serves to counter the narrative according to which those who lost their homes during the crisis had simply over-stretched themselves financially or were living 'beyond their means', and were thus at least partly to blame for the predicament in which they found themselves.[12] And yet Fallarás cannot escape a certain sense of guilt over her sacking, as she is left asking herself '¿Por qué a mí?' (43 ff.), a question which she gradually comes to understand is revealing of a lack of solidarity and conceals an unwillingness (or inability) to question the way in which the neoliberal world works: 'cuando te dan la patada no te preguntas por qué se dan patadas en este mundo cruel, oh, sino por qué la patada le ha tocado a tu culo' (46).

The author's sacking is depicted as a traumatic event that provokes a series of feelings typical of a grieving process: shock, disbelief, denial,

12 Alonso and colleagues (2016) note, in a qualitative, focus-group-based study on social perceptions of the 2008 crisis, that 'en todas las dinámicas sigue apareciendo la posición que defiende que "es obvio que hay gente que realmente ha vivido por encima de sus posibilidades" (RG9-Becarios). Las posiciones moralistas que critican la falta de educación y de cultura entre quienes se endeudaron en exceso sigue muy activa [...]' (358). The study goes on to add, however, that this initially dominant perception – amplified by some sectors of the media – has been modified over time, as citizens became more aware of the extent of malpractice within the financial sector and more cases of political corruption were exposed.

anger, sadness and guilt. What the narrator is mourning in the immediate aftermath of losing her job is not so much the job itself or the income it secured, but her sense of herself as a successful and respected journalist and author. In order to counter this identity crisis, she feels the need to 'enumerar sin descanso todo lo que sabes, lo que eres, lo que quieres. Es tu lucha contra la muerte' (44). Another coping strategy mobilised at this stage of the fall – the first year, when she is still receiving unemployment benefits and the scope of the 2008 crisis is still unknown – is to keep doing things, in the belief that it may be possible to reverse or at least stop or slow down the fall by attempting to pedal her way back up the Niesen staircase. These activities range from keeping an active social media profile, to blogging, to the occasional paid appearance at roundtable discussions and, finally, to incursions in what the narrator defines as journalistic prostitution, that is, the writing of supposedly independent articles that are in fact thinly disguised marketing exercises. There is even an interlude in the first year (2009) in which it seems the narrator might manage to defy gravity and avoid the fall altogether, as she is briefly employed by a new online media outlet which folds before it launches. Despite the guilt and grief that the narrator feels during this first year, there is still hope and an energy reminiscent of the enthusiasm characteristic of creative and precarious professionals, and on which Remedios Zafra has written at length (2017). For while the sacking has knocked the narrator's self-confidence, she still has (some) faith in the system and hence in the possibility of reversing her current situation.

The second year, we are told from the outset of the chapter which covers that period, is different: as paid work and even the prospect of paid work disappear, unemployment payments dry up and savings are exhausted, 'se multiplican los episodios de ansiedad, el vértigo, las horas del lobo, las noches en vela, la agresividad y ciertos gestos de humillación ante amigos con cargos en empresas' (2013: 67). It is during this second year that the narrator loses her faith in the system, as she realises that 'todo estaba roto. Y no hablo de mi casa, sino del mecanismo democrático al que no habíamos prestado demasiada atención, porque parecía que ya iba solo' (75). This insight coincides with what is described as her first 'ruptura absoluta' (68), as she is forced to admit her lack of prospects and her inability to plan for or indeed think about the future, about a future beyond the increasingly challenging task of meeting her own and her children's basic needs. The Spanish phrase 'ganarse la vida' (to earn a living) appears to the narrator as particularly revealing at this juncture, as she comes to realise that life is not a right in itself, but something that must be earned, fought for. The surge in unemployment and the welfare cuts resulting from the austerity policies implemented in the wake of the 2008 crisis are presented as threatening not just individuals' purchasing capacity or general prospects, but the very lives of those affected, as illustrated by the first reported eviction-related suicide in November 2010 (85).[13] In this context, the unwillingness or inability of the Spanish government to intervene is depicted, if implicitly, as a breach of the social contract which seriously undermines democratic legitimacy. David Becerra maintains that Spanish crisis texts (including Fallarás') often have as their underlying premise the belief that

> [l]a 'clase media', que se autopercibe como un estrato intermedio de la sociedad situado entre los que poseen los medios de producción y la clase obrera, había confiado tradicionalmente en el cumplimiento del pacto tácito que había firmado con la sociedad: si cumplían con su función social iban a ver realizada la promesa de progreso, bienestar, estabilidad y consumo. (2018: 46)

The 'función social' of the middle class mentioned by Becerra in the lines above is identified, via Esteban Hernández (2014), as 'garantizar la "paz social" del sistema' (47), eschewing demands for a more egalitarian social order so long as their (relative) privileges – welfare, security, purchasing power – were preserved. The crisis of 2008 and the ensuing austerity policies are perceived as a betrayal of that promise, a widely shared perception in Spain at the time, which manifested itself in disparate ways. One of the more visible reactions to that sense of betrayal was the re-politicisation of wide sectors of Spanish society, which took to the streets to demand that their political representatives defend the interests of the majority, rather than those of the oligarchy, in street protests that eventually coalesced in the 15M movement. But such discontent also led to a questioning of the notion of (national) belonging, and helped fuel the pro-independence movement in Catalonia, as discussed in the Introduction. In the case of the narrator of *A la puta calle*, the experience leads to the emergence of a new subjectivity: that of a 'pesada, beligerante, furbiunda y piquetera individual' (2013: 77), ready

13 Fallarás describes how 'el 11 de noviembre de aquel 2010 apareció en los diarios la noticia de un hombre que se había suicidado en la calle Juan de Juanes del polígono Gornal de Hospitalet, Barcelona' (85), and states that this marked 'el primer suicidio derivado de los desahucios' (85). While Fallarás does not mention any specific newspaper, the news was covered by, among others, *La Vanguardia*, in this article: https://www.lavanguardia.com/sucesos/20101111/54067710058/un-padre-de-familia-a-punto-de-ser-desahuciado-se-ahorca-en-plena-calle.html. The site #15M-Pedia also lists this suicide as the first in the wake of the Great Recession (see https://15mpedia.org/wiki/Lista_de_suicidios_relacionados_con_desahucios_en_Espa%C3%B1a).

to break the law and join one of the many squatter communities which were coming into existence in post-2008 Barcelona.

However, and in spite of her fairly early realisation regarding the unfulfilled promise of material prosperity and stability, the narrator's transformation is a long, drawn-out process. At this point, during her second year of unemployment, she is still primarily engaged in an at times seemingly illogical headlong rush, as she embarks on the writing of two novels in the hope of winning literary prize money. Against her own expectations, in the third year (2011) of her fall the narrator wins the two literary prizes she had entered. The prize money buys her some time, but given the size of her debt with the bank, and the debts contracted with others – children's school meals, loans owed to family members – she very quickly finds herself in the same situation as before: unable to meet her mortgage payments. Yet during the brief reprieve, she is able to look around her and notice that '[a]llá afuera había sucedido algo, algo que con el nombre de 15M y Spanish Revolution e Indignados daba la vuelta al mundo' (104). Her initial response to this phenomenon is one of incomprehension as she finds the protest 'irritantemente pacífica' (104), and scepticism, since her own experience has led her to doubt that those who face complete destitution can afford to practise solidarity. This third year closes with the narrator in a similarly desperate position to that she faced a year earlier, before being awarded the literary prizes. And, as before, despite an increasing awareness that 'ya no hay nada que hacer' (119), she insists that her 'única salida es seguir remando, seguir pedaleando, aferrarte a lo que te has inventado para adaptarte, aunque sea de mentira: las normas de un mundo que no existe ya' (116). This world that no longer exists is, of course, that pre-dating the crisis – a context characterised not only by greater economic prosperity, but also by widespread confidence in the economic and political establishments and by a belief in merit and in the power of each individual in terms of shaping their own fate.

By the final year of her descent down the Niesen staircase (2012), the narrator feels not just that her situation is irreversible, but that '[e]ste lugar empieza a desaparecer' (123). It is worth noting how, once again, the situation of crisis is expressed in spatial terms, even if the space alluded to here is deliberately vague, as there is no referent for 'este lugar'. It is thus left up to the reader to decide whether the narrator is referring to her home (at risk of eviction), her life (in seemingly unstoppable free-fall), a country that she struggles to recognise or indeed the very space of enunciation – as her situation of destitution threatens her ability to complete her chronicle, and because the impending experience of homelessness may resist verbalisation due to its deeply traumatic nature.

Before the enunciative space comes to a close, the narrator depicts her radicalisation, which, though a gradual process, finds its completion in this fourth year of 2012, when she is approached by another mother at her children's school, also facing eviction, and they discuss the possibility of joining Barcelona's growing squatter community. This moment is described as a turning point, as she realises that

> Habían hecho falta cuatro años de empobrecimiento radical y de maltrato a la sociedad por parte de sus políticos para que recuperara aquello que tuve. Para que el tercer crac me rompiera lo que quedaba de entonces. Y de nuevo tuve que enunciarlo para que sucediera, porque ya estaba dentro, por supuesto que estaba; pero lo que no se enuncia, de alguna manera, no existe.
>
> Tuve que escribir que yo ya no soy una mujer pacífica [...]. (2013: 147–48)

The 'aquello que tuve' in the first sentence quoted refers to the narrator's youthful rebelliousness, to her early years in Barcelona, in the late 1980s, when, as a university student, she had flirted with the squatter movement. It is only after four years of progressive but unforgiving impoverishment that she remembers 'que no se debe obedecer lo que no se cree justo, y que las autoridades sólo tendrán respeto si se lo merecen' (147). Only at this point is her faith in the system (or what remains of it) completely destroyed – a process that, crucially, can only culminate through the enunciation of this feeling or insight. In this context, rebelliousness against authority and even violence appear as, if not legitimate, at least understandable responses to a situation of utter desperation and destitution. By the end of the text, the narrator explains her decision to not attend a protest held at Madrid's Congreso in September 2012 in the following terms: 'No ir [al Congreso] fue la única manera que encontré de evitar la agresión física' (148).

Rather than cede to those violent impulses, Fallarás, conscious of the importance of narrative, of enunciation, embarks on what Becerra describes as the articulation of a 'voz subalterna' (2018: 56), which he qualifies as 'un acto subversivo' (56). Indeed, in the opening lines the narrator defiantly addresses an 'ustedes' comprised of economists and politicians who theorise about the 2008 crisis, but have not had to suffer its effects, and states: 'Ustedes acostumbran a pensar que los pobres y desahuciados no saben escribir ni expresarse' (2013: 12). Writing is thus portrayed here as an act that allows the destitute to defy media portrayals of the poor as ignorant and illiterate, to counter a narrative that posits that they have nothing because they have nothing to offer, no skillset.[14] A few pages later, the narrator states the impossibility of accurately depicting destitution from the distance afforded by a minimal degree of comfort and financial security. Her enunciation is valorised here for its unique testimonial value, for its veracity (29). Later on, the enumeration of one's skills is mentioned as a coping mechanism following the loss of employment (44). Putting things into words is also depicted as an often-painful awareness-raising mechanism – 'saber las cosas que pasan es un paso de algodón. El hierro, el filo, está en enunciarlas' (68) – and as a resistance strategy, as it '[s]ignifica que aún puedes luchar' (129–30).

This insistence on the importance of putting experience into words, of narrativising, could also be read as a compensatory act. The close connection between home and narrative has been noted by critics such as Angelika Bammer, who argues that 'what "home" means to us is shaped at once by the material circumstances of our experience and by the various narratives that attempt to define and interpret that experience for us' (1992: ix); or Dietmar Dath, who describes homes as 'origins stories' (Naficy 1999: 68). In a context in which the material, physical home is threatened, the impulse to chronicle the loss of the home could thus be regarded as not only a testimonial act of resistance, but also as a symbolic attempt to build an alternative dwelling space (the text), if not for one's body, then at least for one's subjectivity. But because eviction, in post-2008 Spain, constitutes a shared, collective experience affecting a considerable number of individuals, and because the text has been written to be circulated, this subjectivity is not necessarily conceived of as individual, as that of its narrator alone; instead, it can be read as an attempt or a first step towards the construction of a collective identity – that of the desahuciado, or 'evictee'. This collective – and hence political – dimension of the text can help explain some of the noticeable omissions within it: the barely perceptible presence of the narrator's partner and the scarcity of details concerning her children or wider family;[15] or, more glaringly, the

14 The Spanish philosopher Adela Cortina coined the term 'aporofobia' (often translated into English as 'aporophobia') in the 1990s to refer to what she identified as a fear, aversion and/or hatred of the poor that was distinct from other forms of hatred such as xenophobia. This prejudice is based, at least in part, on the type of stereotype of the poor as illiterate (and having nothing to offer) mobilised by Fallarás here. Cortina discusses the notion at length in the article 'Aporofobia', published by Spanish daily *El País* in 2000, and available at https://elpais.com/diario/2000/03/07/opinion/952383603_850215.html.

15 Babych interprets the absence of the partner as a strategy that 'deprives him of the phallocentric role in the story' (2018: 150), an interesting reading which,

missing climax – as the moment of the physical removal of the narrator and her family from their home is left out of the chronicle. Such details have been omitted, it would appear, to avoid the dual trap of presenting this story as singular in its specificities or sensational in its denouement. Instead, Fallarás' text strikes a delicate balance, offering a stark depiction of the experience of eviction and its effects on herself and her family, without sliding into self-pity or self-victimisation. The effectiveness of this chronicle, and its emancipatory potential, reside in its deft use of a series of rhetorical strategies, such as the mobilisation of verifiable data, the selective deployment of a corrosive irony that testifies simultaneously to the narrator's anger and to her sense of humour, and the at times brutal or hyperbolic, but never moralising, frankness of the tone employed. Such strategies allow the author to vividly describe an individual experience while alluding to its collective dimension and lucidly pointing to some of its structural causes. They also contribute to making this a text in crisis, that is, a text that resits straightforward generic classifications and univocal readings.

Tiempo de encierro (2013)

Published in the same year as *A la puta calle*, Doménico Chiappe's novel *Tiempo de encierro* also describes an eviction process which affects a middle-class couple that has become rapidly impoverished because of the 2008 crisis. The plot, based on a real story, is set in motion when Igrid, a freelance digital media consultant and publisher, receives, at 16-weeks pregnant, an early loan termination notification – in practice, an eviction notice – from her bank for the mortgage on the house she owns and occupies with her partner, Maelo. Igrid's reaction to this news is to barricade herself inside the house, located within an eerily empty, newly built housing development on the outskirts of Madrid. Maelo, meanwhile, frantically tries to stop the eviction process, and when this proves impossible, seeks help from the growing (and increasingly well-organised) squatter movement in central Madrid. If the staircase on Mount Niesen and the chronologically linear chapters provided *A la puta calle* with a chronotope that helped structure the text, here it is Igrid's pregnancy – chapter titles chart its progression, from Semana 16 to Igrid's early labour at Semana 34 – and the house in which it develops that provide an analogous

however, seems somewhat undermined by the fact that he is not entirely absent, and that the first of the two mentions he receives in the text sees him tasked with taking full care of the house and children so that the narrator can complete her novels (Fallarás 2013: 85).

structuring device. Interspersed with these chapters, strongly focalised on the figure of Igrid, and in which omniscient third-person narration coexists with monologues from Igrid to her unborn child, are fragments (numbered one to six) focusing on Maelo and his experiences, over a decade earlier, as a Peruvian-Venezuelan immigrant arriving in a then-prosperous Spain. These chapters have the particularity of being formed by a succession of short infinitive constructions:

> Emigrar, llegar.
> Pero antes, partir.
> Renunciar al trabajo.
> Vender el automóvil.
> Empacar. (Chiappe 2013: 47)

For Babych, '[s]uch unusual grammar points to the inability to finish or conclude any process in his [Maelo's] existence as an immigrant in Spain' (2018: 34), although Igrid's depiction of their relationship and plans at the outset of the novel – before the arrival of the eviction notice – suggests that Maelo has indeed succeeded in building a life, a home and a family in Spain. A further possible explanation for this striking choice is that, through the use of a non-personal verb form, the actions depicted here appear as de-coupled from the figure carrying them out, hence allowing the collective dimension of Maelo's migratory experience to be underlined.

Space is a central motif in the narrative, as exemplified by Igrid's words to her unborn child in the initial pages of the text, where she describes the house to her and explains that '[e]ste es el espacio que habitamos. Yo habito esta casa; tú me habitas a mí' (Chiappe 2013: 10). Igrid's words highlight the connection between dwelling and living, between home and body. As in the previous text discussed, the loss of the home is thus implicitly presented as an existential threat; and, as such, Igrid's decision to confine herself to the house to avoid and resist eviction appears as an understandable, if ultimately pointless, decision. Despite the narrative's focus on enclosed and potentially claustrophobic spaces (the house, the womb, Igrid's mind), the novel expands its scope beyond the individual and private realms, as Igrid's use of digital devices enables her to remain connected to the outside world. The irruption of news from friends and from events taking place in Spain, the visits to the house by Maelo and the artist Bi (with whom Igrid is working), as well as the integration of a dystopic TV series, *Los Caníbales*, which Igrid watches and relays to her unborn child, contribute to the emergence of a polyphonic narrative that amplifies the detailed and subtle portrayal of the mental and psychological processes set in motion in Igrid's mind following the eviction notice.[16]

The author has explained that he chose to focus on one particular eviction story – that of Igrid and Maelo – in order to metonymically 'contar el todo (la crisis española y su salvajismo hacia el individuo, mientras es demasiado permisiva con las instituciones y grandes empresas) por la parte (una persona afectada por el bache)' (Anon. 2013: online). Such an approach allows him to offer a detailed account both of the legal procedures relating to an eviction process – often presented as shambolic and morally bankrupt – as well as of the physical and mental effects that the process has on Igrid. This approach also enables an exploration of different forms of what the author elsewhere describes as 'rebelión particular' (Chiappe in González 2013: online), that is, of different individual rebellion strategies mobilised against a system perceived as unfair, and against a set of circumstances considered unbearable. These strategies range from suicide, as exemplified by the deaths of Igrid's ex-boyfriend Lucas, and of Martina, her former pilates teacher; to Igrid's decision to confine herself to her home in order to resist eviction; to Maelo's various attempts to find a way out (first by legally contesting the eviction, later by occupying an empty flat); or indeed, meta-textually, to the author's decision to write a novel depicting the effects of the global 2008 crisis in Spain. However, the author is careful not to present certain strategies as more effective or preferable than others; rather, he is concerned with vindicating the individual freedom to rebel – a prerequisite in order to combat the prevailing 'desmoralización colectiva [...] que es la estrategia del poder para hacer cualquier cosa' (González 2013: online). Individual acts of rebellion may appear pointless, 'abocados al fracaso', in Chiappe's own words (González 2013: online), yet they testify to the existence of a civic consciousness with the potential to question the legitimacy of certain processes, practices and rules – hence potentially, eventually, contributing to undermine their apparent inevitability. This subversive potential of the act of questioning is put forward by Igrid, as she tells her unborn child: 'Te diré una de las pocas cosas que sé con certeza: En esta sociedad embrutecedora, preguntar ya constituye una rebelión. Una rebelión privada, la más difícil. [...] Hay que hacerse preguntas, criatura. Hay

16 The title of the TV series, which Igrid narrates to her unborn child (191–94, 198–201, 210–14, 218–21, 224–27) and which features a besieged city in which cannibalism has become commonplace, is reminiscent of Germán Labrador's theorisation of the 'temporality of crisis' (2014) through the prisms of gastronomy and anthropophagy.

que formularlas, expresarlas aunque la respuesta no exista o ya la conozcas' (Chiappe 2013: 19).

It is worth noting that Igrid utters these words, and those quoted below, before she receives her eviction notice, but after learning about Lucas' suicide, which is presented as, at least in part, a result of the crisis. Among the questions Igrid asks herself at this point are some relating to the media coverage of the effects of the 2008 downturn:

> ¿Y ese lenguaje? ¿salvar al euro, rescatar al país? ¿de qué superhéroe con capa hablan? Superhéroes del equívoco, defensores del error y la prepotencia, envestidos de supremacía moral sufragada con fondos públicos, preconizadores de la desigualdad. Y nada se informa sobre Lucas, ni sobre las personas. Solo hay demagogia encubierta. Excusas para allanar el camino a una ideología, la misma que nos ha metido en este lío. (19)

There are echoes, in Igrid's characterisation of the media coverage of the crisis as a superhero epic, of Alain Badiou's 2008 article 'De quel réel cette crise est-elle le spectacle?', published by *Le Monde* a month after the collapse of Lehman Brothers, and in which he likens media portrayals of the financial crisis to the disaster movie genre – a linguistic and generic-stylistic choice that Badiou, like Igrid, sees as having a markedly ideological intent: to present the policies set in motion to respond to the 2008 downturn – which is itself referred to as a natural disaster that no-one could have foreseen or prevented, and for which therefore no-one can be held accountable – as a painful but inevitable corrective to avert an even larger catastrophe. The disaster narrative rhetoric mobilised in such media coverage contributes to extend fear and uncertainty so that any meaningful questioning of the measures adopted in the wake of the crisis, or of its root causes, is either entirely dissuaded or indefinitely postponed.

Despite Igrid's questioning of the legitimacy of political and economic leaders, despite her criticism of the media coverage on the crisis – a position she holds even before she herself becomes directly affected by it – she does not, at this point or indeed at any point in the narrative, take part in collective action. In fact, she comments on the 15M phenomenon, telling her unborn baby how '[t]u padre y yo vimos toda la movida del 15M por televisión. Nos emocionó pero no llegamos a ir a Sol' (37). There are several possible explanations for this passivity: firstly, Chiappe explains that Igrid and Maelo's decision to stay home and not join the 15M protest 'es la actitud mayoritaria en casi todas las manifestaciones democráticas' (García Márquez 2014: online); hence their attitude could be seen as indicative of the novel's ambition to construct a plausible, realistic story – a narrative with which its largely educated, middle-class (if precariously or aspiringly so) readership can identify. Secondly, Igrid's chosen form of protest, her voluntary confinement in the house, seems intended to set a contrast with Maelo's more conventional resistance strategies, and thus to underline that rebellion or resistance can take a multiplicity of forms, depending on the circumstances, skills and proclivities of each individual. As such, Igrid's attitude once she decides to confine herself to the house should not be read as a passive stance, nor as a seclusion within the private/domestic realm that affords her an escape from a hostile socio-political climate – an interpretation to which Babych (2018: 40) comes perilously close when he identifies the male storyline (Maelo's) with the political, and Igrid's narrative with the domestic. Such an identification, as well as uncritically reproducing a gender(ed) scheme which posits the domestic as a private and female realm and the public sphere as a political and male territory, risks de-politicising the private, the domestic, the individual – precisely the very move the novel seeks to challenge, as exemplified by Igrid's assertion that '[e]n la vida todo es personal' (2013: 55). Finally, as well as contributing to problematise the distinction between the private and the public, the individual and the social, Igrid's reluctance to join or endorse a specific group or initiative could be seen as, ironically, an implicit nod to the plurality of the 15M phenomenon, which eschewed conventional political labels (such as left/right, progressive/conservative) and frameworks (such as the hierarchically organised party) in favour of more direct and horizontal forms of citizen engagement.[17] While Chiappe's novel is set barely a year after the 15M events, there is already a sense, on Igrid's part, that the phenomenon is at risk of becoming absorbed and neutralised by the system, as she explains her reluctance to use the term 'indignada' as follows: '[m]e niego a definirme a partir de la estrategia de marketing de una editorial poderosa, que aprovechó la concentración en la plaza para vender un libro que nadie allí había leído' (154).[18]

Unlike in *A la puta calle*, the protagonists of *Tiempo de encierro* are not unemployed, but rather under-employed. Igrid has seen her freelance work dry up as a result of the crisis, while Maelo has had his teaching hours –

17 Due to space constraints, I cannot offer a detailed account of the initiatives related to 15M here, but such an account can be found in the volume edited by Benjamín Tejerina and Ignacia Perugorría, *Crisis and Social Mobilization in Contemporary Spain: The 15M Movement* (Abingdon and New York: Routledge, 2018).

18 Igrid is of course referring to Stéphane Hessel's *Indignez-vous!* (2010), translated into Spanish as *¡Indignaos!* (2011) here, but her comment alludes to a pattern of commodification that can potentially extend to other forms or gestures of protest, such as 15M.

and hence his salary – significantly reduced. The protagonists of Chiappe's text hence embody a different facet of the crisis: the vulnerability of a liberal-professional precariat whose exposure to economic fluctuations had, in the years in which Spain's economy was booming, been presented as a competitive advantage, a sign of flexibility and adaptability to a continuously changing environment, and a condition which could, moreover, afford its members an increased sense of personal freedom. The global economic crisis of 2008 revealed such freedom as illusory, and it quickly highlighted how precarious the apparent prosperity of the preceding years had been, as many lost contracts and commissions, and others were forced to close shop or fell into debt – in some cases, as in Chiappe's text, putting themselves and their families at risk of eviction. The question of the personal responsibility of all those who got into debt (often in the form of mortgages) in the years prior to the crisis, and were then rendered incapable of meeting repayments is not avoided: Igrid herself admits, before she becomes aware of her own financial problems, that '[v]ivimos bien. [...] ...usufructuamos el despilfarro como cualquier ciudadano de esta comunidad, país, continente' (24). Latent in her words is a sense that the years preceding the crisis were a time characterised by 'despilfarro', by a generalised squandering of money in which she and Maelo, like everybody else in the Western world, also took part. At this early point in the narrative, Igrid shows no regret, as she almost defiantly states that '[v]ivimos bien y no hay nada de lo que arrepentirse' (24). Yet once the eviction notice arrives, she cannot help but blame herself for having taken out the mortgage, for having fallen prey to the generalised optimism of the early 2000s. Later on, she admits her complicity with a system she knew was flawed, as she admits to Bi that

> Yo conocía el sistema, y preferí obviar sus consecuencias. No soy la dama inocente a la que desvirga el monstruo. ¿Sabes lo que me desconcertó? No fueron la incapacidad, la ociosa ineptitud, la corrupción de las autoridades ni el marco legal que ya estipulaba la posibilidad de aplastarme. Me perturbó que la letra pequeña me alcanzase. A mí. A otros, sí, qué se le va a hacer, pero ¿a mí?' (156)

The quote above resonates with Fallarás' remarks regarding the pointless but unavoidable question that courts her mind following her dismissal, '¿Por qué a mí?' – a question which she comes to realise is revealing of a degree of selfish, or at least self-centred complicity with a system that both Igrid and Fallarás recognise as unfair, but have been willing to accept and abide by, so long as its unfairness did not directly affect them. Yet despite this sense of personal guilt, Igrid's denunciation of a political class that has proven at best impotent against, and at worst complicit with, the abuses perpetrated within the global financial sector is far more scathing:

> Los antaños [*sic*] dictadores son ahora altavoces de sátrapas invisibles. Más Pétain que Hitler. Cierran los ojos ante la invasión y colaboran para salvar sus pellejos. El mercado, un eufemismo para camuflar un puñado de compañías, es un ejército invasor que ametralla a los civiles desprotegidos. (56)

Igrid's words, directed to the child she is expecting, cast politicians as willing and necessary collaborators of the perpetrators of a legally sanctioned plundering of the welfare state: the handful of companies (mostly banks and other financial institutions) which had to be shored up by substantial injections of public money in the wake of 2008. The analogy established with Second World War figures such as Hitler and Pétain serves the dual purpose of clarifying their role and of highlighting – to a deliberately hyperbolic degree – both the opportunistic and cowardly nature of their actions, and the dire consequences of those actions on the defenceless civilian population they supposedly represent. While such outbursts on Igrid's part may appear as facile exercises in banker-bashing, Chiappe takes care not to cede to moralising or propagandistic temptations, carefully framing such fragments within the context of Igrid's fluctuating moods and increasing desperation. Further, Igrid's – and, we might be tempted to presuppose, Chiappe's – criticism extends far beyond the financial sector and the political class: we already mentioned Igrid's attack on the media coverage of the crisis above; and the creative and cultural industries (in which Igrid works) are not spared, as Igrid decries the conservatism of publishers (23) and mocks the attitude of writers and intellectuals who

> creen que la consagración está en una reseña en *Babelia*, en una foto de Mordzinski, en un escaparate comprado en La Casa del Libro, en un premio otorgado a dedo por el gurú de turno, en participar gratis en el Hay Festival, en responder con grosería al becario del Cervantes. (80)

While the lines above display more than a hint of embittered self-righteousness, the fact that they are intoned 'con voz de proclama y mitin' (80) suggests a degree of irony on Igrid's part that points to her self-awareness regarding her own role in and complicity with at least some of the mechanisms she attacks. Indeed, her relationship with the artist Bi, with whom she sets out to collaborate at the beginning of the novel, offers some revealing insights in terms of the perverse power dynamics that articulate not just the economic and political spheres, but permeate also a creative-cultural establishment shown to be dominated by the same exploitative logic.

Bi is an internationally renowned visual and performance artist who approaches Igrid to collaborate on a new project. Igrid is initially intrigued by Bi and her project, and given her financial circumstances, she is also grateful at the prospect of paid work. From the outset, Bi is described as barely human, resembling 'una fotografía en blanco y negro, una puesta en escena adobada de simbolismo y metáfora, la obra perfecta de Abramovic o cualquier otra artista que se exhibe como obra' (151) – a characterisation that aligns with her enigmatic and unusual name, with its suggestions of both duality and duplicity. Her apparent concern for Igrid's financial troubles is quickly revealed as self-interested, as she hopes to mobilise Igrid's rage for her own work, and she barely conceals the parasitic relationship she envisages, telling Igrid she intends to '[c]hupar tu sangre, beber to dolor, mamar de tus lagrimales. [...] ...eso es lo que quiero hacer. Lo necesito' (155–56). The bodily references in her words quickly prove to be not merely metaphorical, as Bi instigates a sexual encounter with Igrid which has clear abusive traits, and which serves to further reaffirm the power imbalance between them (163 ff.). Elsewhere, Chiappe has explained that

> Bi encarna el poder, es el único [personaje] en toda la narración que lo hace, y muestra cómo puede llegar a ser esa relación entre el poderoso y una persona que está a su merced. El poder no se ejerce necesariamente con violencia. Aquí se muestra cómo logra fascinar y subyugar. Y es así como logra mantener el poder. (González 2013: online)

The relationship between Igrid and Bi simultaneously illustrates Igrid's vulnerability – for, despite her vocal criticism of the political, economic and media establishments, she cannot stand up to Bi, as she cannot afford to lose her sole source of income – as well as the fact that 'power' in the abstract can take many different guises and operate in ways that do not conform to conventional definitions of violence or force. Chiappe's decision to personify power in the figure of a radical female avant-garde artist lends itself to multiple readings: firstly, as the author states in the quote above, Bi exemplifies how those in power often resort to seduction, fascination or flattery, among other strategies, to secure the subservience of those they seek to control. Secondly, Bi's anti-system rhetoric – her ultimate goal, she tells Igrid, is to replace the current system, run by 'machos cocainómanos' (2013: 157), with a matriarchy of her own making – stands in contrast with her own actions and attitude, as exemplified not only in her domineering (if not abusive) attitude towards Igrid, but also in her unfeeling reaction to her assistant's suicide ('No quiero hablar de eso. Ahora está a cargo Xing Chin. Más joven, más internacional, la mitad de comisión', 159). Bi's figure can thus also be interpreted as a critique directed towards an artistic-cultural elite that might outwardly mock, parody or decry the shortcomings and abuses of the socio-political and economic order it inhabits, but which, inwardly, is governed by the same principles of exportability and profitability, and thus proves just as inhumane. Finally, Bi's figure might also act as a warning against supposedly radical or emancipatory figures or discourses which, in fact, contribute to perpetuate the status quo while providing an illusion of change. It is interesting to note how, despite her self-proclaimed radical feminism and anti-establishment ideas, and despite the supposedly corrosively critical nature of her work, Bi has thrived because she has been able and willing to unscrupulously exploit those around her to further her own career. Her success, rather than undermine the system, in fact contributes to its perpetuation, providing it with a necessary other, with an outspoken but manageable dissident who helps to create an illusion of plurality. Bi's willingness to act as ruthlessly as those who she attacks disqualifies her discourse, showing it for what it is: mere rhetoric.

In a review for *El Cultural*, Sanz Villanueva defined *Tiempo de encierro* as '[a] la vez novela social e intelectual' (2014: online), perhaps so as to underline that, while this text closely reflects a specific social landscape (post-2008 Spain) and issue (evictions resulting from mortgage payment defaults), its scope is far broader than a mere denunciation of the effects of the crisis. As well as offering a detailed account of the effect of the threat of eviction over Igrid and Maelo – with Igrid's thought processes portrayed in particular depth – the text includes reflections on art, media, the experience of migration, parenthood, the kind of society in which we live and the kind in which we might aspire to live. Chiappe has been reluctant to label his work as political or ideological, presumably due to the widely held assumption that such texts inevitably compromise their literary or aesthetic value in order to articulate a univocal message that can reach a broad readership and thus contribute to social transformations. While the recent wave of authors critically engaging with Spain's contemporary realities (many of them featured in this monograph) disprove the myth that such texts cannot also be aesthetically daring, Chiappe's preference to describe *Tiempo de encierro* as 'una novela cívica' (González 2013: online) points to the author's reluctance to align the text's critical content with a specific political creed. Indeed, many of the questions which Igrid asks herself transcend the political to touch on the existential ('¿No es preservar la especie el principal fin de un ser vivo? ¿O, en este momento de la historia, tener hijos es una inmoralidad?', 2013: 18), the aesthetic ('¿Por qué ya no es belleza aquello que representa fertilidad y asentamiento?', 26) and the ethical ('¿Cuál es el mejor regalo que puedo dejarte? ¿Confianza en ti misma?', 261). Indeed, the three realms are seen as inextricably linked, for existential decisions – such as whether or not to procreate – are conditioned by economic, social and political factors; aesthetic preferences and choices are, at least in part, socially and historically determined; and ethical principles, while in theory underlying social and political systems, are often, in practice, eroded by those very systems. Within this interdependent web of questions, education and critical thinking are identified as the key tools to ensure the survival of democracy post-2008, as Igrid rhetorically asks '¿No es la educación, el pensamiento, la inteligencia, lo único que puede frenar que claven el puñal al único sistema capaz, la democracia, de bloquear un riesgo esencial: la acumulación de poder, el endiosamiento?' (261). Igrid's questions are directed, within the novel, to her unborn daughter; yet the reader also feels directly interpellated by them, as well as by Igrid's exhortation to her unborn baby: '[e]scucha estas preguntas. Y piensa, piensa por ti misma. También escucha las pausas, como si leyeras entrelíneas. Porque ahí, en los silencios, existo' (262). This desire to encourage readers to think independently and critically can help explain the novel's lack of resolution, both in terms of offering any answers to the myriad of questions uttered by Igrid throughout the text, and in terms of the text's open ending – which has Igrid going into labour and finally, it seems, putting an end to her voluntary seclusion in the home. Critics including Babych (2018) and Sanz Villanueva (2014) have commented on the positive or hopeful nature of this ending; and Chiappe has remarked that, underlying the dire circumstances faced by the main characters, there is a certain optimism, in as much as they are able to resist and rebel (Sainz Borgo 2013: online). However, readers are not given a comforting or reassuring ending: the text closes with Igrid going into labour prematurely, and her fate and that of her baby are omitted from the narrative, beyond Igrid's call for help to the emergency services. Even if we presume that they are both fine post-labour, there is a marked sense that this event, though joyful, will not be exempt from difficulties, as Igrid notes that her decision to call for help in order to ensure a safe delivery 'nos obligará a buscar otra forma de resistir' (2013: 281). It is left to the reader to imagine what shape such a new form of resistance may take.

Desahucios. Los escenarios del horror (2013)

Carlos Luján's photo-journalism project *Desahucios. Los escenarios del horror* consists of a series of seven images depicting five locations in which eviction-related suicides have taken place. A brief text accompanies each image or pair of images, providing a basic description of the event that has taken place at each location: the name, age and profession of the victim, the date of the event and some of the circumstances leading up to it (unemployment, receipt of eviction or debt repayment notices). The project was originally published in the weekly magazine *XL Semanal* – a publication distributed as a weekend magazine accompanying 23 regional diaries owned by media group Vocento – on 31 March 2013, and can be accessed at present through the website of NoPhoto, a collective of Spanish photographers to which Luján belongs.[19] Despite the sensational dubbing of these spaces as 'escenarios del horror' in the work's title, Luján's images stand out for the apparent mundanity of the settings depicted: the buildings and streets featured in the series seem utterly unremarkable. Luján thus establishes a suggestive tension between the apparent normality of these scenarios and the horrific events which we know, from the title, have taken place within them – a tension echoed in the captions provided for each image, which combine an almost forensically detached tone with the rendition of seemingly trivial or inconsequential details – such as the football matches which two of the deceased are known to have watched on the eve of their deaths. This tension between the factual documentation of events and the mobilisation of details that encourage an affective response or identification from viewers/readers is reminiscent of Barthes' (1981) distinction between *studium* ('a [visual] field, which I perceive quite familiarly as a consequence of my knowledge, my culture', 25) and *punctum*, the accident or detail that can prick (and indeed wound) the viewer (27). Such details, which include both visual elements in the images and textual cues in the captions, testify to the photographer's intention to transcend the purely testimonial in order to elicit certain emotions from the viewer – but rather than a visceral reaction to a graphic depiction of suffering, they invite (again, following Barthes) a pensive response, as their disturbing elements or qualities are not immediately obvious – therefore arguably making them all the more haunting.

At first glance, the images depict a series of buildings in a detached, factual manner reminiscent of the New Topographics movement's 'stylistic anonymity' (Jenkins 1975: 7). The framing varies from image to image: the images corresponding to the first and third locations (Córdoba, Francisco Lema and Granada, José Miguel Domingo, respectively), for instance, have been taken at an angle and from a distance which allow the photographer to feature two sides of the building, with their meeting point (a corner of the

19 The images can be viewed at http://nophoto.org/desahucios [last accessed 19 August 2024].

building) occupying the centre of the image. In the second (Basauri, Iñaki Vesga) and fourth (Cartagena, Guillermo Santos) images, by contrast, the buildings are depicted frontally; that is, the camera appears to have been positioned immediately opposite the buildings, and hence the resulting images appear flatter, lacking the perspectival depth of other images in the series. The fifth and final setting (Baracaldo, Amaia Egaña) stands out inasmuch as the camera's focus appears to have shifted from the building – which is only depicted fragmentally, unlike in the other images, where buildings are featured in their entirety (or almost) – to the streets around and below it. While the buildings featured in the series vary in shape and size – from a mid-rise four-storey apartment block in the first image, to high-rise blocks of flats in the second and fifth photographs, to the single-storey terraced house in the fourth image – they are all recognisably working-class or lower-middle-class dwellings, as evidenced by their appearance and surroundings. There are other elements that confer on the series a degree of visual coherence, despite the already-mentioned differences in terms of the buildings featured. Chief among these is the light – all images are taken during the day and in natural light, against grey, overcast skies which contribute to endow them with a sense of melancholy.

There is a glaring absence at the heart of the images – that of the deceased individuals who ended their lives at these locations. This absence is made perceptible primarily through the texts accompanying the images, but also, in the first and final locations featured in the series, through the inclusion of two additional photographs (hence the series totalling seven images, despite covering five locations) of the street below the buildings – the spot where the bodies of Francisco Lema and Amaia Egaña were once located. In both cases, these fragments of pavement appear to be wet or stained, presumably as a result of recent rain, though this coincidence also acts as a poignant reminder (a punctum?) of the fact that these spaces would have been cleaned to erase the traces of the suicides in their aftermath, a gesture undermined in the case of Francisco Lema by a graffiti that spells out, in red letters, its memorialising intent: 'Fran no te olvidar'. Interestingly, the final word of that statement is interrupted by the edge of the image, thus introducing a degree of ambiguity as the verb's conjugation marks are left out, making it impossible to know whether the refusal to forget is expressed as an individual (olvidaré) or a collective (olvidaremos) gesture. Given that the photograph is the work of an experienced professional photographer, it seems unlikely that this cut is a mere unintended accident or mistake, and not a deliberate choice. Taken as owing to its author's deliberate intent, then, the break in the final word may be interpreted as a subtle visual metaphor about the fragility and fragmentary nature of memory itself – for despite the graffiti's defiant memorialising declaration not to forget (a declaration which is, moreover, performative: it has been inscribed in the pavement, it has left a physical mark), memories inevitably fade and become confused over time. The decision to miss out part of the final word also acquires a self-reflexive dimension: the notion of the photograph as true, objective, reliable and transparent transposition of reality is thrown into question, as part of the object depicted here (the graffiti) is deliberately hidden from our view, hinting not only at the constructed and mediated nature of every form of representation, including photography, but also at the limitations of the medium as a means to document and convey the suffering caused by the Spanish eviction crisis.

Yet despite this awareness, Luján persists, insisting on turning his camera to these scenarios of eviction-related suicides. Given the carefully articulated, contained, almost austere visual style of the images, it seems obvious that the project does not intend merely to satisfy the public's morbid curiosity. Neither does it make any claim or attempt to be exhaustive: according to data gathered by #15Mpedia, an online project resulting from the 15M movement, there were seven reported eviction-related suicides and one suicide attempt in 2012 and 15 eviction-related suicides, one suicide attempt and one eviction-related death in 2013.[20] It is difficult to determine Luján's selection criteria in terms of the cases and locations featured in his series, although it is noteworthy that all took place within a narrow time frame of almost exactly four months (between 25 October 2012 and 26 February 2013), and the original photographic feature was first published at the end of March 2013. However, the possible documentary intent of the project seems undermined by the fact that these images are not arranged in chronological order or according to any other discernible pattern, such as geographical location or profile of the victim. Rather than a purely factual, informative

20 The data is obtained by collating newspaper articles reporting these suicides, mostly from local and regional press. However, its creators emphasise that the list may not be exhaustive, as only those deaths that triggered media coverage have been included – and indeed, when last checked in November 2023, the site did not list one of the suicides included in Luján's photographic series (that of Guillermo Santos in Cartagena on 26 February 2013). It should also be noted that the site lists not only suicides but also suicide attempts and eviction-related deaths, such as that of a recently evicted man who died in the street, where he was sleeping, in March 2013. Full details can be accessed at https://15mpedia.org/wiki/Lista_de_suicidios_relacionados_con_desahucios_en_Espa%C3%B1a [last accessed 4 September 2024]. It should be noted, however, that this site has not been updated since 2018, in spite of further cases being reported in the media, such as that of Segundo Fuentes in June 2021, reported by *Ctxt* this article: https://ctxt.es/es/20210601/Firmas/36425/suicidios-desahucios-salud-mental-catalunya.htm.

or classificatory approach, Luján seems interested, on the one hand, in the small details concerning these cases that can provoke an affective, empathetic response from viewers; and on the other hand, on the reactions that these events have sparked both at a local level and beyond. For instance, as well as depicting the memorialising graffiti described above, Luján notes how Francisco Lema's suicide 'conmovió al país' – not least because Lema had been featured in a short documentary in which he detailed his personal situation and described an earlier suicide attempt.[21]

The second case featured, that of Iñaki Vesga, acquired additional significance retrospectively, as four Spaniards took their own lives in the same week of February before they were evicted from their homes. Additionally, Vesga's suicide took place on the eve of the Spanish parliament agreeing to consider a Popular Legislative Initiative (PLI) against evictions, coordinated by anti-eviction activists – an approval that only came after an eleventh-hour U-turn from the then-ruling conservative Popular Party in the face of mounting public pressure around the issue of evictions.[22] José Miguel Domingo's death, the third case featured (though the first to take place chronologically, in October 2012) constituted, according to *El Mundo* journalist José A. Cano, 'el primer caso de trascendencia de un suicidio provocado por un desahucio inminente' (Cano 2013: online) and his funeral culminated in one of the first public marches against evictions in Spain, in his native Granada.[23] The suicide of Guillermo Santos, who had been involved in unemployment protests in his native Cartagena (Murcia) on the eve of his death, led to spontaneous demonstrations in his hometown. The final case depicted (although the second in chronological terms), that of Amaia Egaña, led to the acting judge charged with recording the death, Juan Carlos Mediavilla, calling for a change in mortgage legislation to avoid further tragedies – a call supported by other judges which eventually resulted in the passing of the Ley 1/2013, de 14 de mayo, de medidas para reforzar la

21 The documentary, titled 'Con la sangre al cuello', filmed and released in the summer of 2011, can be viewed at https://www.youtube.com/watch?v=fUsZ45u1Nsw [last accessed 13 November 2023].

22 For more information, see http://www.rtve.es/noticias/20130213/congreso-aprueba-tramitar-ilp-sobre-dacion-pago-tras-rectificacion-del-pp/607896.shtml.

23 Although Cano is right in signalling that Domingo's death sparked an unprecedented public reaction, his was not the first-known or first-media-reported eviction-related suicide in the wake of the 2008 crisis. The first such case is believed to have taken place in November 2010, as reported in this article published by *La Vanguardia* on 11 November 2010: https://www.lavanguardia.com/sucesos/20101111/54067710058/un-padre-de-familia-a-punto-de-ser-desahuciado-se-ahorca-en-plena-calle.html. This suicide is also mentioned in Cristina Fallarás' *A la puta calle* (2013: 85).

protección a los deudores hipotecarios, reestructuración de deuda y alquiler social. Although this law was deemed insufficient by anti-eviction activists, as explained earlier in this chapter, the circumstances of its passing – with the then Spanish government forced to veer course due to popular pressure – speak of the potential of grassroots initiatives and mobilisations in terms of achieving at least some level of change. Read in this light, Luján's decision to produce and publish the series could be interpreted as an act of resistance, or at least an act intended to incite viewers to exercise their civic rights to organise and mobilise – even if (or perhaps precisely because) the absent figures at the heart of each image hauntingly testify to their inability to carry on fighting individually.

Susan Sontag famously wrote that '[p]hotographing is essentially an act of non-intervention' (2005 [1977]: 8), yet Luján's series does not, as this analysis has made clear, have a purely informative or documentary purpose, despite the strategic mobilisation of a seemingly detached visual style. In fact, Luján seeks to intervene by provoking a response in viewers/readers that is simultaneously affective and reflective. His careful staging of a tension or dialectic between the seemingly objective and detached visual style of the images and the information offered in the accompanying captions, as well as his inclusion of unsettling visual details, such as the wet pavement and the graffiti fragment, that further throw into question the superficial appearance of normality of these settings, force viewers/readers to reflect upon the invisibility – or very tenuous visibility – of much of the suffering resulting from the 2008 crisis. Implicit in such an exercise is also a recognition of the limits of photography in terms of re-presenting such suffering; yet Luján's work is effective precisely because of its acknowledgement of its own limitations, as it speaks not only of the precarity and vulnerability of the subjects featured, but also of the medium through which they are depicted.

Aquí vivió. Historia de un desahucio (2016)

The graphic novel *Aquí vivió. Historia de un desahucio*, a collaboration between the Spanish author Isaac Rosa and the illustrator Cristina Bueno, contrasts with the two preceding literary texts on multiple levels. Unlike in *A la puta calle* and *Tiempo de encierro*, the focal point of the narrative is not an individual or a family at risk of eviction, but a teenage girl who discovers that the previous owners of the flat into which she and her mother have recently moved, following her parents' divorce, were evicted from the property. This discovery leads Alicia, the teenage protagonist, to find out more about the issue of eviction, and ultimately, to participate in anti-eviction initiatives, as she becomes aware both of the similarities between herself and her family and the previous occupants of the house, and of the abusive and inhumane attitude of the banks towards hundreds of thousands of families at risk of eviction. The visual nature of this text – a graphic novel in which description is superseded by image – also sets it apart from the two other narrative texts discussed in this chapter. And while Rosa and Bueno do offer some insights into Alicia's thoughts and feelings, the spaces she frequents – her room, her flat, her grandmother's house, her school, her *barrio* – arguably take centre stage. In other words, if in the preceding texts we found detailed psychological studies of individuals at risk of or affected by eviction – though these individual personal stories were always shown as indissociable from wider social processes – here the emphasis is on the transformations of Alicia's surroundings – transformations which are shown to be neither accidental nor inconsequential.

The text opens with one of the more visually striking frames in the entire novel: six figures whose close proximity is exacerbated by the lens in the spyhole through which they are seen. The only textual element in this page is the onomatopoeic '¡¡¡DRRRRRIIIING!!!' (Rosa and Bueno 2016: 5) of the doorbell, which helps readers interpret the scene, as it makes clear that these individuals are seeking entry into somebody's flat. The stern expression of the six figures – three of which are dressed in uniform and hence presumably police – and the way in which they visually cram the frame of the lens as they stand in two rows, almost as in formation, together with the text, in block capitals and framed by multiple exclamation marks, contribute to a create a sense of intimidation in the reader, and are indicative of the ominous nature of the occasion. This is confirmed in the following pages, which feature the description of an eviction attempt which is only stopped because the homeowner manages to prove that the officials are at the wrong address. This opening scene, while not relevant to the main plot line, serves the purpose of highlighting, from the very outset of the text, the brutal nature of eviction procedures – the court officials and police featured refuse to listen to the homeowner, who has to go to court to prove their mistake and halt the procedure – their widespread nature and the fact that their effects are beginning to be felt, if in different ways, by an increasing number of Spanish citizens.

This 'no desahucio' (9) is an anecdote told at work by a colleague of Carmen, Alicia's mother. From this story, the narrative attention shifts to Carmen, in the process of moving to a new flat, the plan of which is featured in the text (10–12) framed by Carmen's and Alicia's arguments regarding the suitability of the property, which Alicia complains is claustrophobically small. We then follow Alicia as she moves into the new flat and is greeted with the unexplained hostility of neighbours; as she visits her father (living with his mother, Alicia's grandmother, in the wake of the separation from his wife); and as she returns to her former residence, a house with a garden in a low-rise, residential area of the city. The new flat and the old house, the new *barrio* and the old neighbourhood, are set in contrast to one another: the spacious family home with a garden has been traded for a small flat, the pleasant suburb for a densely built working-class district. Whether the change of circumstances in Alicia's life is the result of her parents' marital breakup or whether the breakup itself is the result of financial difficulties which are also driving the house move is left unexplained.

Alicia's initial complaints about the diminutive size of her new home give way to an increasing sense of unease, as her new neighbours are repeatedly and inexplicably unfriendly, and she is confronted with reminders and remainders of the home's past: a dent in one wall, presumably resulting from an impact (20); damp stains that seem to acquire an uncannily anthropomorphic shape at night (20, 56, 124); pencil marks on a door frame charting a child's growth (and leading Alicia to deduce the past presence of a child of roughly her age in the house) (29); and a mysterious diary that describes a family's confinement, and which is later identified, by Alicia's father, as copied excerpts from Anne Frank's diary (32–47). Despite Alicia's father's assertion that the supposed diary must be nothing more than 'un trabajo de clase' (47), Alicia remains convinced that there is more to the notebook than a mere selection of quotes for a school project. She is proven right by the sudden appearance of Carmen, an elderly lady who enters the flat in which Alicia and her mother are living while they sleep. The frail and confused Carmen insists this flat is her home, and mistakes Alicia for her own granddaughter (also named Alicia). All the elements cited, and particularly the emergence of these 'doubles' of the mother and daughter at the centre of the story, are suggestive of the Freudian notion of the *unheimlich* or uncanny – a term which in the original German has a clear association with the home. For Freud, 'the unheimlich is what was once heimisch, homelike, familiar; the prefix "un" is the token of repression' (1919: 15).

The repression that turns the familiar into the uncanny is, in this context, associated with the trauma experienced by the elderly Carmen as a result of her eviction. Her story is brought to light by the neighbours, who recognise Carmen and explain to Alicia and her mother how, after Carmen, her son, daughter-in-law and granddaughter were evicted, they illegally re-entered the vacant flat and secretly occupied it for a few months, with the help of their neighbours. At this stage, the parallels between Anne Frank's story and that of the 'other' Alicia (absent from the narrative until the very end, but mentioned repeatedly) become clear. The trauma experienced by Carmen and her family is also associated with another historical (and therefore collectively experienced) trauma, that of the brutal repression of the post-war years in Spain, as Alicia's paternal grandmother relates it to the experience of a relative who had to live in hiding for two years after the end of the Civil War. Rosa's tracing of such links could appear hyperbolic or sensationalist, in so far as he appears to equate the effects of two protracted armed conflicts (the Spanish Civil War and the Second World War) with those of a global financial crisis which, while severely impacting on living standards across large swathes of Spanish society, appears far less brutal, or at least less bloody. Yet as Slavoj Žižek's work on violence (2008) reminds us, such a distinction is both illusory and ideologically driven; indeed, for the Slovene critic, objective violence – that is, the violence required to maintain the status quo – is 'the highest form of violence' (68), even if (or rather, precisely because) it is not perceived as such. Subjective violence – the type of acts that we do regard as violent: terrorist acts, riots, attacks by individuals or groups on others – is a reaction against 'the [objective] violence inherent to this "normal" state of things' (2) and 'an implicit admission of impotence' (80–81) vis-à-vis objective violence. Read through this Žižekean lens, Rosa's mobilisation of excerpts from Anne Frank's diary and the inclusion of a story of Francoist repression within the narrative can be interpreted as an attempt by the author to use the past as a means to expose objective violence. In the same way as the suffering of Anne Frank and that of the victims of Francoist repression remained invisible while Nazism and Francoism, respectively, constituted the hegemonic ideologies/ regimes of their time, the struggles of those affected by the effects of the 2008 crisis have been, if not overlooked, then at least frequently presented as self-inflicted (the 'living beyond their means' narrative to which I alluded earlier in this chapter) or minimised (the 'surely it can't be that bad/true' reaction discussed in relation to Fallarás' text). In the context of Peninsular Hispanic studies, Alison Ribeiro de Menezes (2017) has proposed that the memory of Spain's recent and troubled past – the Civil War, the Franco regime and the country's Transition to democracy – can serve as 'a productive disruption of seemingly self-evident assumptions with a view to imagining alternative vistas on the future' (899), and it seems Rosa's mobilisation of the past here serves precisely that purpose.

One apparently obvious difference between the examples of historical trauma featured in the text and the effects of the 2008 crisis is related to responsibility and guilt. If in the case of Anne Frank or of Alicia's relative, Emilio, apportioning responsibility for their suffering seems straightforward – both were victims of authoritarian, cruel and inhumane regimes (Nazism and Francoism, respectively) – in the case of those affected by the 2008 economic downturn, things are far less clear. While many initially blamed the crisis on the reckless, irresponsible or downright fraudulent practices within the financial sector (Stiglitz 2010), others soon pointed their finger at the regulatory deficiencies that had allowed such behaviour to go on unnoticed, and thus at a political class seen as increasingly powerless within a context of global capital flows and economic interdependence (cf. Bauman and Bordoni 2014; Tooze 2018). In Rosa's text, explicit criticism of the financial sector – in the form of a page that succinctly and graphically illustrates its contradictions, as the local bank branch manager's self-exculpatory speech is depicted against a background of different posters encouraging customers to take out all manner of mortgages (2016: 137) – goes hand in hand with a more subtle critique of the readiness with which most of us living in the so-called First World had been willing, in the years leading up to the crisis, to accept a system that fosters social inequality, for as long as we prospered under it. Alicia voices this criticism towards her mother once they learn about the flat's history, as she asks her: '¿No te pareció extraño que [el piso] fuese tan barato? [...] ¿Lo habrías comprador de haberlo sabido [de haber sabido que sus anteriores dueños habían sido desahuciados]?' (150). Alicia's mother adopts a defensive attitude, telling her daughter that they are not to blame for the previous owners' eviction, and insisting that 'cada uno toma sus decisiones en la vida' (151), a statement which she illustrates through reference to her own difficulties: 'Yo misma, por ejemplo. Tuvimos que malvender una casa estupenda, y no fue una decisión fácil. [...] Si no hubiésemos tomado la decisión, quién sabe, igual habríamos perdido también la casa' (151). Her words and her attitude seem reasonable and as readers, we can empathise with her; however, the fact that Alicia remains unconvinced by her mother's reasoning seems indicative of Rosa's aforementioned criticism of the willingness of most to accept inequality if they can, at an individual level, be spared from its negative effects. In contrast, Alicia only manages to deal with the profound unease she feels over her new home's past by overcoming the individualism voiced by her mother ('cada uno toma sus decisiones') and taking part in the actions of her local PAH anti-eviction grassroots group, which she initially contacts in order to locate Carmen's family.

Alicia's involvement with her local PAH branch enables her to learn more about the issue of eviction in Spain: she hears the testimonies of different individuals and families affected, tales of hardship and desperation – but also the hopeful stories of those who have managed to fight back, in large part thanks to the support from the PAH and through the pressure exerted on their banks through collective actions.[24] Although she is met with hostility

24 Alicia's engagement with the Plataforma de Afectados por la Hipoteca (PAH) mirrors Rosa's own, as he explained in an interview with Mélanie Valle Detry

when it becomes clear that her mother has bought a flat from which the previous owners were evicted, Alicia nevertheless remains interested in the issue. She befriends a young activist named Iván, who tells her more about his experiences – pointing out, for instance, the difficulty in establishing the total number of evicted households since 2008 (a problem which is noted in the opening section of this chapter), as well as the fact that the district through which they are walking has come to be known as 'Villa Desahucios' (Eviction Village), a reference that allows readers to identify the until-that-point-indeterminate setting of the story as Barcelona's Ciutat Meridiana district, which was given that nickname by the press due to the high number of evictions taking place within it.[25] Alicia also carries out her own research, delving into Spain's past, from the 1957 pledge by the first-ever housing minister in Spain, José Luis Arrese, that Spain would become a country 'no [...] de proletarios, sino [...] de propietarios' (225; also cited in Colau and Alemany 2012: 34), to the mass-scale urban development in Spanish towns and cities throughout the 1960s and on to the early 2000s, when the Spanish construction boom meant that more housing was built in the country than in Germany, France and Italy combined (227; also cited in Colau and Alemany 2012: 28). This clearly unsustainable path towards economic growth was propped up by the mantra, repeated incessantly by politicians, economists, developers and journalists – and hence largely believed by the wider public – that '[e]l precio de los pisos nunca baja' (229–30). This segment, shaded in black and white to indicate its retrospective nature, serves to undermine

published in 2021. In that interview, Rosa highlighted the importance of that experience within his trajectory as an author, stating that 'la sacudida y el aprendizaje que me supuso el contacto con las gentes de la PAH, gentes que tras una experiencia durísima no se permiten el pesimismo' (2021: 173) led to a turning point in his literary production, as he consciously veered away from the pessimism that had characterised some of his earlier works.

25 The first reference to Ciutat Meridiana as 'Villa Desahucio' that I have been able to find is in an article by Patricia Gabancho, published in Spanish daily *El País* on 3 December 2012 and available at https://elpais.com/ccaa/2012/12/02/catalunya/1354480579_174304.html, although an article by Clara Blanchar published by the same newspaper in July 2012 already dubs the district 'ciudad desahucio' (https://elpais.com/ccaa/2012/07/21/catalunya/1342895388_879265.html). There are further such identifications of Ciutat Meridiana as 'Villa Desahucio' or 'Villa Desahucios' in articles published in *La Vanguardia* (https://www.lavanguardia.com/local/barcelona/20180116/4449466158/ciutat-meridiana-mercado.html) and *El Periódico* (https://www.elperiodico.com/es/barcelona/20121230/ayudar-a-villa-desahucio-3965495). Perhaps unsurprisingly, these pieces note that the district has the lowest per capita income in Barcelona and an immigrant population (40%) double the average for the city as a whole.

Alicia's mother's earlier contention that 'cada uno toma sus decisiones en la vida' (151), illustrating how such individual decisions do not occur in a vacuum, but within a specific context that conditions them; in other words, seemingly free individual choices are here revealed as, at least in part, shaped by a series of social discourses and practices involved in what the Italian thinker Antonio Gramsci (1971) termed the manufacture of consent. But following Gramsci, precisely because consent is manufactured, because it is the result of collective everyday practices, it can also be questioned and undermined – as Alicia establishes after witnessing an action of civil disobedience coordinated by anti-eviction activists to prevent an eviction from taking place (184–92).

Alicia's initial contact with her local PAH branch is motivated by her desire to locate Carmen's family, which is made all the more pressing once Carmen goes missing from the flat Alicia shares with her mother. Eventually, Alicia tracks down the 'other' Alicia and the two young girls have a brief and awkward meeting during which it transpires that Carmen passed away shortly after her eviction – thus suggesting the figure encountered by the protagonist Alicia was in fact a ghost or spectre. This plot twist is highly suggestive as it lends itself to a reading along Derridean lines – perhaps as a warning by Rosa and Bueno about the dangers for Spain's future of repressing or supressing from public discourse the trauma of 'evictees' (and, more generally, of those who have suffered as a result of the 2008 crisis) – a risk that both Alicias appear to seek to avert at the end of the text, as they meet again at a public gathering organised by anti-eviction activists in order to install a plaque to commemorate the life – and eviction – of the late Carmen (251–55), in a memorialising gesture that is meta-textually paralleled in Rosa and Bueno's decision to put eviction at the centre of this graphic novel.

Like the story written for *Aquí vivió* by Isaac Rosa and discussed at length above, the visual language used by Cristina Bueno to tell that story is marked by its deceptive simplicity. On the surface, Bueno deploys a realistic and almost austere visual style, yet there are some very interesting details that merit attention. Chief among them is the subtle relationship of homology established between the frames used as structuring devices in the graphic novel (and typical of comics more generally) and some of the physical, urban spaces depicted, such as the floorplan of the flat (10–11, 146), the bank (136) and the multiple frames depicting buildings featuring square windows (41, 53, 55, 105, 143, 200, 250–51, 255), as well as a map of the district (203). The link established between comic frame and the physical space in which the narrative takes place suggests that the built environment portrayed in the text is not a mere setting, but also (like the comic frame) a narrative space. Framing (or its absence) is also used to express proximity or suggest the formation of collective spaces and identities: for instance, in the segment of text depicting Alicia's visit to a PAH assembly (169–80), framing is dispensed with – perhaps as an indication of the open and collective nature of this space. Similarly, towards the end of the story, when the plaque in Carmen's memory is placed on her old block of flats (252), anti-eviction activists Víctor and Iván and residents of the block are depicted in two separate frames at the top of the page; below, in two further separate frames, we see the two Alicias with their respective families – though a strong sense of contiguity is achieved here, as Alicia's grandmother appears in both frames; at the bottom of the page, all figures are shown together, suggesting their coming together and joining forces for a common purpose: honouring Carmen's memory. For Łukasz Smuga (2022), this memorialising gesture is suggestive of 'un espacio que remite a realidades reemplazadas por otras' (79), and he thus proposes a reading of both Alicia's and Carmen's flat, and, more broadly, of Spanish cities at a time of crisis, as heterotopic spaces, following Foucault.

The use of a green filter in many of the frames is intended, according to Bueno herself, as a nod to the PAH, which uses that colour as its emblem (J. Jiménez 2016: online). But the colour filter also has a narratological function, as the frames in which it is not used correspond to stories taking place within the story (and hence in the past); and when green is deployed not as filter, but to delineate figures, it denotes scenes as imagined by the characters in the story. However, towards the end of the narrative some of these visual-narrative conventions are abandoned, and hence it becomes increasingly difficult for the reader to distinguish actual events from what Alicia dreams, thinks or plans – a powerful if subtle reminder of the importance of narrative devices and conventions in mediating our knowledge of the world, and our interactions within it.

This concern is present also in two of the other texts discussed: for instance, when Fallarás remarks, upon receiving her eviction notice: '[m]e detengo a pensar que el nombre del demandante y el de la procuradora están escritos en mayúsculas y el mío en minúsculas' (2013: 16) – a detail upon which she does not elaborate, but whose symbolic charge is clear to the reader. In Chiappe's text, Igrid discusses the mortgage agreement with her unborn child, remarking:

> ¿Y sabes en qué me fijo? [...] En que el contrato que firmamos está repleto de errores ortográficos y de sintaxis. Y pienso que debería ser posible impugnar una ley o cualquier documento legal con faltas, porque cada errata da cuenta de la capacidad de quien redactó las frases. Y pienso que ningún escrito que destruya el lenguaje puede ser bueno para una sociedad. (Chiappe 2013: 153)

It could be tempting to dismiss such reflections as mere linguistic pedantry; yet these statements and the interest in form and language they share reveal something other, or beyond, a simple concern for correct language usage. All three texts share an awareness of the importance of *how* these eviction stories are told, of the fact that the language, the structure and the narrative devices deployed are not innocent, simple vehicles to convey meaning, but are ideologically determined and ideologically charged. Such (self-)awareness is evident in some of the features shared by these texts, such as their lack of closure; their meta-literary digressions on language and narrative; and their incorporation of elements (surrealist interludes in Fallarás' text; fragments from legal documents concerning a real eviction case in the case of Chiappe; intertexts and visual segments of ambiguous status in Rosa and Bueno's graphic novel) that complicate univocal readings and problematise generic adscription. Likewise, in Luján's photographic project on eviction sites, the apparently detached visual style of the images is undercut by the accompanying captions and a series of subtle visual details that lend the photographs an unsettling effect, while also throwing into question the medium's perceived mimetic prowess and neutrality. Thanks to the problematisation of the act of showing, telling and narrating that these four texts implicitly carry out, they transcend the testimonial, inviting readers to reflect critically both on the socio-economic context they inhabit and on the ways in which narrative – in its broadest sense – is used to construct, justify or contest that reality.

CHAPTER THREE

Body

Precarious Lives: Biopolitical Effects and Affects of the 2008 Crisis in Pablo Gutiérrez's Democracia *(2012), Elvira Navarro's* La trabajadora *(2014), Belén Gopegui's* El comité de la noche *(2014) and Marta Sanz's* Clavícula *(2017)*

The four literary texts analysed in this chapter chart the physical and mental (ill) effects of the 2008 financial crisis – and of ensuing austerity policies adopted in Spain and elsewhere – on four protagonists, all of whom are highly educated liberal professionals. While the focus of my analysis is upon the bodily afflictions or threats experienced by the central character in each text, such symptoms are represented as resulting from a process of precarisation that antedates the 2008 downturn and which also affects other areas of their lives – such as their relationship with urban space; their geographical re- or dislocation; as well as their interactions with others. If the texts analysed in the previous chapters implicitly point to the unsustainability of a system that destroys natural environments, and the inhumanity of a framework which would sooner render thousands homeless than risk upsetting 'free' market capitalism, respectively, those included here question the very liveability of a socio-economic order that makes people unwell. As with the works selected for analysis elsewhere, the four texts featured in this chapter challenge formal and narrative conventions, transcending the purely testimonial – Becerra's 'relato desde la pérdida' (2015: 21–22), encouraging instead more reflective and critical reading practices. This chapter opens with an overview of the explosion in critical engagements with notions of precariousness, precarity and vulnerability in recent decades, in Spain and beyond, before presenting the individual analyses of each text. The closing section of the chapter considers the four texts collectively, suggesting a reading of their destabilisation of literary conventions as displacements which contribute to a redefinition of the notions of body and self.

The theoretical preoccupation with the precariousness and vulnerability of human life in late-capitalist, globalised societies pre-dates the 2008 economic crisis, as exemplified, for instance, by Judith Butler's *Precarious Life* (2004), among others. In that work, as well as in *Frames of War* (2010), Butler explores the inherently fragile and interdependent nature of human existence and considers the ethical and political implications that can be derived from such an awareness of our vulnerability. In parallel to this more metaphysical approach, we see a proliferation of works concerning the material and existential precariousness resulting from a neoliberal order that has eroded the welfare state since at least the end of the Cold War (*Precarias a la deriva* 2004; Tsianos and Papadopoulos 2006; Standing 2011). The dismantling of the welfare state in the West gathers pace in the wake of 2008 due to the austerity policies implemented globally, but which have particularly afflicted Spain and other southern European states. Álvarez Blanco and Gómez López-Quiñones correctly note that these two strands of criticism are rooted in different disciplinary traditions (philosophy and critical theory in the first instance; sociology and political science in the second) and that they respond to different events (the increasing emphasis on security, particularly in the wake of 9/11, in the first case; the effects of globalisation on labour practices and the 2008 downturn, in the second), and therefore warn of the dangers of collapsing these approaches (2016: 10). However, these authors also recognise the potential for establishing meaningful connections between these two discourses – the work of Isabell Lorey (2010), for instance, mobilises Butler's ideas in an analysis of social movements emerging across Europe in the first decade of the twenty-first century.

Within Spain, the work of philosopher Marina Garcés can also help make sense of the four works analysed in this chapter. Following Giorgio Agamben (1998) and Achille Mbembé (2003), Garcés argues that the role of the state is no longer managing life, as Michel Foucault contended through his examination of what he termed biopower and biopolitics; increasingly, the role of the state is administering death – what she terms the 'necro-political' turn – in a manner that secures the perpetuation of the status quo (2017). This administration of death takes on different guises: at its most extreme, we can think – and this is the context in which Garcés makes her diagnosis – of restrictive immigration policies in Europe and beyond that often result in the loss of life.[1] But it is possible also to see

1 The tragedy at El Tarajal in February 2014 is a graphic example of how the mobilisation of measures to restrict access to Spain resulted in the loss of life, as 15 people died when police fired rubber bullets at swimmers trying to make it from Morocco into the Spanish enclave of Ceuta in Northern Africa. At the time of writing in 2023, no-one has been held accountable for those deaths. See https://www.es.amnesty.org/en-que-estamos/blog/historia/articulo/justicia-tragedia-tarajal/ for further details. In a separate and more recent incident in June 2022, at least 24

something of this necropolitical turn in Lauren Berlant's notion of 'slow death'. Writing in 2007, Berlant defines 'slow death' as 'the physical wearing out of a population and the deterioration of people in that population that is very nearly a defining condition of their experience and historical existence' (2007: 754).[2] Similarly, the German-based Korean philosopher Byung-Chul Han writes about our inhabiting a 'burnout society' (2015). For Han, who, like Garcés, uses Foucault as a point of departure, we no longer inhabit a Foucauldian disciplinary society, but rather an achievement society shaped not by prohibitions but by the compulsion to meet targets, come up with new initiatives and reach novel goals. Han also argues that

> [d]isciplinary society is still governed by no. Its negativity produces madmen and criminals. In contrast, achievement society creates depressives and losers. [...] The depressive human being is an *animal laborans* that exploits itself – and it does so voluntarily without external constraints. It is predator and prey at once. (2015: 8–10)

If Foucault had advocated that the shift from classical sovereign power to biopower consisted in a shift from the sovereign's right to take life or to let live to the state's ability to make live or let die (Foucault 2003: 240–41), then theorists such as Garcés, Berlant and Han destabilise those distinctions, suggesting that the manner in which life is currently administered constitutes, in fact, a threat to existence. Put bluntly, for these theorists, the administering of life in contemporary neoliberal societies involves in fact an administering of death – a slow death through burnout for certain population groups, and a more immediate and violent death for others, particularly those not regarded as 'citizens'.

Along similar lines, Germán Labrador seeks to define – borrowing a financial term – what he calls 'subprime lives', that is, lives 'en situación de grave riesgo biopolítico' because of 'las condiciones originadas por el último ciclo económico' (2012: 570). For Labrador, the global financial downturn of 2007–8 has led to a transformation, within the public

migrants died (local NGOs raise that number to 37) and over 200 were injured in Melilla while trying to cross from Morocco to Spain. More details can be found at https://www.bbc.com/mundo/noticias-internacional-63477686.

2 Berlant's concept and definition of 'slow death' finds further echo in Rob Nixon's work on 'slow violence' (2011); however, there is a different focus, as Berlant (like Han) centres her analysis on labour and consumption practices in 'Western' societies, whereas Nixon's work highlights the (neo)colonial policies and discourses that make specific populations in poorer countries particularly vulnerable to forms of violence resulting from slowly unfolding environmental degradation.

sphere, of the perception of issues such as suicide. Where these were once considered private and individual tragedies, more recently they have come to be regarded as 'muertes políticas' (563), in the sense that the destitution faced by individuals is seen as a decisive factor leading to their demise. The emphasis and focus of Labrador is slightly different from that of the theorists mentioned before – for one, the Spanish critic sees the events of 2007–8, and particularly the popular protests linked to the *indignados* movement in Spain and to the Arab Spring in 2011, as a turning point in terms of leading to explicitly bio- or necropolitical readings of individual suffering. Moreover, Labrador's attention is centred on the political potential of what he terms 'historias de vida' – that is, usually orally transmitted life stories of individuals and/or communities who have traditionally lacked 'formas autorizadas de contar públicamente sus vidas' (564). For the Spanish critic, the increased circulation of such testimonies in the wake of 2007–8 has the potential to reveal the structural causes of precariousness and to encourage the creation of broad social coalitions to address them.

In contrast to Labrador's positive (or at least hopeful) valorisation of the circulation of precarious life stories, other critics point to the potential pitfalls of this emphasis on vulnerability. For one, in insisting that precariousness is a universally shared human condition, the risk arises that we overlook how our exposure to various threats (and our ability to overcome them) will significantly vary depending on geopolitical and socio-economic factors. Butler addresses this risk by coining an alternative term, 'precarity'. While precariousness is an ontological trait, precarity is socially and politically determined, as it refers to 'that politically induced condition in which certain populations suffer from failing social and economic networks of support and become differentially exposed to injury, violence, and death' (2010: 34). This distinction allows Butler to acknowledge the different degrees of hardship endured by specific groups and individuals, while retaining precariousness as a condition common to all humans – and one which, therefore, has the potential of overcoming the limits of identity politics. A further reservation in relation to precariousness and vulnerability as frameworks, voiced by critics such as Slavoj Žižek (2005) and Alain Badiou (2002), among others, stems from the extent to which such a focus might undermine individual agency. What happens to individual autonomy and decision-making within a framework that appears to privilege interdependency and heteronomy? Can we imagine a precarious subject that is also a militant one? Amador Fernández-Savater has attempted precisely such a definition in his exploration of what he conceives as 'una fuerza vulnerable' (2011) or 'la fuerza de los débiles' (2021); yet his work takes the 15M or *indignados* phenomenon in Spain as exemplary of such a force at work, while also acknowledging the movement's failure. For other critics, such as Gómez López-Quiñones (2016), precariousness risks offering a rather convenient alibi to absolve ourselves from taking part in political (or any other form of collective) action.

It falls beyond the remit of this work to offer a detailed discussion of different theoretical positions in relation to such questions – an impossible task, as this debate is still unfolding and will no doubt evolve further in response to the Covid-19 pandemic and the climate crisis. What I do want to explore, rather, is how these questions, and the tensions upon which they rest – between precariousness and precarity; between agency and injurability; between autonomy and interdependency – are reflected and negotiated in four recent Spanish novels. My aim in so doing is not to offer a verdict on the questions above, but rather, to consider what the symptoms and strategies featured and mobilised in each text can tell us about both contemporary Spain and the potential of cultural texts to propose imaginative responses in a context of crisis. As Christian Claesson reminds us,

> [e]l potencial de la ficción política se detecta en su capacidad para crear un espacio de subjetivación, interrumpir el relato dominante y cambiar las formas de pensar y percibir el mundo. En la ficción tenemos la libertad de imaginarnos situaciones imposibles para nuestra identidad, origen o condición; con ella podemos desestabilizar las estructuras de pensamiento y dar la vuelta a lo individual y lo común, lo propio y lo impropio, lo compartido y lo transversal – lo tuyo y lo mío. (2019: 19)

The four novels discussed in this chapter do not set out a roadmap to end precarity; neither do they constitute a call to arms for members of the precariat (Standing 2011). Yet these texts are not mere portrayals of individual experiences of precariousness and precarity, either. Instead, the existential uncertainty faced by the protagonists affects (infects?) the structure of the texts, disrupting narrative linearity and integrity. My analysis of the novels, which will proceed individually and chronologically (starting with Pablo Gutiérrez's *Democracia* from 2012 and closing with Marta Sanz's *Clavícula* from 2017), considers how these texts attempt to reframe or contest hegemonic narratives on pain and vulnerability – and how they succeed in doing so by destabilising literary and generic conventions.

Democracia (2012)

Like the other three novels discussed in this chapter, Pablo Gutiérrez's *Democracia* (2012) pushes at the limits of generic conventions: narrative fragments following the trajectory of the text's protagonist, Marco, are interspersed with secondary, seemingly disjointed plot lines – one of them featuring a character called George Soros and modelled on the Hungarian-American financier – and with quotes from a variety of sources, from philosophical treaties to primary-school textbooks. The event that sets the narrative in motion is Marco's sacking from his job as a draftsman, which coincides exactly with the implosion of Lehman Brothers. This '[c]oincidencia cósmica' (11), as the narrator describes it, sets the tone for a novel that explores and exposes the effects and resonances of the macro-political over individual lives. Such an intent is already apparent in the choice of the protagonist's name: 'Marco' literally means 'frame' in Spanish, and, as Matos-Martín (2017) argues, it points to the character's metonymic function, which is explicitly alluded to in at least two instances in the novel (cf. 2012: 158 and 195). Not only is it possible to read Marco as a symbol of 'the process of becoming precarious', as Matos-Martín suggests (2017: 526); the character also exemplifies the extent to which our subjectivity is moulded by the socio-cultural and economic conditionings which frame our experiences. For instance, readers learn that, long before the 2008 crisis, in spite of Marco's artistic aptitudes and contrary to his mother's wishes (as she had projected her own thwarted aspirations for an unconventional life onto her child), Marco decides not to pursue a career as an artist. Instead, he puts his creative ability to the service of profit, via his work at a real estate and property construction company. While Marco's career choice could be attributed to a personal lack of daring or confidence in his talent, the inclusion of school textbook fragments outlining the individual and social dimensions of labour (2012: 25–27) alert us to the fact that his decision is not made in a vacuum, but within a discursive and ideological matrix which favours values such as stability, responsibility and material wellbeing.

Preceding these schoolbook citations is the story of Marco's antagonist and former boss, Gonzalo (or Talo), a young, successful entrepreneur. Gonzalo's trajectory stands in contrast to Marco's: while Marco, a mediocre student, quietly applied himself to obtain a qualification that would allow him to make a living, Gonzalo was expelled from several elite schools due to his disruptive behaviour. While Marco went for the 'safe' option of becoming a draftsman rather than an artist, Gonzalo – bankrolled by his wealthy family – took the risky decision of setting up his own business, and the even riskier one of investing his profits in high-yield packages that would go up in smoke after the collapse of Lehman Brothers. The juxtaposition of Marco's and Gonzalo's trajectories, punctuated by the textbook quotations, lays bare the irony of a system that preaches stability but rewards risk, and which ultimately punishes – indeed, crushes – those who, like Marco, had played by its ostensible rules. Yet Marco is not presented as a passive victim of an unfair system, but as someone who actively believed and participated in that system until he lost his job. Indeed, Marco's acceptance of hegemonic capitalist narratives of success, with home ownership at their core, causes a rift in his relationship with his mother, Cloe (100–4). Hernández Herrero thus reads Marco as a metonym for an aspirational Spanish middle class who was 'víctima, pero a la vez también causante' (2013: 16) of the crisis, in a diagnosis reminiscent of Han's verdict that *homo laborans* is simultaneously predator and prey. Marco's sudden and unexpected sacking in September 2008, however, changes him – first, he plunges into a depressive state, not knowing how to fill the hours. For the first time in his life, Marco finds himself without a schedule, without a structure, with no deadlines. Yet far from being enjoyable, this newfound freedom leads him to despair. Eventually, he revolts: his 'primera victoria contra el orden establecido' (2012: 77), though described in grandiloquent terms, takes on the rather modest form of a violent reaction to an angry waiter at a café, who objects to Marco drawing on the establishment's paper napkins. This seemingly trivial incident nonetheless marks a turning point for Marco, a law-abiding, conforming, passively acquiescent figure up until then, who goes on to become an artist-activist first, and, eventually, an outcast willing to turn his rage into acts of violence.

Marco's first transformation, following the incident at a bar, is the result of a visit to his childhood neighbourhood which leads him, seemingly by chance, to come into contact with poetry – specifically, the work of Baudelaire, Alberti and Miguel Hernández, authors available from his old local bookshop. Reading their poetry is the catalyst for a project that enables him to overcome his depressive state, and which he will name 'La Ciudad':

> a diferencia de tantos otros marcos de vida destruida, el verdadero Marco-Banksy tiene una escapatoria y se abrazará a ella como un monje oriental, hará que cada una de sus acciones cobre sentido en torno a una idea superior, como un yihadista. La idea superior es La Ciudad, aún inconclusa, La Ciudad que ocultará la ciudad. (2012: 158)

In the lines above, Marco's destitution is playfully framed within a context in which the destruction of life – or, at least, of life prospects – is commonplace ('tantos otros marcos de vida destruida'); yet Marco can find a way out through his 'idea superior', ironically likened in the quote to a religious calling ('monje oriental', 'yihadista'). Marco's notion of La Ciudad to replace la ciudad consists, as its name suggests, of an intervention in urban space:

under cover of darkness, Marco will proceed to cover his city in verses and drawings. The transformative potential of poetry – at once redeeming and subversive – is alluded to elsewhere in the text, becoming one of the threads within a narrative that is otherwise fragmented. For instance, Marco's wife Julia is emboldened in her resolve to abandon her dysfunctional family as a teenager in part thanks to her reading of the work of Pedro Salinas, inspired in turn by her college teacher, who takes his leave from the class telling his students:

> vosotros, muchachos, vosotros que leéis con ojos vivaces e ignoráis lo que os espera, vosotros tan ingenuos aún, salvaos, huid de este país antes de que os devore, llevad en los bolsillos el libro de algún poeta honesto, no son muchos, la lista se enumera con los dedos, apuntad. (2012: 86)

Both Julia and Marco are characterised as not particularly intellectual, and as somewhat reluctant or accidental readers of poetry; yet both seem to heed Julia's teacher's advice and turn to poetry at critical junctures in their lives. There is a third character, the presenter of a daytime TV programme watched by the unemployed Marco, who experiences a similar poetry-induced epiphany. After one of her guests quotes some verses by Rubén Darío on air, the presenter, an obsessive reader of the Nicaraguan poet in her adolescence, realises she is wasting her life making inane TV and quits her show. However, her concept for a new cultural TV programme is ridiculed and she eventually questions her decision to quit her breakfast show.

It would be an overstatement to suggest that poetry – or literature, more broadly – is presented, within the text, as having the power to solve characters' problems or to transform their living conditions. Rather, poetry appears as a necessary but insufficient condition for change, which is why it is particularly effective at times of crisis. This mirrors Pablo Gutiérrez's own belief in the power of the word as a catalyst: 'La palabra es el arma más contundente. Una palabra sirve para ejecutar o para perpetuar, las palabras pueden hacer que una nación entera estalle, o que se quede en casa' (Gutiérrez in C. Jiménez 2013: online). Here, Gutiérrez expresses a faith in the power not just of poetry or literary language, but of rhetoric more broadly, which explains the inclusion, within the novel, of fragments from media reports, textbooks, philosophy treatises and political speeches; as well as the profuse references to popular culture texts (videogames, Tolkien texts, Star Wars characters, etc.). Gutiérrez's mobilisation of these references and intertexts can be read as an attempt to delineate the ideological matrix which contributes to shape the choices made by his characters, as we saw in the case of Marco's decision not to pursue an artistic career. In some instances, however, they are used also to question hegemonic narratives. The most salient example of this is in the use of strikethrough within the text: '[Marco y Julia] ...compraron su piso-nido en el apogeo ~~de la estafa~~ del mercado inmobiliario, precio astronómico y cepo a perpetuidad' (56). In this case, strikethrough serves to provide a counter-hegemonic viewpoint (the real estate market as a swindle); elsewhere, it is deployed to question the notion of democracy, which is rendered as 'demo~~cracia~~' (69, 73). In this case, the strikethrough suggests that democracy is illusory; a 'demo' – a term borrowed from the world of videogames, which denotes a limited version of a game, used to entice potential buyers to purchase it – of the 'real' thing. In other words, contemporary democracies are presented as limited versions of actual democracy – limited in as much as they are subjected to macro-economic diktats – yet invested in projecting to citizens the illusion of freedom and choice so that the status quo can be preserved.

Marco's second transformation, from solitary graffiti artist to radical activist, takes place as he is approached by three alter-globalists who have identified him as the author of La Ciudad. Together, they form an unofficial alliance, as Marco's three new 'friends' appreciate the potential of his work: 'El descubrimiento de los dibujos de Marco alivió la urgencia, dulcificó el combate, la poesía hace eso con las cosas hostiles, un poema para resucitar, otro para enardecer, otro para justificar el crimen' (2012: 176). Once again, poetry is alluded to in the text, and defined as a multi-purpose tool that can inspire, revive, console or inflame readers, depending on the poem. Yet once he joins the so-called 'Comité', Marco's attention appears to shift from his poetic urban intervention project to the participation in direct urban guerrilla actions in the context of a variety of demonstrations and protests. It is during one of several confrontations with riot police that Marco will discover his 'habilidad especial' (183) or specialist skill, in his ability to transform his rage into uncontainable outbursts of violence. The sweet, anxious, law-abiding citizen at the outset of the narrative is thus replaced, by this point in the story, by a furious man willing and able to hurt others.

Collective action is depicted as impossible within Gutiérrez's text – not just due to the repression it faces from the forces of law and order, but also, and more perversely, because it is shown to reproduce some of the very power dynamics it denounces. For instance, in the activist cell that Marco comes to lead, the sole female member, Alicia, is relegated to a secondary role, and is mainly valorised as a vehicle for the sexual release of its male members. Further, the dissolution of the cell is precipitated by Marco's rape by a fellow member of the committee. While this scene could be read as an allegory for a struggle for leadership within the group, it is described in explicit terms and qualified as 'verdadero', in contrast to other episodes in the text, which are presented as the product of Marco's fantasy or hallucinations (cf. 195–97). Along similar lines, the protests of 15M are presented as ineffective and as constituting nothing else than, in the words of one of the committee's activists, 'otro recurso de válvula de escape generado por el propio ejem Sistema para liberar una presión social que, bien dirigida, podría hacer que todo estallara' (194). This description of the *indignados* movement in Spain curiously echoes the Foucauldian notion of the dispositif as disparate discourses and practices that contribute to perpetuate the status quo. Within the Spanish context, Amador Fernández-Savater links Foucault's concept to what he terms the contemporary 'crisis of presence' (2011: online), and which Lauren Berlant identifies elsewhere as 'exhausted practical sovereignty' (2011: 119). In a contemporary context in which individuals experience a diminishing sense of their presence and/or of their ability to act sovereignly, 'dispositifs' perpetuate the status quo in part by offering some relief (or release) to individuals, even if short-lived. Gutiérrez's depiction of the 15M protests as 'dispositivos' seems ironic, given that for Fernández-Savater (2021), the 2011 events constituted a – temporary – overcoming of the logic of the dispositif. This differing diagnosis of the 15M movement seems to stem from their contrasting views on collective action: while for Fernández-Savater grassroots, non-hierarchical, affectively charged collective experiences such as 15M embody what he terms 'la fuerza de los débiles', which has the potential to change existing frameworks (2021), for Gutiérrez, it inevitably reproduces existing power dynamics.

Once the committee is dissolved, and collective action is revealed as an impossibility, Marco finds himself once again alone, more broke – and, arguably, more broken – than ever before. In his pitiful state, he lacks the energy to resume his La Ciudad project – until a chance encounter with his former boss Gonzalo presents him with an opportunity for revenge. This fragment is titled 'El carro de Aquiles' (2012: 200), a reference to one of the most violent episodes in the *Iliad* (Hector's dismemberment, resulting from his being tied to Achilles' chariot), hinting at Gonzalo's bloody ending. In contrast to that Classical reference, the climactic scene in which Marco steals a van and embarks on a crazed pursuit of his former boss Gonzalo, which will culminate in Gonzalo's violent death, is given the title 'Mario Bros Racing' (202), in reference to the popular videogame. These title choices not only illustrate the very broad and diverse repertoire of cultural references mobilised by Gutiérrez throughout the text, but also serve as framing devices, in the Butlerian sense (2004). In the case of the first fragment, the title serves to establish an identification between Marco and Achilles, thus presenting the text's protagonist as a hero; in the second, the potential for pathos resulting from Gonzalo's death is neutralised as the title likens the scene to a videogame.

But the framing for this key scene extends beyond the title choice: the two quotes mobilised immediately before and after it are also highly significant. A quote by Schopenhauer precedes it: '*El estado no es más que el bozal que tiene por objeto volver inofensivo a ese animal carnicero, el hombre, y hacer que tenga aspecto herbívoro*' (2012: 202; italics in the original); and a second, longer quote from Marvin Harris' *Antropología general* follows. If Schopenhauer's words set out the state's primeval role as 'domesticating' humans, keeping their violent instincts under control through the establishment and enforcement of a social contract, then Harris' lengthier quote, concerned with the Aztec praxis of human sacrifice, suggests that the 'civilising' role of any belief system or culture is ultimately subordinated to the fulfilment of the basic needs of the members of a community. Read in their new context, the quotes – as well as the climactic scene itself, which culminates Marco's transformation from law-abiding citizen to homicidal outcast – can be seen as a warning, a cautionary tale of how individuals (and communities) whose needs are neglected may become ungovernable – or, at least, ungovernable in a manner compatible with the preservation of democracy, whether in 'demo' or 'full' mode. In this regard, Gutiérrez's diagnosis foretells developments that have thrown into question the nature of Spanish democracy, such as the passing in 2015 of the Ley Orgánica de protección de la seguridad ciudadana, commonly known as the Ley Mordaza or Gag Law, which significantly increases police powers and curbs civic rights, including the right to demonstrate. Although we are not (yet) at the point of embracing cannibalism as a cultural practice, Gutiérrez appears to imply that the impassibility of Western governments in the face of glaring (and growing) socio-economic inequality and dwindling resources is setting us on that path.[3]

While Marco's story occupies centre stage in the novel, there are several interweaved secondary plot strands, such as that of Gina Monk, a (fictional) US congresswoman who attempts to challenge George Soros during his (real) appearance before the US Congress in November 2008, and who goes on to suffer a nervous breakdown. The TV presenter of a daytime programme assiduously watched by Marco, whose reignited love for poetry leads her to abandon her successful breakfast show, ends up jobless, alone and fighting cancer. The therapist and TV self-help guru featured in the aforementioned

3 Readers will recall that the trope of cannibalism is mobilised also in Doménico Chiappe's *Tiempo de encierro* (2013), analysed in the previous chapter, and used by Germán Labrador (2014) in his own analysis of cultural and discursive practices in post-2008 Spain.

programme, and whose help is sought by Marco at one point, is abandoned by her husband, an event that unravels her seemingly successful life. George Soros flees to a far-flung location on the banks of the river Nung, a nod to Francis Ford Coppola's *Apocalypse Now* (1979), which is developed further as the *New Yorker* hack sent to locate him is named Oliver Willard, after the film's Captain Benjamin Willard.[4] However, rather than murder Soros upon finding him, Oliver Willard and the financier in fact fall in love and start a family, a new species of *homo economicus*. Tellingly, most members of the ensemble cast of characters in *Democracia* meet an unhappy ending: Gina Monk, the TV presenter and the therapist, all of whom had enjoyed a considerable degree of professional success, end up paying a costly personal price; Gonzalo, Marco's boss, is killed; Marco has to flee justice and lead a clandestine existence; and Alicia and the other Comité members end up in prison. The only exceptions to this pattern are Soros and Willard, and Julia and her new romantic partner. The former couple represent a comically exaggerated, utterly implausible adaptation process, leading to the appearance of a completely new species; while Julia's happy ending is made possible because her boyfriend renounces his activism in favour of a political appointment. As before, this denouement appears to anticipate the fate of the 15M movement, with its (mis)translation – to borrow Fernández-Savater's conceptualisation (2021: 85 ff.) – from grassroots phenomenon to formal political party allowing some to prosper professionally on an individual level, but at the price of neutralising its emancipatory potential and mainstream appeal.

Due to the brutal or violent fates faced by most of its characters, the novel has been regarded by some critics as so pessimistic as to invite passivity from readers (cf. Ibáñez 2012; Zamarreño Méndez 2016). Yet I believe another, more hopeful interpretation is possible, if we focus on the novel's closing fragment and on its – for want of a better term – rhetorical exuberance or excess, and read both through the prism of some of Fernández-Savater's ideas. In 'Demo', the final fragment in the novel, we get a glimpse of Marco's existence after his murderous pursuit of Gonzalo: he has evaded arrest, has found a hiding place and is in the process of forging a new life for himself. He succeeds in doing so because he does not remain alone, but finds help from an unusual family who are squatting nearby. Marco is first drawn to the woman, whom he nicknames 'Linda' due to her prettiness, but he quickly also becomes acquainted with her partner (nicknamed 'Serio-Severo') and

4 The change of name, from Benjamin to Oliver Willard, is likely a further nod to a popular culture reference, namely, the 1980s football-themed Japanese anime series *Captain Tsubasa*, known in Spain as *Oliver y Benji*.

their strange child, known simply as 'La Niña'. Eventually, and for reasons left unexplained, Linda and Serio-Severo flee, leaving Marco to look after La Niña. Rather than allow her to be taken into the care system, Marco 'la protegerá de la Democracia y del Estado del Bienestar' (2012: 234), teaching her to draw and making her the co-author of La Ciudad Nueva, a new exercise in urban intervention similar to his earlier attempt. The closing lines of the text describe the project in the following terms:

> Las cuadrillas de limpieza usan cloro y disolvente, Marco y La Niña usan tiempo y nadaquehacer, el combate es desigual. La Ciudad Nueva crece cada noche, como una demo que enseguida termina pero que permite reiniciar el juego y repetir mil veces la misma partida. (234)

It is worth noting that this ending entails one more transformation for Marco: he is no longer (just) the raging, desperate man who has pushed his former boss off the road, causing his death. While those actions have led him to become a social outcast, this ending suggests that he has found a new purpose through his role as a carer to La Niña and through his creative work. As elsewhere in the text, the closing of the novel makes a scathing critique of democracy and of the welfare state, which are presented, in the quote included above, as something from which individuals ought to be protected, rather than as elements affording them protection. Yet as well as denouncing the system, the ending implies that it may be possible to live differently, to remain outside of it. The existence of Marco and La Niña is, of course, a marginal and precarious one; yet they seem both capable of and intent on avoiding detection and assimilation. Similarly, their project of La Ciudad Nueva is described as an unequal struggle against the groups of cleaners who set about erasing their work on a daily basis; yet Marco and La Niña nevertheless persevere in their task. Where the emphasis of El Comité had been to confront what Fernández-Savater describes as the 'force of the strong' (i.e. the state) on its own terms, through open violent confrontation, La Nueva Ciudad can be read as an example of the 'force of the weak' – a force that is limited and aware of its limitations, but nonetheless perseveres. Because its victory is not defined in terms of defeating an opponent and assuming its place – that would require it to become what it seeks to oppose – but, rather, in terms of duration. The aim is therefore '[r]esistir sin imitar aquello a lo que resistimos' (Fernández-Savater 2021: 38) – and Marco and La Niña certainly seem an embodiment of such a resistance.

Democracia's baroqueness – its mobilisation of a wealth of intertexts and cultural references (both highbrow and popular); its inclusion of caricaturised versions of 'real-world' figures such as George Soros; or its interweaving of multiple, interconnected plot lines – can also be read as a form of resistance. The novel defies genre conventions and its 'retórica hiperabundante' (Gutiérrez: online), as the author himself describes the text's exuberance, resists univocal readings, or indeed – to borrow again from Fernández-Savater's theorisation – any straightforward and normalising 'translation'. It is thus possible to simultaneously read this text as a cautionary tale on the effects of the state's failure to protect individuals from the ravages of late-stage capitalism; as a call to arms directed at those disenfranchised in the wake of 2008 (in quite a literal sense, as Marco, the hero, resorts to violence in revenge for his sacking); as a vindication of alternative forms of life, kinship and resistance to the system; or, indeed, as the author suggests in a blog entry, as simply a joke, a parodic approximation to the reality of post-crisis Spain. Rather than reading the author's refusal to put forward 'una sentencia optimista y reconfortante, un alivio o una tesis' (Gutiérrez: online) as a sign of dejected or powerless pessimism, such an authorial choice can be interpreted as a means to avoid co-optation, to prevent the work from becoming a(nother) Foucauldian dispositif. Instead, readers are confronted with a host of characters that reflect the type of unflattering compromises with which they will be all too familiar – between political principles and life choices or aspirations, between wanting to change the system and needing to exist within it. As such, the novel makes for a disquieting read, pointing to our complicity with unfair power structures and suggesting that a radical break with those structures – whether effected through creative or violent means – while possible, comes at a very high price indeed.

El comité de la noche (2014)

If a real-life event – the collapse of Lehman Brothers in September 2008 – set the narrative in motion in *Democracia*, in Belén Gopegui's *El comité de la noche* a real news item from April 2012 is taken as the point of departure, with its headline appearing as a paratext at the start of the novel. The headline details the proposal, by a pharmaceutical multinational company, to pay a weekly wage of 70 euro to the unemployed in exchange for blood 'donations'.[5] The biopolitical – and bioethical – issues at the heart of this text are thus clear from the outset; yet the possibility of selling blood to counter economic

5 Gopegui cites a news item from Europa Press, which I have not been able to locate. Its contents, however, are reproduced in this article, published on the same date (17 April 2012) as the Europa Press piece: https://www.publico.es/espana/farmaceutica-plantea-pagar-70-euros.html.

destitution is not treated in isolation, but as part of an extractive continuum, with blood substituting for labour force. Thus, rather than presenting the marketisation of blood as an isolated ethical aberration, or focusing primarily on the ethical quandaries deriving from such a measure, Gopegui sees in this development a very graphic illustration of Marx's characterisation of capital as 'vampire-like', and situates it within a broader context of the dismantling of the welfare state through the privatisation of basic services.[6] In my analysis of Gopegui's novel, I will consider how the author mobilises blood as a very powerful symbol of the ethically problematic nature of capitalism as a whole. Further, I will analyse the ways in which the text explores the potential of both collective action and of writing as means to challenge the status quo and to start imagining alternatives. Gopegui's mobilisation of the trope of the vampire is both connected to and combined with – as will become clearer later in my analysis – the ghostly or spectral, in ways which are reminiscent of Mark Fisher's work (2009; 2014).

El comité de la noche is divided into three sections, introduced by a one-page note that describes the subsequent parts as a 'documentos durmientes' that an unnamed organisation has decided to 'activate' (i.e. publish) (2014: 11). The first part, 'De Álex', is a first-person account by an unemployed haematologist in her thirties, who has had to return to live at her parents' home in Madrid with her young daughter due to her dire financial situation. This section is mostly descriptive, as we follow Álex's routines, and as she reflects on her own predicament and her decision to become involved in clandestine forms of activism. As Lizarte Fernández perceptively notes, 'el ritmo narrativo es [...] muy lento. El tiempo está casi detenido porque intenta recrear la percepción temporal de lo que significa no tener empleo' (2022: 403). As well as encapsulating Álex's experience of unemployment, the slow narrative pace in this opening section also serves other purposes: it helps explain some of the character's actions and motivations later on in the text; and it also provides a theoretical framing or counterpart to the action-packed, thriller-like second (and longest) part of the novel. As Álex states, this opening section can be read as simultaneously 'una tregua y [...] un manifiesto' (2014: 16). The second section, 'De Carla', is dialogical: an unnamed 'escribiente' (as opposed to 'escritor') transcribes Carla's oral narration of her experiences in Bratislava, where she was forced to emigrate

6 Marx deploys the trope of the vampire several times in *Capital*, but the best-known instance, and the most relevant in this context, seems to be in his definition of capital at the end of the first volume: 'Capital is dead labour, that, vampire-like, only lives by sucking living labour, and lives the more, the more labour it sucks' (*Capital* vol. I, chapter 10, Section 1).

due to her lack of employment prospects in Spain. Like Álex, Carla is a haematologist, and she comes to the transcriber because she wants him to record her story: her move to Bratislava, her romantic relationship with Michal and the bond that she establishes with Michal's half-sister Elenka, who suffers from a hepatic condition that means she is in need of a liver transplant. Carla's happy, relatively uneventful existence is thrown off course when her boss at Pharmen Laboratories, Gustav, asks her to falsify the results of blood products received from the state-run blood donation service, in a move conceived to precipitate a change in legislation to allow for the marketisation of blood. Although Carla refuses her boss's request, he goes on to blackmail her, hinting that he has the means to make Elenka's transplant a reality (or, alternatively, to delay it indefinitely, potentially causing Elenka's death). At this point, Carla reluctantly agrees to fulfil Gustav's requests. Carla is then approached by Álex, who has travelled to Bratislava from Madrid, and by a local man, Uno – both of them are part of a larger clandestine network of activists (the eponymous *comité de la noche*) working to expose the dirty tricks of Pharmen and other companies and to stop their attempts to privatise healthcare. Though initially unwilling to take part, for fear of risking Elenka's life, Carla eventually agrees to cooperate with them and provides crucial evidence, which, when made public, results in the blocking of legislation to allow for the sale of blood, as well as in the expropriation of Pharmen.

The last of the three documents that comprise the novel is embedded within Carla's story, and is a letter from Uno addressed to the organisation with which he has been collaborating. This ten-page text interrupts Carla's story and broadens the focus of the novel, for Uno's experiences as an almost 60-year-old Slovakian man are markedly different from those of Álex and Carla. In his letter, and in a similar manner to Álex's first-person narration at the outset, Uno explains the reasons for his actions, which he presents as inextricably linked to his personal trajectory. A former doctor in Communist Czechoslovakia, by the turn of the millennium Uno quits his medical career, disgusted and demoralised by the parallel defunding and privatisation of healthcare in the country. After a number of years working as a swimming instructor and later as a heavy for hire by those facing extortion or injustice, he starts to collaborate with a local branch of a broader clandestine network in an attempt to overcome his feelings of isolation and loneliness. In his letter, Uno explains that he feels compelled by a sense of urgency, which leads him to defy the committee's call for caution, and to knowingly risk his life in order to protect Carla, defend his ideals and further the aims of the organisation. As we find out later through Carla's retelling, he succeeds in his aims, but pays for it with his life.

genre, the interweaving of action and commentary, plot and metadiegetic discussion, point to a resistance, on Gopegui's part, to eschew activism in favour of literature, or vice versa. And her refusal to provide us with either an unequivocally happy ending or with a clearly negative, cautionary closing suggests a view of political struggle as open-ended, in line with Harvey's idea of the 'long revolution'. That words, language, narrative and the lived experience to which they give shape are presented as the basic tools for any such revolution is, ultimately, a democratising and hopeful sign, given that language is a universally accessible resource, and that it is collectively transformed over time.

La trabajadora (Elvira Navarro, 2014)

Like the protagonists of *Democracia* and *El comité de la noche*, the narrator–protagonist of *La trabajadora*, Elisa Núñez, is a young, urban-dwelling, highly educated liberal professional. Elisa's increasingly precarious work situation as a freelance editor and writer forces her first to move from her central Madrid home to the periphery of Aluche, and then to sublet the spare room in her rental flat. The character's occupation and name – the initials of which coincide with the author's – are suggestive of certain parallels between narrator and author, although as Vicente Luis Mora notes (2014) this is not a fully autofictional text. Navarro's novel is structured in three parts: the first section has Elisa reconstruct a story told to her by her flatmate, Susana, concerning the latter's 'madness'. The veracity of the account, however, is thrown into question not only by Susana's unreliability as a narrator, but also by the fact that Elisa is, at the time when she hears Susana's story, medicated to alleviate her own mental health problems, as she acknowledges when reconstructing Susana's story. The second and longest part of the novel opens with a short story originally published by Navarro in a Spanish newspaper in 2010 (but which, in a further autofictional nod, is presented as Elisa's work within the novel). This section traces Elisa's gradual mental health deterioration over several months, which coincides with the worsening of her working conditions and financial situation. The final part, a barely two-page-long dialogue between Elisa and her therapist, throws into question the possibility of resolving or overcoming the precariousness and vulnerability portrayed throughout the preceding pages.

Elvira Navarro's novel has attracted considerable critical attention, from favourable early reviews by renowned cultural critics including David Becerra (2014), Fernando Broncano (2014) and Vicente Luis Mora (2014) to lengthier engagements with the text in scholarly articles by Furió Sancho (2015), Suárez García (2016), Martínez Rubio (2016) and Gallego Dueñas

(2018), among others. As well as its engagement with twenty-first-century job insecurity from a gendered perspective, the novel's portrayal of urban space has attracted considerable critical attention. For Martínez Rubio, for example, Elisa's move from her city-centre flat in Tirso de Molina to the periphery of Aluche should be read 'como signo de la marginalización o de la exclusión en términos urbanos de esa pretendida clase media española representada por la protagonista' (2016: 294), a view shared also by Furió Sancho, who describes that move as a metaphor for 'el fracaso de las expectativas socioprofesionales de la protagonista' (2015: 13). Gallego Dueñas (2018) further notes how Elisa's mental health problems first manifest themselves spatially, as her perception of the surrounding urban space is destabilised – and, in fact, her first acute nervous breakdown occurs while on a bus, as an anodyne city scene (a group of elderly men congregated around some benches) becomes distorted (cf. Navarro 2014: 83). The treatment of urban space in this novel, however, is markedly different from that of *Democracia*: while Marco intervenes in and transforms the urban space he inhabits through his graffiti, Elisa simply traverses her *barrio* whilst experiencing varying levels of threat – most notably from a gang of scrap and cardboard collectors. Elisa's fear while walking around the city streets points to the gendered dimension of her experience of urban space, as the gang targets young women in particular: 'A veces me cruzaba con los del camión. Me arrebujaba en el abrigo para que no me insultaran. [...] Eran casi unos niños, todos gitanos; recogían cartones y les gritaban a las mujeres jóvenes que se encontraban' (57). In response to such intimidating encounters, Elisa feels increasingly unable to leave her flat, until her medication finally enables her to overcome that fear, at least partially or temporarily. While other critics have read Navarro's text as 'una novela sobre una ciudad en crisis y una crisis en la ciudad' (Gallego Dueñas 2018: 121), the gendered and embodied dimension of its protagonist's experiences has not always been sufficiently accounted for. In my own analysis of the novel, I consider how urban space, gender and creative work intersect to offer an unsettling diagnosis on twenty-first-century precarity – and I deliberately use Butler's neologism to denote that Elisa's predicament is the result of socio-economic factors, rather than of an inherent personal weakness.

Elisa Núñez, the titular working woman in Navarro's novel, is a precariously employed, underpaid, yet fiercely competitive worker. As such, at the outset of the text she offers a perfect illustration of what Byung-Chul Han (2015) defines as the *animal laborans* characteristic of our achievement society. When the company for which she works starts to struggle, Elisa's financial destitution and the cutthroat atmosphere of her workplace preclude any form of protest or collective action:

> Tras mis prácticas encadené tres contratos temporales, y luego todo se precipitó: la empresa debía hacer frente a una deuda cuantiosa y comenzaron los recortes salariales y la conversión de los que estábamos contratados temporalmente en colaboradores externos. Eso implicaba, aparte de cobrar menos, corregir no solo para el sello donde había trabajado, sino también para la colección de bolsillo, en la que se editaban libros de todo tipo, incluyendo primeras ediciones. Al principio no me quejé, ni busqué la solidaridad de nadie. [...] Tampoco mantuve el contacto con ninguno de mis antiguos compañeros de mesa. Nuestra amistad, si es que podía llamarse así, la atravesaba la punta filosa de la competición [...]. (Navarro 2014: 63)

This quote makes clear that the protagonist's unstable employment conditions are not merely a result of the global economic downturn of 2007–8, but in fact pre-date it – even before the crisis, she had been employed on rolling temporary contracts. The crisis only exacerbates or accelerates ('todo se precipitó') a pre-existing trend. Left with no other choice given her precarious finances, Elisa reluctantly sublets her small spare room to the mysterious Susana, who has just returned to Spain after living in the Netherlands for several years. While both Susana and Elisa face similar challenges – uncertain or underpaid employment leading to financial hardship, which contributes to isolate them from others and provokes or worsens their mental health problems – they are presented as very different characters. Elisa is cash poor but holds a certain degree of cultural capital which Susana, at least at the outset of the narrative, can only dream of achieving – a difference of which both women are acutely aware. Elisa describes Susana's 'notoria obsession por ceñirse a temas culturales a pesar de no ser una persona realmente culta' (54) and, when Susana discovers that Elisa published a novel some years prior, the latter describes Susana's curiosity in relation to that fact as 'codicia' (61) directed at finding out how to become an agent within the cultural sphere. If Elisa appears dismissive of Susana's efforts to enter a cultural field that she herself feels entitled to inhabit, she also, however, envies the regular working hours and more secure income that Susana derives from her job at a call centre. This lack of homogeneity among the precariously employed is tackled head-on in the collective work *Precarias a la deriva* (2004), when its authors incisively remark on the social prestige ascribed to different forms of immaterial labour which 'establece una diferencia irreductible entre hacerle una paja a un cliente y diseñar una página web' (2004: 22). Such differences mark the relationship between Elisa and Susana as one of mistrust, and prevent them from developing a proper friendship, or even a sense of solidarity. Carmentxu, Elisa's unofficial boss at the publishing house, remarks sardonically on this lack of solidarity or ability for empathy as she recounts an anecdote that occurred during a work trip, as a flight cancellation led to a collective response from passengers demanding a solution. However, once individual solutions were offered selectively to certain passengers, these were quick to accept, privileging their own comfort over the collective demands of the group. For Carmentxu, that experience epitomises the problem with precariously employed freelancers such as Elisa: their pitiful working conditions cannot be overcome, in part at least, due to the rapaciously individualistic attitude of those concerned. As Han states, such individuals are simultaneously predator and prey (2015: 10).

A further difference between the characters, noted by critic Fernando Broncano (2014), pertains to how the two women in Navarro's novel each deal with their mental health problems. Susana is open about her mental health history and diagnosis, which she considers a personal trait akin to her height or her taste in music. This openness surprises and disconcerts Elisa, who, upon listening to Susana's narration of her first nervous breakdown, wavers between disbelief and envy for 'la libertad que ella [Susana] se daba para construirse' (Navarro 2014: 14). In contrast, Elisa, the protagonist-narrator, endeavours throughout the text to regain a sense of 'normality' or stability after experiencing what she describes as a 'desbarajuste absoluto de mi sistema nervioso' (83). Elisa looks to her friend Germán for help, who arranges an appointment with Elisa's GP so that she can be referred for psychiatric care. The GP also extends a prescription for bromazepam (lexatin) to help Elisa cope (or rather, to ensure she can continue working) while she waits for her specialist appointment. This band-aid approach, focussed on managing symptoms to guarantee workers' productivity, is reminiscent of David Harvey's contention that 'sickness is defined under capitalism broadly as inability to work' (2000: 106). While I agree with Broncano's view that Navarro's text confronts us with 'dos fenomenologías de la soledad' (2014: online), I also believe that the characters' differing – and fluctuating – attitudes towards their predicaments can be best understood by recourse to Lauren Berlant's notion of cruel optimism, which she defines in the following terms:

> A relation of cruel optimism exists when something you desire is actually an obstacle to your flourishing. It might involve food, or a kind of love; it might be a fantasy of the good life, or a political project. [...] These kinds of optimistic relations are not inherently cruel. They become cruel only when the object that draws your attachment actively impedes the aim that brought you to it initially. (2011: 1)

In Elisa's case, it seems clear that her attachment to an ideal of professional stability, achievement and recognition is undermining her wellbeing and her mental health, ironically preventing her from completing the tasks assigned to her by Carmentxu. When asked by her therapist about her job-related expectations, Elisa responds:

> Me gustaría que me pagaran lo que me deben, que subieran las tarifas de corrección, que no me sobrecargaran de trabajo, que por el número de horas que corrijo (son muchas aunque pierda el tiempo) pudiera pagar tranquilamente un apartamento para mí sola en el centro, tener un mes de vacaciones y no llevarme un disgusto ni recurrir a mi padre cada vez que se me rompen los cristales de las gafas. Supongo que tendría que ser emprendedora, como dicen los manuales de los cursos para autónomos que he hecho, pero ahora estoy demasiado deprimida y acobardada. (Navarro 2014: 115)

While these aspirations might seem quite modest, they are nonetheless beyond Elisa's reach, due to circumstances entirely beyond her control – the liquidity crisis afflicting her employer, which, in turn, is linked to a broader context of the global economic recession of 2007–8. Yet she has so internalised a neoliberal 'optimistic' discourse that posits individuals as masters of their own destiny that she cannot let go of her attachment to the notion of a 'good life' and, further, she blames herself ('supongo que tendría que ser emprendedora') for her failure to achieve that goal. However, Elisa's use of the verb 'supongo' already alerts us as readers to her wavering faith in some of the cruelly optimistic narratives on professional success to which she has previously unquestioningly adhered.

In contrast to Elisa, who is still invested in an attachment that is harmful to her, Susana appears free from such expectations.

> Susana nunca se comportaba como cabía esperar de alguien que no había dado más que tumbos, que no había conseguido nada de lo que ansiaba, que casi en la cincuentena vivía en una precariedad poco envidiable. Lo que me había parecido irritante y estrafalario de ella, y me había llevado a suponer que tenía menos años, era lo que al mismo tiempo admiraba, pues esa forma de conducirse no dejaba de ser una resistencia. (142)

For Elisa, then, Susana's unconventionality is rooted in her seeming disregard for social expectations and narratives around success: she seems unflustered by how little she has achieved, professionally and financially. Elisa finds that stance simultaneously irritating – as she herself cannot physical pain is linked simultaneously to professional activities and the demands they place on our bodies, and to the role of language and literary representation in mediating our understanding of and relationship to it. For, when the pain is felt for the first time, the narrator is not only halfway across the ocean: she is also reading the memoirs of Lillian Hellman, specifically the section in which Hellman details Dashiell Hammett's lung cancer (Sanz 2017: 13). As in her earlier autofictional work *La lección de anatomía* (2008), by framing her individual experience in this manner, Marta Sanz endeavours to 'hablar del yo desde el nosotras' (Sanz in Bonet 2016: online), problematising, in the process, the boundary between individual subjectivity and the collectively experienced socio-historical and cultural coordinates that contribute to articulate that subjectivity. Sanz reinforces this idea elsewhere, where she argues for a form of autobiography which

> desdiga el tópico de la vanidad. Una autobiografía donde interese el paisaje, el fondo, que siluetea al cuerpo en primer plano. Me interesan los textos que desde lo singular se insertan en lo plural: una autobiografía de las cosas comunes que saque la palabra literatura del terreno de prestigio de 'lo extraordinario'. (Sanz in Rovecchio 2017: online)

Clavícula is thus explicitly autobiographical, yet Sanz avoids the narcissism often associated with the genre by deliberately choosing to portray herself and her life 'en un momento poco fotogénico' (Cruz 2017: online), that of the menopause, and by mobilising her trademark boldness as a writer:

> El climaterio es un asunto interior y pornográfico. No es sólo una cuestión de imagen o de sequedad de piel, paulatina pobreza capilar, arañas vasculares en las mejillas, bolsas en los ojos, retículas de arrugas como el velo de un sombrerito chic. Sí, en todo ese me fijo, y a ratos me importa. [...] Sin embargo, lo peor es que la menopausia provoca un estado de sensibilidad que te induce a creerte vulnerable y, consecuentemente, a serlo. (Sanz 2017: 28–29)

In the lines above, Sanz gives a detailed and unforgiving account of the physical changes that she has experienced, or is experiencing, as part of the menopause – transformations which are not exclusive to her but which will be recognisable to many female readers of a similar age. Yet beyond those symptoms, she tells us, lies something even worse: a sense of vulnerability that results not only from bodily changes, but also from broader, social-contextual phenomena. On the one hand, as Sanz states elsewhere, 'el cuerpo de las mujeres ha sido objetualizado de una manera perversa' (Sanz and Landero 2018: online), and part of the taboo surrounding the menopause relates to an identification of the female body as either an object of (male) desire or as a maternal body – and the menopausal body fits neither ideal. The narrator, keenly conscious of this, rebels: 'No me da la gana de responder a estos modelos ni forzarme para estar permanentemente pizpireta y operativa' (2017: 30). On the other hand, however, the narrator's vulnerability is linked also to a context of economic crisis, within which her husband has become unemployed – a predicament which threatens the couple's financial security, and which the narrator does not have the power to alter.

After multiple fruitless medical examinations, it becomes increasingly clear to the narrator that her pain is likely to have not just a physical cause, but that it is also a manifestation of her worries and anxieties, as she realises that

> [l]a vida consiste en trabajar todo el día y culparse por esos momentos en los que no se está trabajando. Hay una desproporción, un inmenso desajuste entre esfuerzo y remuneración que me obliga a multiplicar el número de mis trabajos para poder mantener mi nivelito de vida. [...] Mi dolor es una letra que se escribe cuando tengo miedo de no poder pagar las facturas o subvencionarme una vejez sin olor a vieja. (69)

While the pressures inherent to the 'achievement society' (Han 2015) we inhabit affect both men and women, the narrator notes how women feel its consequences more acutely: 'descubro que casi todo el mundo ha pasado por lo mismo que yo [...]. Echo cuentas y me salen más mujeres. No creo que sea cuestión de debilidad, sino de incremento de la presión' (2017: 95). For Sanz, this additional pressure exerted on women – resulting from greater exposure to uncertain employment conditions, as well as to the so-called 'second shift' of reproductive labour mostly undertaken by women – manifests itself in certain medical conditions, such as fibromyalgia, which overwhelmingly affect women.[9] This recognition of the gendered dimension of precariousness echoes the work of the aforementioned collective *Precarias*

9 The term 'second shift' was coined by Arlie Russell Hochschild and Anne Machung, authors of an influential 1989 book, *The Second Shift: Working Parents and the Revolution at Home* (New York: Avon Books). Silvia Federici touched on some of the same ideas (though deploying a Marxist-inflected historicising approach, rather than a sociological one) in her seminal *Caliban and the Witch* (2004). In that text, Federici distinguishes between productive labour (the only form of labour recognised within the formal economy) and reproductive labour, that is, unpaid and unrecognised work necessary to preserve life (housework, caregiving, etc.), normally and historically undertaken by women.

a la deriva (2004), as well as that of Remedios Zafra (2017), for whom gender and social class are two key vectors in determining job inequality and exposure to precarity (cf. Zafra 2017: 24). And yet, perversely, Sanz argues in the text, gendered prejudices prevent adequate recognition of, and research into, these complaints, as the women experiencing them are all too often dismissed as 'locas' or 'flojas' (cf. 2017: 96–97).

Throughout the text, Sanz denounces the persistent blind spots of modern medicine in relation to women, acerbically noting how even today, '[l]os calvarios de las hembras de la especie son jodidamente naturales' (31). Elsewhere, the narrator recounts the experience of several women friends misdiagnosed by physicians (96–97, 134–36, 186–87) who attributed their symptoms to weakness or anxiety, and she traces this tendency to minimise women's pain to Nietzsche's mocking of the suffering of bourgeois ladies (cf. 98–99). The diagnosis for the narrator's own ailment also proves elusive, and the pages of the text bear witness to her pilgrimage from medical specialist to medical specialist. In the final pages, the narrator can finally put a name to her condition: 'una retracción pulmonar ante un proceso de inflamación de la clavícula' (189). Yet the cause of that inflammation of the clavicle remains somewhat hazy – perhaps over-exertion, maybe a side effect of the menopause – and the naming of her condition does little to alleviate her symptoms. This is probably because, by the time the diagnosis arrives, the narrator has come to understand the contextual factors underlying her illness, which no medical treatment can 'cure':

> Enfermo del miedo a enfermar y del miedo a no poder enfermar. A que se hunda el mundo. A que la enfermedad se relacione con la imposibilidad de pagar las facturas. Durante un rato tengo la certeza de que mi temor es razonable y de que estoy condenada a pensar con retruécanos como Santa Teresa de Jesús. (54)

> Sin darnos cuenta, nos resistimos al neoliberalismo somatizándolo y nuestras somatizaciones se transforman en un interesado misterio de la ciencia. (135)

This realisation of the social dimension of pain goes beyond the recognition that external factors beyond our control (such as job or income security) can and do affect our physical and mental health. The narrator of *Clavícula* is also acutely aware of the effect that her suffering is having on others: '[e]l dolor no es íntimo. Es un calambre público que se refleja en el modo que los otros, los que más quieres, tienen de mirarte' (89). The gaze of others not only reflects her pain back to her, but also makes her aware of the negative effect that her condition is having on her loved ones (her husband, her parents). This leads to feelings of guilt – both at the suffering she may be inflicting on family and friends, and at the relative degree of privilege she enjoys. The narrator acknowledges her condition as a middle-class liberal professional (albeit a precarised one) living in the West. The inclusion of a free-verse poem chronicling her encounter with a mendicant child upon her arrival in Manila serves as a poignant illustration of her own (relative) privilege (173–79), but also of how awareness of one's privilege should not neutralise one's right to protest, but in fact drive it, an idea Sanz has also expressed elsewhere (cf. Cruz 2017: online).

The vindication of one's right to protest about living conditions that are causing harm coexists, as mentioned, with guilt and doubt. At one point in the text, for instance, the narrator tells us how she cannot feel calm in spite of the gradual ruling out of serious illnesses (cancer, emphysema), and adds:

> [l]uego me vienen a la mente las depauperadas caritas de los niños calvos y, pese al dolor, me siento una impostora. Enseguida me rebelo: yo también tengo derecho. A mi dolor. A mi propia y quizá no tan frívola aflicción. Siento otra punzada: el adjetivo *frívola* me duele tanto que casi rompo a llorar. (Sanz 2017: 166)

Here, Sanz's use of the adjective 'frivolous' points to her own internalisation of some of the narratives around pain – specifically, around female middle-class pain – critiqued elsewhere in the text in relation to Nietzsche and to (some) medical professionals; yet her close attention to language (and to its effects: 'casi rompo a llorar') contributes to highlight its ideological and affective dimensions. Words can name and explain, but they can also deceive and damage – and the narrative fearlessly explores and exposes that tension, questioning its own legitimacy in the process: 'Y me pregunto: ¿Es legítimo dañar a los otros compartiendo tus temores, la china de tu zapato?' (155).

In this text, as in *La trabajadora*, there is a vindication of writing as a means to navigate and understand (if not necessarily overcome) physical and psychological pain: 'La escritura araña la entropía como una cucharilla de café el muro de la prisión' (51). Here, writing is presented as a blunt and woefully limited instrument (cucharilla de café) against the surrounding chaos, yet it is also the only tool at the narrator's disposal. While acknowledging this limited scope of writing, throughout the pages of *Clavícula*, Marta Sanz explores, and seeks to expand, its disruptive potential. The structure of the text is fragmentary, disjointed, as if mimicking the havoc caused by the mysterious pain over the narrator's body (a relationship made explicit as the narrator observes how '[e]l dolor me afea la letra', 86). There is a deliberate refusal to comply with certain narrative conventions – suspense in particular is eschewed, as the narrator feels that recounting her experience in a neat, linear manner leading to a clear resolution would betray her experience of '[e]l terror y lo cotidiano' (165). In fact, terror and the everyday are conflated, as the narrator realises that her physical complaint is not the result of a mystery, rare illness, but is instead connected to her experience of an everyday that appears increasingly hostile and uncertain. The opening lines of the text already advance that possibility: 'Voy a contar lo que me ha pasado y lo que no me ha pasado. La posibilidad de que no me haya pasado nada es la que más me estremece' (11). This citation connects Sanz's enunciation with Alain Badiou's notion of the event or *l'événement* (Badiou 2002). For Badiou, beyond what we commonly conceive of as 'reality' lies a supplement or void which an event can make visible. This supplement aligns with Lacan's notion of the Real as that which transcends the Imaginary and the Symbolic; and its sudden eruption as event therefore sets in motion a truth-process with the power to destabilise or perforate existing and accepted knowledge (cf. Badiou 2002: 45–53). In *Clavícula*, the narrator's pain could be read as an event in Badiou's terms, inasmuch as it sets in motion a truth-process that forces the protagonist to reassess what she does and what she believes. Sanz certainly describes her objective in writing the novel in such terms:

> Yo cuando estaba escribiendo *Clavícula* [...], yo aspiraba a algo que ahora está muy, muy, poco de moda; aspiraba a contar la verdad. [...] ...yo quería arañar la verdad de lo que a mí me había pasado en un momento crítico de mi vida. (Sanz 2017b: online)

For Badiou, however, '[w]hat arises from a truth-process [...] cannot be communicated' (2002: 51), it must be encountered. Sanz, by contrast, expresses, in the lines above, her faith in language to at least approximate ('arañar') the truth. In spite of this seeming divergence of opinion, Sanz proceeds in a manner that resonates with Badiou's concept of 'the ethic of a truth: "Do all you can to persevere in what exceeds your perseverance. Persevere in the interruption. Seize in your being that which has seized and broken you"' (2002: 47). Perseverance and interruption are two central features of this text, as the narrator repeatedly struggles to find the appropriate words to describe and name her pain:

> ¿Han probado a buscar las palabras exactas para describir ese dolor, convertido en síntoma, que ayuda a los médicos a diagnosticar? [...] "Mi dolor es..." Nudo, corbata, pajarita, calambre, ausencia, hueco invertido, cucharada de aire, vacío de hacer al vacío, blanco metafísico, succión,

> opresión, mordisco de roedor, de pato, de comadreja, carga, mareo, ardor [...]. Tengo tantas palabras que no puedo decir ninguna. Conozco bien el lenguaje y sus figuras retóricas. Pero soy tan imprecisa. [...] No hay mentiras ni metáforas para expresar mi dolor. (2017: 61)

In spite of this impossibility of accurately describing her pain, the narrator nevertheless strives throughout the novel to negotiate the unbridgeable gap 'entre sentir el dolor y no poder contarlo' (Buczek and Pietrak 2021: 56). Sanz has explained how writing *Clavícula* was, in the first instance, a therapeutic exercise, an attempt to understand what she was experiencing and to counter the de-structuring effect of pain. Yet she soon realised the social or collective dimension of her experience, the fact that 'todo eso que me está doliendo por dentro, no me duele solo a mí' (Sanz 2017b: online). That awareness of the collective nature of her pain explains the narrator's oscillations from the individual and personal – the localised pain affecting a specific area of her body – to the social, as she shares with the reader reflections on her own (self-)exploitation, particularly now her husband is unemployed; or on the downward social mobility experienced by many in Spain in the wake of the global 2008 recession. If physical pain is the Badiouan event that sets the enunciation (or truth-process, following the French philosopher) in motion, then the shattering conclusion at which the narrative voice arrives at the end of the text is that '[n]os hemos hecho viejos antes de tiempo por culpa de la reforma laboral' (2017: 197); that 'todos somos víctimas del capitalismo avanzado' (Sanz 2017b: online).

Several critics have noted how, in spite of *Clavícula*'s fragmented structure, the text is impressively coherent (Portela 2017; Ballarín Aguarón 2020). I would contend that the text's coherence or consistency lies precisely in its perseverance in the interruption, to paraphrase Badiou. For the vulnerable, aching narrative voice in *Clavícula* to articulate a linear, univocal discourse would have entailed a degree of construction which, the narrator argues in the text, would have produced something different, something other – perhaps a detective fiction (cf. Sanz 2017: 164–65). The narrator makes explicit her refusal to produce pages that are 'convencionalmente interesantes' (165), conceived to please or draw in the reader; instead, the enunciation is set out as an enquiry (a truth-process, in other words) that operates as '[u]n trépano o un berbiquí' (165), that is, as a sharp, perforating tool capable of uncovering unpalatable truths. In fact, and as if following Badiou's dictum about the un-communicability of the event, *Clavícula* does more than merely critique late-stage capitalism or describe its effects on an individual. The narrator places disparate materials before the reader, such as email correspondence between her and her husband, photographs taken by the author, a summary of the narrator's fluctuating monthly income, and metafictional digressions on her reasons for writing, among others. These fragments – which vary in length and form from aphoristic one-liners, to several-page-long epistolary interludes, to one-paragraph, diary-like entries – are not connected to one another; the only link between them is the experience of pain, and the inquiry about its origins and effects. As such, *Clavícula* could be read as an example of 'lateral writing', following (and adapting) Lauren Berlant's notion of 'lateral politics'. For Berlant, lateral politics is a practice which is 'mimetic of the historical sensorium [...] of the present moment', a moment in which the West has been 'forced to adjust emotionally to the process of living with the political depression produced by brutal relations of ownership, control, security, and their fantasmatic justifications in liberal political economies' (2011: 261). Lateral politics departs from conventional and formal politics in that it does away with the illusion of sovereignty, without therefore entirely renouncing agency. In other words, lateral politics recognises that a radical break with the present order may be impossible, but it nevertheless strives to erode that order by focussing on specific acts of solidarity and localised interventions that can foster a sense of community and a new imaginary. In an analogous manner, *Clavícula* does not offer the illusion that it can save us readers from the ravages of late-stage capitalism – rather, in confronting us with the suffering of its narrator, it makes for a disquieting read. Neither does the text suggest that writing can cure the narrator: in fact, the text ends in a somewhat circular manner, with the narrator once again on an aeroplane, as in the opening. Upon a well-meaning but unfortunate comment from a cabin crewmember to her elderly parents, the narrator declares: '[y]o, sin fijarme mucho, me doy cuenta de todo y me llevo los dedos al Bósforo de Almasy' (2017: 201). The narrator's gesture hints at the return of the physical pain that has been plaguing her, and which is localised around her clavicle. The words that precede the description of that gesture point to an unsettling connection, suggested elsewhere in the text (cf. '[e]l gen de la infelicidad. El ojo sucio', 173), between the narrator's lucidity ('me doy cuenta de todo') and her suffering. Yet that painful lucidity coexists with what Sanz elsewhere describes as 'mi optimismo respecto a las posibilidades comunicativas y sociales de los textos literarios' (Rovecchio 2017: online); that is, with a belief that language, and particularly literary language, has the potential to challenge hegemonic narratives and, in so doing, effect some change – even if of a limited nature – upon the social sphere.

In the four texts analysed in this chapter, the 2007–8 downturn is not presented as an anomaly or malfunction of the global capitalist system, but rather as part of its logical development; in Berlantian terms, the process of 'slow death', which the American critic had identified in 2007, simply gathers pace in the following years, as rising unemployment leads to an increase in mortgage foreclosures and evictions, and, in some cases, to eviction-related suicides, as seen in the preceding chapter. This deterioration of living conditions is further exacerbated by austerity policies that result in funding cuts for basic services (health, social care, education). In the novels discussed, the economic crisis of 2007–8 and its consequences are no longer portrayed as events that take place in the background, or that merely influence their protagonists' lives. Instead, in these novels the financial crisis and its effects have, in a literal, etymological sense, been incorporated by the main characters – that is, these events have entered their bodies, affecting their physical and mental health and compromising their bodily integrity.

The foregrounding of the body in these texts does not, therefore, present it as the last bastion of personal, individual autonomy or resistance, but rather as a site of struggle in which the contradictions, excesses and violence of late-stage capitalism are reproduced, with pathogenic consequences. In their privileging of permeability, and their implicit questioning of the boundaries between the body and the space(s) which that body inhabits and traverses, these narratives destabilise categories such as inside/outside, self/other or individual/collective. Unlike what some critics of vulnerability frameworks might have feared (cf. Gómez López-Quiñones 2016), however, this move does not lead to either a self-indulgent and narcissistic exhibition of individual suffering, or to powerlessness and paralysis. Rather, the emphasis on the porosity (and thus vulnerability) of the human body and of the self results in the problematisation of the neoliberal dogma of individual agency and self-determination. In all four novels, the protagonists come to realise that the challenges they face – unemployment or work in exploitative conditions, financial insecurity, loneliness, illness and pain – are not the result of their individual flaws, or of their poor decision-making (as the hegemonic neoliberal discourse would want them to believe), but rather structural or systemic side effects. Yet instead of leading to a resigned, if dejected, acceptance of the status quo, their breaking with dominant narratives on individual agency and personal responsibility in fact leads these characters to engage in different forms of collective (or at least dialogical) action.

In *Democracia* and *La trabajadora*, such action is of an explicitly spatial nature. Marco's project of La Ciudad (later La Ciudad Nueva) constitutes an intervention in urban space intended to present an alternative to what exists ('La Ciudad que ocultará la ciudad', Gutiérrez 2012: 158). While, as the narrator of *Democracia* concedes, this aim might be ultimately unattainable, at least if taken literally, the novel nonetheless suggests such acts of resistance have an effect on others – the members of the Comité in the first instance, but also other inhabitants of Marco's city (166). Significantly, once protest and violence (or the combination of both) are proven ineffective, Marco returns to his graffitied calligrams in a modest but persistent attempt to transform the surrounding built environment – and, hopefully, the mindset of those who traverse it. In *La trabajadora*, Susana's disrupted maps of Madrid not only provide her with a creative outlet that allows her to regain some stability (and, eventually, recognition); they also have a powerful effect on Elisa, as they confront her with a visual and graphic representation of a city in crisis, thus arguably helping her realise the structural underpinnings to her problems. Elisa's own walks through an impoverished Madrid populated by discreet squatters and menacing scrap collectors further reinforce that realisation.

The spatial dimension of *El comité de la noche* is perhaps less obvious, yet the mobility of its protagonists, primarily between Madrid and Bratislava, serves to highlight the global nature of some of the threats posed by neoliberal policies in Spain and beyond. Moreover, the novel explores the possibilities for collective, non-hierarchical action (and reflection) opened up by cyberspace. There is no naïve cyber-utopianism here, however; rather, Gopegui is interested in the interface between physical and virtual space, in how the internet can expand or extend the reach and possibilities of 'conventional' or 'analogue' activism. In that sense, the potential of virtual space is presented as akin to that of literary writing, as they can both encourage 'una misma impugnación de lo que hay, de lo que impone su existencia sin permitir que nadie pondere su utilidad o su sentido' (Gopegui 2014: 36). Writing and the internet may not have the power to change the world, but they can certainly challenge and disrupt meaning-making processes, and thus hegemonic narratives – a necessary first step for any emancipatory movement.

Finally, in *Clavícula*, the spatial translocations of its narrator–protagonist (from Madrid to Puerto Rico at the outset; from St Petersburg to Madrid at the end, with trips to Paris, Mexico, Manila and several destinations within Spain interspersed throughout) are presented as simultaneously indicative of the degree of success and privilege which she has achieved, and as a factor contributing to her ill health. With devastating irony, the protagonist remarks: 'Tengo una vida maravillosa. [...] Mi sueño se ha cumplido. Espero no asfixiarme. Y poder dormir' (Sanz 2017: 60). This dual role of travel as both a marker of success and a cause of ill health helps uncover what Lauren Berlant termed 'the fantasy of the good life' – that is, the enduring belief that personal long-lasting happiness and stability can be attained in spite of contextual factors that preclude it, and which include job insecurity, growing economic inequality and the loosening of familial and community bonds (cf. Berlant 2011: 2–3). In Sanz's text, spatial mobility can thus be read as a metaphor for the illusory nature of the ideal of the good life, and for the potential cost of our persistent investment in that ideal: it denotes that the protagonist has fulfilled her professional goals, yet it also leads to her physical and mental exhaustion, to the point where she is not just unable to enjoy her success, but can barely function.

In my preceding analysis of each text, I have remarked upon how each of them formally or structurally integrates some of the elements explored at the level of the plot. While this is achieved through a variety of discursive strategies, as my individual analysis of each text illustrates, it is nonetheless possible to conceptualise these as displacements. In *Democracia*, for instance, Marco's deteriorating mental health is mirrored in the structural fragmentation of the text, which takes place through the displacement of the central narrative strand via the incorporation of intertextual materials and secondary plot lines. In *El comité de la noche* there is a displacement of both narrative voice (as several narrators coexist and part of the narration is dialogical) and of verisimilitude, which is truncated at the end of the text through the revelation that Carla is a ghost. While there is a single narrator in *La trabajadora* – Elisa, the novel's protagonist – the form of narration oscillates between a monologic central second part and the dialogic opening and closing sections. Lastly, in *Clavícula* there is a displacement at the level of genre: an autobiography according to its author, the text has also been read as a novel and as a work of poetry, due to its inclusion of heterogeneous materials, including a short story, a poem, personal correspondence and photographs. These formal-structural displacements challenge the notion of literary text in a manner that is analogous to the redefinition of the body undertaken within the four novels. If the (re)definition of the individual body and psyche as permeable to its surroundings (and thus not fully autonomous) throws into question notions such as personal autonomy and individual agency, then the narrative structures and voices deployed, in their diversity, heterogeneity and unconventionality, can be interpreted as attempts to imagine the ways in which a heteronomous subject might begin to break with (or through) literary and discursive conventions. That the success of such an endeavour is inevitably always contingent does not lead these authors to resignation or silence; rather, it spurs them on to experiment with new forms of writing.

globalised, late-capitalist, neoliberal paradigm is unsustainable and that an alternative is needed urgently. The task of devising and implementing such an alternative is primarily a political one; but, as thinkers such as Rancière (2017) have argued, creativity and the imagination – in other words, art and culture, understood in the broadest possible terms – have a crucial role to play in any such process, as they can (re)shape subjectivities and modify social discourses and imaginaries – and thus also, potentially, collective practices. Attempting to identify such changes seems premature; and, moreover, it would fall beyond the scope of this work, which is engaged in a cultural, rather than sociological, analysis. However, it seems fitting to close this book with a brief outline of some of the discursive trends that have developed in the wake of the end point of this study (2017) and which can be seen as further manifestations of the movement away from (or against) the non-ideological, as defined by Becerra, or the CT paradigm, as theorised by Guillem Martínez and colleagues (2012).

In spatial terms, and beyond the texts analysed in this study, the most significant development in recent years is the return of (or to) the rural in contemporary Spanish fiction. If this phenomenon has not been included in this monograph, it is for two reasons: first, most recent rural narratives do not establish a link between rurality and crisis, even though Ibarretxe and Delgado (2022) do suggest such a link exists, as they argue that at times of crisis, Spain looks to the countryside – and they posit the revalorisation of the (Castilian) countryside in the wake of the 'disaster' of 1898 as an example which prefigures the contemporary, renewed interest in the rural in the aftermath of the 2008 downturn and the Covid pandemic. Second, many – though not all – contemporary texts on the rural were published after the period under analysis (2007–17), as the publication and editorial success of Sergio del Molino's essay *La España vacía* (2016) placed the rural at the centre of public debate in Spain, sparking a boom in rural narratives in the following years.[1] As I argued in connection with the narrativisation of the transformation of coastal landscapes in the first chapter, this renewed preoccupation with physical spaces – in this case, rural and mostly interior – does not merely query their configuration; rather, the rural is understood

1 As examples of this boom, we might think of Jesús Carrasco's novels *Intemperie* (2013), *La tierra que pisamos* (2016) and *Llévame a casa* (2022); Santiago Lorenzo's *Los asquerosos* (2018); Sara Mesa's *Un amor* (2020); Ana Iris Simón's *Feria* (2020); or Rosa Montero's *La buena suerte* (2020), among many others. The resurgence of the rural has also found filmic expression in titles such as Icíar Bollaín's *El olivo* (2016); Carla Simón's *Estiu 1993* (2017) and *Alcarràs* (2022); Óliver Laxe's *O que arde* (2019); Rodrigo Sorogoyen's *As bestas* (2022), among others. For an overview of recent rural cinema, see González del Pozo 2021.

and explored as a way of life, as a milieu in which alternative forms of existence and relationality may be possible.[2]

This (re)turn of the rural can be read as, in part at least, a reaction against a socio-economic framework increasingly perceived as unsustainable and damaging – a perception that also permeates other recent texts which draw connections between different forms of violence. Edurne Portela's *Mejor la ausencia* (2016) and *Formas de estar lejos* (2019), for instance, explore (and expose) the links between political, structural, workplace-based and domestic forms of violence; Cristina Morales' misleadingly titled *Lectura fácil* (2018) examines institutional and symbolic forms of violence, and their role in the disciplinary control and containment of non-normative behaviours and identities; while Begoña Méndez's essay *Lodo* (2023) draws on the parallels between environmental and gendered violence. Social inequality – and particularly the re-emergence of a working-class consciousness – is at the heart of texts such as José Ignacio Carnero's *Ama* (2019), Andrea Abreu's *Panza de burro* (2020) and Bibiana Collado's *Yeguas exhaustas* (2023). In all three novels, the working-class identity of their protagonists and/or narrators is presented as articulated in connection to specific spaces (the Basque Country; the rural, interior Canary Islands; and the region of Valencia, respectively), and thus class, place and belonging – or non-belonging – are presented as inextricably enmeshed.

A further and as yet under-studied trend in contemporary Spain is the marked proliferation of mental health narratives – that is, of cultural texts which chronicle an experience of nervous breakdown, offering a critical portrayal of mental health services in post-austerity Spain, and in some cases undertaking a broader questioning of mental health frameworks and protocols. Certain texts included in the final chapter of this study – *Democracia*, *La trabajadora* and *Clavícula* – foreground this boom in stories in which mental ill health is depicted as connected to broader, collective issues, and thus 'seemingly personal suffering always-already enunciates a certain truth of the socioeconomic condition' (Tomšič 2020: 17).[3] This boom in stories which reframe mental ill health is particularly noticeable in the field of comics and graphic novels, with notable examples including Bea Lema's *El cuerpo de Cristo* (2023), Fran Ferriz's *Yo también tengo miedo* (2023), Borja Sumozas' *Pesimismo mágico* (2022) and *Manicomio: una historia real* (2019)

2 For an overview of different approaches within the contemporary Spanish 'rural turn', see Usoz de la Fuente and Miguélez-Carballeira (2024).

3 Tomšič is writing about the work of Freud and Lacan, rather than about any specific cultural works in Spain or beyond; however, his insights about psychoanalytical theory resonate with how many contemporary Spanish authors choose to depict and frame experiences of mental health crises.

by Montse Batalla and Xevidom. While not directly engaging with space, these titles nonetheless invite critical reflection on how environments – in the broadest sense – can impact individual experiences and perceptions, leading, in some cases, to nervous or psychotic breakdown. In many of these texts, dissociation from reality is presented not as the result of a chemical imbalance in the brain that can be easily fixed via medical means, but rather as an understandable – some would argue even rational – response to an unbearable and seemingly inescapable situation.

If the aforementioned titles reflect a discontent with the current status quo, revealing the human and environmental costs of late-stage neoliberal capitalism, as well as the hollowness of its promise of individual freedom and upward social mobility, some authors are beginning to attempt to imagine alternatives. Belén Gopegui's 2021 novel, *Existiríamos el mar*, explores new forms of kinship, in line with Donna Haraway's call to 'make kin, not babies' (2018). The text features a group of middle-aged characters who cohabit in a framework other than that of the conventional, nuclear, biological family or of the purely utilitarian, needs-driven flat-share. Instead, Gopegui's ensemble cast chooses to live together because its members value and appreciate each other, and they recognise the benefits derived from such an arrangement, such as companionship, resource efficiency and the ability to draw from an expanded skillset when needed. Their set-up, however, is very different from that of a hippy, utopian commune: all characters have (or aspire to have) regular jobs and lead relatively conventional lives, and the strength of the text lies precisely in Gopegui's clear-eyed depiction of the tensions and contradictions which the characters must negotiate in order to sustain their alternative living arrangement within a system which does not support or recognise it. Aixa de la Cruz's *Las herederas* (2022), meanwhile, imagines the conversion of an old countryside family house into an unconventional sanctuary for several women from the same family: a metaphor for how we might transform problematic legacies – genetic, material, affective, historic – into a collectively built and sustained, and more hopeful, future. The collectively authored graphic work *Ecotopías* (Adanti et al. 2024), meanwhile, endeavours to 'imaginar el futuro para cambiar el presente'[4] by projecting onto an imagined future alternative ways of organising collective life which are possible, sustainable and desirable. The different stories featured reimagine various aspects of everyday life, including the layout of towns and cities, housing, transportation, healthcare,

4 This motto is used as the subtitle of the work and thus appears on its title page, which is why I have not provided a page number.

medicine and education, in an attempt to present imaginative but realisable alternatives.

The texts analysed in this monograph depict the destructive effects of the hegemonic economic order over different spaces – Spain's landscapes, the home, the body, as well as the cultural texts themselves, which often (as discussed in the central chapters) also bear signs of dislocation and discontinuity. The more recent trends outlined above share this concern with spatiality – whether through a (re)turn to the rural; via the establishment of connections between events or phenomena taking place at different scales; through the foregrounding of the importance of place in the articulation of personal identity; through the connection they explicitly or implicitly establish between lived environments and mental health; or through the positing of new forms of communal living, which entail a new relationship to (and redefinition of) notions such as private and public (or communally managed) space and property. Obviously not all post-2007 cultural production in Spain is concerned with spatiality; neither are all texts always necessarily emancipatory in their intent. As argued in the Introduction, the banner of *literatura de la crisis* led to the circulation of many narratives that sought to reinforce, rather than challenge, the status quo, by presenting the downturn of 2007–8 as an anomaly, as the result either of a technical glitch or of human foibles for which a technocratic fix could be found. Similarly, in the case of the more recent rural (re)turn, progressive approaches which see in the rural a repository of sustainable and collective practices coexist with regressive idealisations nostalgic for a rural world imagined as homogenous and free of conflict; as well as with problematic remnants of the *España negra* tradition, which present the rural as brutal and primitive.[5] Second, and as Gutiérrez (2017) notes when he provocatively posits the picaresque tradition as part of the so-called *literatura de la crisis*, there is a long tradition of socially critical literature in Spain. My contention throughout these pages is not, therefore, that the global financial crisis of 2007–8 inaugurated, or even revived, that tradition; but rather, that the post-2008 socio-economic context of austerity led to changes within the Spanish literary field, whereby the pre-eminence of the 'non-ideological' novel, as well as of the 1990s and 2000s historical memory boom, was displaced by texts anchored in specific – and often contested or problematised – spaces in the present, and with a markedly critical slant.

Throughout this book, I have shown how the wide-ranging economic, political and social effects of the Great Recession of 2007–8 had an effect

5 Helena Miguélez-Carballeira (2024) identifies features of the *España negra* tradition in Sorogoyen's film *As bestas* (2022), for example.

over the Spanish cultural field – displacing certain actors and inviting new readings, or reassessments, of other, hitherto 'peripheral' figures; as well as inspiring some writers to produce the genre-defying, richly complex works explored at length in this study. Yet given that the outlook in Spain (and globally) at the time of writing in late 2025 seems more fractious than that of the mid-2010s, when most of the texts under study here were first published and read, the question of the extent to which these titles have had an effect over the Spanish public sphere seems pertinent, particularly given that, while some of the works discussed in this volume have proven influential in critical and academic circles, their sales figures (and, thus, presumably, their readership) remain relatively modest – with the exception of Rafael Chirbes, whose *Crematorio* was adapted for TV in 2011. Indeed, several of the authors featured in this study have admitted a degree of scepticism in relation to the role and influence of literature – and culture, more broadly – in today's world. Isaac Rosa, for example, has repeatedly referred to an unacknowledged 'crisis de la literatura', that is, to literature occupying an increasingly marginal position in terms of its reach (Anon. 2014: online; Usoz de la Fuente, Gustrán Loscos and Blanco Muñoz 2020b: 67–72), although interestingly, he has nuanced his views more recently (Montano 2022: online). Meanwhile, Marta Sanz has written about how her literary texts constitute

> un oxímoron: textos que parten de la radical convicción de que la literatura ya no le importa a casi nadie y que a la vez pretenden hablar de la literatura desde un lugar que no sea su templo, su jardín vallado, su paraíso perdido. (Sanz 2014: 8)

Similarly, in a 2020 interview, Belén Gopegui defines the influence of literature as 'almost non-existent' in present-day Spain, but is quick to add that 'that "almost" defines a responsibility' (Usoz de la Fuente, Gustrán Loscos and Blanco Muñoz 2020: 61). Rafael Chirbes, meanwhile, conceives of the impact of narrative in qualitative rather than quantitative terms, as he argues that '[n]o importa tanto el número de lectores a corto plazo que tenga un libro, lo que importa es que alguna vez el mundo ha sido contemplado desde un lugar nuevo' (2002: 27); yet he also acknowledges that, in contemporary societies, literature does not enjoy the influential position it once did, as nowadays 'la lucha por el control del relato toma la forma de la lucha por el control de los medios de comunicación de masas: el cine y, muy especialmente, la prensa escrita, la radio y la televisión' (2010: 235). In spite of this awareness of the diminished, or diminishing, sphere of influence of literature, the authors cited all persevere in their efforts to 'llegar a la médula del tiempo que nos ha tocado vivir' (Chirbes 2010: 37). Such stubbornness – as well as the texts resulting from it – might be read as both a recognition and vindication of literary fiction as an instrument of enquiry and of social intervention; and as a form of resistance against a capitalist logic that privileges the quantitative over the qualitative; speed over durability; and impulse or reaction over reflection.

References

Abreu, Andrea. *Panza de burro* (Seville: Editorial Barrett, 2020).

Adanti, Darío, Flavita Banana, Miguel Brieva et al. *Ecotopías. Imaginar el futuro para cambiar el presente* (Bilbao: Astiberri, 2024).

Agamben, Giorgio, trans. Daniel Heller-Roazen. *Homo Sacer: Sovereign Power and Bare Life* (Stanford: Stanford University Press, 1998).

Albrecht, Glenn. '"Solastalgia": A New Concept in Health and Identity', *PAN: Philosophy Activism Nature*, 3 (2005): 41–55.

Alonso, Luis Enrique, Carlos Jesús Fernández Rodríguez and Rafael Ibáñez Rojo. 'De la moral del sacrificio a la conciencia de la precariedad. Un análisis cualitativo de los discursos sobre la evolución de la crisis en España', *Política y Sociedad*, 53:2 (2016): 353–79.

Alonso, Pedro. 'Contra el ruido y el silencio: los espacios narrativos de la memoria de la posguerra española', in María Teresa Ibáñez Ehrlich (ed.), *Ensayos sobre Rafael Chirbes* (Madrid: Iberoamericana Vervuert, 2006), 11–19.

Álvarez-Blanco, Palmar and Antonio Gómez López-Quiñones (coord.). *La imaginación hipotecada. Aportaciones al debate sobre la precariedad del presente* (Madrid: Libros en Acción, 2016).

Andrade Blanco, Juan Antonio and Josep Fontana i Lázaro. *El PCE y el PSOE en (la) transición: la evolución ideológica de la izquierda durante el proceso de cambio político* (Madrid: Siglo XXI de España, 2012).

Angulo Egea, María. 'La construcción del discurso de la crisis: Los desahuciados y el caso de Cristina Fallarás', *IC – Revista Científica de Información y Comunicación*, 14 (2017): 159–89.

——. *Los discursos mediáticos de la crisis: escenarios, retratos y narraciones del desencanto (2008–2016)*, PhD thesis (Universidad de Málaga, 2019).

Anon. 'Doménico Chiappe hace literatura desde las fronteras', *EntornoInteligente.com*, 18/11/2013 (2013), available at https://www.domenicochiappe.com/wp-content/uploads/2013/01/Dossier-de-prensa_Tiempo-de-encierro_OK.pdf [last accessed 13 September 2024].

Anon. 'Entrevista a Isaac Rosa', *Quimera*, 22/01/2014 (2014), available at https://www.revistaquimera.com/entrevista-a-isaac-rosa/ [last accessed 9 September 2025].

Anon. 'Pablo Iglesias (Podemos): "La casta quiere mantener un sistema que nos lleva al desastre"', *La Vanguardia*, 27/05/2014 (2014b), available at https://www.

lavanguardia.com/politica/elecciones-europeas/20140527/54409339819/pablo-iglesias-podemos-casta-sistema.html [last accessed 19 August 2024].

Anon. 'Nota informativa sobre los procesos de ejecución hipotecaria sobre viviendas', Banco de España, 30/07/2015 (2015), available at https://www.bde.es/f/webbde/GAP/Secciones/SalaPrensa/NotasInformativas/Briefing_notes/es/notabe300715.pdf [last accessed 13 September 2024].

Anon. 'Nota informativa sobre los procesos de ejecución hipotecaria sobre viviendas', Banco de España, 20/07/2016 (2016), available at https://www.bde.es/f/webbde/GAP/Secciones/SalaPrensa/NotasInformativas/Briefing_notes/es/notabe200716.pdf [last accessed 13 September 2024].

Arana, Juan Ramón de. 'La problematización de la clase en *Crematorio*, de Rafael Chirbes', *La nueva literatura hispánica*, 14 (2010): 165–86.

Armada, Alfonso. '"No hay riqueza inocente". Entrevista a Rafael Chirbes', *ABC*, 28/05/2013 (2013), available at https://www.abc.es/cultura/libros/20130526/abci-entrevista-rafael-chirbes-201305241354.html [last accessed 24 November 2023].

Augé, Marc, trans. John Howe. *Non-Places: Introduction to an Anthropology of Supermodernity* (London and New York: Verso, 1992).

Ayala, Luis and Olga Cantó. *Radiografía de medio siglo de desigualdad en España. Características y factores que explican que España sea uno de los países más desiguales de Europa* (Palma: Observatorio Social La Caixa, 2022), available at https://elobservatoriosocial.fundacionlacaixa.org/documents/22890/492074/T01_ID_ES_AyalaCant%C3%B3.pdf/ [last accessed 19 December 2023].

Baba, Naohiko and Frank Packer. 'From Turmoil to Crisis: Dislocations in the FX Swap Market before and after the Failure of Lehman Brothers', *Journal of International Money and Finance*, 28:8 (2009): 1350–74.

Babych, Oleksiy. *Picking up the Pieces: The Economic Crisis and the Transformation of the Contemporary Peninsular Novel*, PhD thesis (University of Toronto, 2018), available at https://tspace.library.utoronto.ca/bitstream/1807/91862/1/Babych_Oleksiy_201811_PhD_thesis.pdf [last accessed 13 September 2024].

Bachelard, Gaston, trans. Ernestina de Champourcin. *La poética del espacio* (Mexico DF: Fondo de Cultura Económica, 1965).

Badiou, Alain, trans. Peter Hallward. *Ethics: An Essay on the Understanding of Evil* (London: Verso, 2002).

——. 'De quel réel cette crise est-elle le spectacle', *Le Monde*, 17/11/2008 (2008), available at https://www.lemonde.fr/idees/article/2008/10/17/de-quel-reel-cette-crise-est-elle-le-spectacle-par-alain-badiou_1108118_3232.html [last accessed 13 September 2024].

Ballarín Aguarón, Víctor. 'Autoficción y autobiografía en Marta Sanz. *Clavícula*', dissertation (2020), available at https://zaguan.unizar.es/record/88778/files/TAZ-TFG-2020-145.pdf [last accessed 28 June 2023].

Bammer, Angelika. 'Editorial', *New Formations*, 17 (1992): ix–x.

Barjau, Teresa and Joaquim Parellada Casas. 'Rafael Chirbes, en Beniarbeig', *Ínsula: revista de letras y ciencias humanas*, 803 (2013): 13–21.

Barthes, Roland, trans. Richard Howard. *Camera Lucida: Reflections on Photography* (New York: Hill & Wang, 1981).

Bauman, Zygmunt. *Liquid Modernity* (London: Polity, 2000).

Bauman, Zygmunt and Carlo Bordoni. *State of Crisis* (Cambridge: Polity, 2014).

Becerra Mayor, David. *La novela de la no-ideología. Introducción a la producción literaria del capitalismo avanzado en España* (Madrid: Tierradenadie Ediciones, 2013).

——. 'Las enfermedades psíquicas que el capitalismo provoca', *Mundo obrero*, 271 (2014), available at https://www.mundoobrero.es/2014/04/23/las-enfermedades-psiquicas-que-el-capitalismo-provoca/ [last accessed 26 June 2023].

—— (ed.). *Convocando al fantasma. Novela crítica en la España actual* (Madrid: Tierradenadie Ediciones, 2015).

——. 'El relato de la pérdida y las representaciones del fin de la clase media en las novelas de la crisis', in Jaume Peris Blanes (ed.), *Cultura e imaginación política* (México/París: RILMA 2/ADEHL, 2018), 45–62.

——. *Después del acontecimiento. El retorno de lo político en la literatura española tras el 15-M* (Manersa: Bellaterra Edicions, 2021).

Benito Mesa, Iris de. 'Y de pronto nos mandaron a la puta calle: el caso Cristina Fallarás', in Claudio Moyano Arellano and Iris de Benito Mesa (eds), *Narrar el conflicto económico: el papel de la economía en la literatura* (Valladolid: Ediciones Universidad de Valladolid, 2021), 59–84.

Berasategui, Blanca. 'Libros. Rafael Chirbes. *Crematorio* era el esplendor y *En la orilla* es la caída', *El Cultural. El Mundo*, 11 (2013).

Berlant, Lauren. 'Slow Death (Sovereignty, Obesity, Lateral Agency)', *Critical Inquiry*, 33:4 (2007): 754–80.

——. *Cruel Optimism* (Durham, NC: Duke University Press, 2011).

Bértolo, Constantino. 'Construir imaginación', *Mundo Obrero*, 24/07/2015 (2015), available at https://www.mundoobrero.es/pl.php?id=4980 [last accessed 13 September 2024].

Bezhanova, Olga. *Literature of Crisis: Spain's Engagement with Liquid Capital* (Lewisburg: Bucknell University Press, 2017).

Bieling, Hans-Jürgen. 'Austerity-induced Populism: The Rise and Transformation of the New Right', in Stephen McBride, Brian Evans and Dieter Plehwe (eds), *The Changing Politics and Policy of Austerity* (Bristol: Policy Press, 2021), 213–29.

Blanchar, Clara. 'Ciutat Meridiana, ciudad desahucio', *El País*, 22/07/2012 (2012), available at https://elpais.com/ccaa/2012/07/21/catalunya/1342895388_879265.html [last accessed 13 September 2024].

Bollaín, Icíar. *El olivo* (2016).

Bonet, Paula. 'Marta Sanz: "Sufrir no nos hace más fuertes, normalmente nos debilita"', *Jot Down* (2016), available at https://www.jotdown.es/2016/03/marta-sanz/ [last accessed 27 June 2023].

Bonvalot, Anne-Laure. 'Nuevas territorialidades y ontologías políticas en la ficción española post 15M: horizontes estéticos y antropológicos de la "literatura indignada"', in Jorge Cagiao and Isabelle Touton (eds), *España después del 15M* (Madrid: Catarata, 2019), 193–201.

Bourdieu, Pierre. 'The Berber House or the World Reversed', *Social Science Information*, 9:2 (1970): 151–70.

——, trans. Susan Emanuel. *The Rules of Art: Genesis and Structure of the Literary Field* (Stanford: Stanford University Press, 1996).

Boym, Svetlana. 'Ruinophilia: Appreciation of Ruins', *Atlas of Transformation* (online: 2011), available at http://monumenttotransformation.org/atlas-of-transformation/html/r/ruinophilia/ruinophilia-appreciation-of-ruins-svetlana-boym.html [last accessed 24 November 2023].

Brazys, Samuel and Niamh Hardiman. 'From "Tiger" to "PIIGS": Ireland and the use of heuristics in comparative political economy', *European Journal of Political Research*, 54:1 (2015): 23–42.

Brenner, Neil (ed.). *Implosions/Explosions: Towards a Study of Planetary Urbanization* (Berlin and Boston: JOVIS, 2013).

Broncano, Fernando. 'Fragilidad del afecto', *El laberinto de la identidad*, 16/02/2014 (2014), available at http://laberintodelaidentidad.blogspot.com/2014/02/fragilidad-del-afecto.html [last accessed 27 June 2023].

Buczek, Olga and Mariola Pietrak. 'El malestar: codificación de la crisis española en *Clavícula* de Marta Sanz', *Études romanes de Brno*, 42 (2021): 51–62.

Butler, Judith. *Precarious Life: The Powers of Mourning and Violence* (New York and London: Verso, 2004).

——. *Frames of War: When is Life Grievable?* (London: Verso, 2010).

Calvo Carilla, José Luis. 'Lecturas críticas sobre la Transición: el caso de Rafael Chirbes', in Calvo Carilla et al., *El relato de la Transición. La Transición como relato* (Zaragoza: Prensas de la Universidad de Zaragoza, 2011), 119–46.

Cano, José A. '"El suicidio de mi hermano sirvió para que se viese el problema"', *El Mundo*, 25/10/2013 (2013), available at https://www.elmundo.es/andalucia/2013/10/25/526ab659684341be558b456e.html [last accessed 13 November 2023].

Carnero, José Ignacio. *Ama* (Madrid: Caballo de Troya, 2019).

Carrasco, Jesús. *Intemperie* (Barcelona: Seix-Barralc, 2013).

——. *La tierra que pisamos* (Barcelona: Seix-Barral, 2016).

——. *Llévame a casa* (Barcelona: Planeta, 2022).

Chiappe, Doménico. *Tiempo de encierro* (Madrid: Lengua de Trapo, 2013).

Chirbes, Rafael. *El novelista perplejo* (Barcelona: Anagrama, 2002).

——. *Crematorio* (Barcelona: Anagrama, 2007).

——. *Por cuenta propia. Leer y escribir* (Barcelona: Anagrama, 2010).

——. *En la orilla* (Barcelona: Anagrama, 2013).

Claesson, Christian (coord.). *Narrativas precarias. Crisis y subjetividad en la cultura española actual* (Xixón: Hoja de Lata, 2019).

Colau, Ada and Adriá Alemany. *Vidas hipotecadas. De la burbuja inmobiliaria al derecho a la vivienda* (Barcelona: Cuadrilátero de Libros, 2012).

——. '2007 – 2012 : Restrospectiva sobre desahucios y ejecuciones hipotecarias en España, estadísticas oficiales e indicadores' (2013), available at https://afectadosporlahipoteca.com//wp-content/uploads/2013/02/RETROSPECTIVA-SOBRE-DESAHUCIOS-Y-EJECUCIONES-HIPOTECARIAS-EN-ESPA%C3%91A-COLAUALEMANY1.pdf [last accessed 13 September 2024].

Collado, Bibiana. *Yeguas exhaustas* (Logroño: Pepitas de calabaza, 2023).

Colomer, Josep M. 'La aventurada apuesta por la independencia de Cataluña', *Revista de Estudios Políticos*, 179 (2018): 267–94.

Corominas i Julián, Jordi. 'Diálogo con Rafael Chirbes', *Revista de Letras*, 27/03/2013 (2013), available at http://revistadeletras.net/dialogo-conrafael-chirbes-por-jordi-corominas-i-julian/ [last accessed 24 November 2023].

Cortina, Adela. 'Aporofobia', *El País*, 06/03/2000 (2000), available at https://elpais.com/diario/2000/03/07/opinion/952383603_850215.html [last accessed 26 February 2026].

Cruz, Aixa de la. *Las herederas* (Barcelona: Alfaguara, 2022).

Cruz, Silvia. 'Marta Sanz: "Sin estabilidad económica es imposible tener un proyecto de vida"', Entrevista con Marta Sanz publicada en *El Español*, 29/03/2017 (2017), available at https://www.elespanol.com/cultura/libros/20170328/204230144_0.html [last accessed 27 June 2023].

Davies, Ann. *Spanish Spaces: Landscape, Space and Place in Contemporary Spanish Culture* (Liverpool: Liverpool University Press, 2012).

Davis, Lewis and Sumit S. Deole. 'Immigration and the Rise of Far-right Parties in Europe', *ifo DICE Report*, 15:4 (2017): 10–15.

Delgado, Luisa Elena. *La nación singular. Fantasías de la normalidad democrática española (1996–2011)* (Madrid: Siglo XXI, 2014).

Derrida, Jacques, trans. Peggy Kamuf. *Spectres of Marx: The State of the Debt, the Work of Mourning and the New International* (London: Routledge, 1994).

Díaz Parra, Ibán and José Candón-Mena. 'Espacio geográfico y ciberespacio en el movimiento 15M', *Scripta Nova: Revista electrónica de geografía y ciencias sociales*, 18:470 (2014).

Diz, Carlos. 'La imaginación de lo público: repensar la ciudad desde una acampada del 15M', *Zainak. Cuadernos de Antropología-Etnografía*, 36 (2013): 75–86.

Domínguez, Íñigo. *Mediterráneo descapotable. Viaje ridículo por aquel país tan feliz* (Madrid: Libros del K.O., 2015).

Douglas, Mary. 'The Idea of Home: A Kind of Space', *Social Research*, 58:1 (Spring 1991): 287–307.

Dowling, Andrew. 'Accounting for the Turn towards Secession in Catalonia', *International Journal of Iberian Studies*, 27:2–3 (2014): 219–34.

Dueñas, Francisco Javier. 'Elvira Navarro: vagar, narrar y repensar la ciudad en crisis', *Intersticios. Revista sociológica de pensamiento crítico*, 12:1 (2018): 113–32.

Etxezarreta, Miren, Francisco Navarro, Ramón Ribera and Victòria Soldevila. 'Boom and (Deep) Crisis in the Spanish Economy: The Role of the EU in its Evolution', Communication for 17th Workshop on Alternative Economic Policy in Europe, Vienna, September 2011, available at https://www2.euromemorandum.eu/uploads/ws1_etxezarreta_et_al._boom_and_deep_crisis_in_the_spanish_economy_the_role_of_the_eu_in_its_evolution.pdf [last accessed 19 October 2023].

Faiola, Anthony. 'Economic Malaise Threatens to Undermine European Unity', *Washington Post*, 11/08/2008 (2008), available at https://www.washingtonpost.com/archive/national/2008/08/12/economic-malaise-threatens-to-undermine-european-unity/9f4d883b-db77-4117-84b8-d05b96d457d6/ [last accessed 19 April 2024].

Fallarás, Cristina. *A la puta calle. Crónica de un desahucio* (Barcelona: Planeta, 2013).

Federici, Silvia. *Caliban and the Witch* (New York: Autonomedia, 2004).

Fernández-Cebrián, Ana. *Fables of Development: Capitalism and Social Imaginaries in Spain (1950–1967)* (Liverpool: Liverpool University Press, 2023).

Fernández Durán, Ramón. *El tsunami urbanizador español y mundial. Sobre sus causas y repercusiones devastadoras y la necesidad de prepararse para el previsible estallido de la burbuja inmobiliaria* (Barcelona: Virus Folletos, 2006), available at https://www.viruseditorial.net/paginas/pdf.php?pdf=el-tsunami-urbanizador-espanol-y-mundial.pdf [last accessed 24 November 2023].

Fernández-Savater, Amador. 'Crisis de presencia. Una lectura de *Tiqqun*', *Espai en Blanc*, 09/07/2011 (2011), available at http://espaienblanc.net/?cat=10 [last accessed 26 June 2023].

——. *La fuerza de los débiles. El 15M en el laberinto español. Un ensayo sobre la eficacia política* (Madrid: Akal, 2021).

Ferrero, Ángel. '"Todas las luchas literarias son luchas políticas", entrevista a Rafael Chirbes', *Sin Permiso*, 20/08/2012 (2012): 1–13, available at https://www.sinpermiso.info/sites/default/files/textos//RChirbes.pdf [last accessed 20 September 2023].

Fisher, Mark. 'Hauntology Now' [blog post], *k-punk*, 17/01/2006 (2006), available at http://k-punk.abstractdynamics.org/archives/007230.html [last accessed 5 September 2024].

——. *Capitalist Realism: Is There Really No Alternative?* (Winchester: Zero Books, 2009).

——. *Ghosts of My Life: Writings on Depression, Hauntology, and Lost Futures* (John Hunt Publishing, 2014).

Foucault, Michel, trans. Jay Miskowiec. 'Of Other Spaces', *Diacritics*, 16:1 (1986): 22–27.

——, trans. David Macey. *Society Must Be Defended: Lectures at the Collège de France, 1975–76* (New York: Picador, 2003).

Freud, Sigmund. 'The Uncanny (1919)', in *The Standard Edition of the Complete Psychological Works of Sigmund Freud*, trans. James Strachey, vol. 17, 1917–19 (London: Hogarth Press, 1971), 217–56.

Friedlander, Eli. 'Some Thoughts on Kitsch', *History and Memory*, 9:1/2 (1997): 376–92.

Friedländer, Saul, et al. 'On Kitsch: A Symposium', *Salmagundi*, 187 (2015).

Furió Sancho, María-José. 'Evocación y reivindicación de las vanguardias artísticas en la arquitectura moderna con ambición social en las novelas *Catálogo de Formas*, de Nicolás Cabral, y *La trabajadora*, de Elvira Navarro', *Dissidences: Hispanic Journal of Theory and Criticism*, 6:11 (2015), available at https://digitalcommons.bowdoin.edu/dissidences/vol6/iss11/3 [last accessed 13 September 2024].

Gabancho, Patricia. '"Villa desahucio"', *El País*, 03/12/2012 (2012), available at https://elpais.com/ccaa/2012/12/02/catalunya/1354480579_174304.html [last accessed 13 September 2024].

Gallego Dueñas, Francisco Javier. 'Elvira Navarro: vagar, narrar y repensar la ciudad en crisis', *Intersticios. Revista sociológica de pensamiento crítico*, 12:1 (2018): 113–32.

Garcés, Marina. *Nueva ilustración radical* (Barcelona: Anagrama, 2017).

García Márquez, Marta. '"Las instituciones son más responsables que los desahuciados que creyeron en ellas". Entrevista a Doménico Chiappe', *El Ideal Gallego.com*, 02/02/2014 (2014), available at https://www.domenicochiappe.com/wp-content/uploads/2013/01/Dossier-de-prensa_Tiempo-de-encierro_OK.pdf [last accessed 13 September 2024].

Geeroms, Maarten. 'La escritura-constelación de Walter Benjamin como alternativa de la historia: *En la orilla* (2013) de Rafael Chirbes', *Bulletin of Hispanic Studies*, 94:7 (2017): 747–64.
Giesz, Ludwig. 'Kitsch-man as tourist', in Gillo Dorfles (ed.), *Kitsch: An Anthology of Bad Taste* (London: Studio Vista, 1969), 156–74.
Gómez López-Quiñones, Antonio. 'La precariedad de la precariedad y el discreto encanto de la culpa política', in Palmar Álvarez-Blanco and Antonio Gómez López-Quiñones (coord.), *La imaginación hipotecada. Aportaciones al debate sobre la precariedad del presente* (Madrid: Libros en Acción, 2016), 133–46.
González, Pilar. '¿Qué es una novela política hoy?', *Letralia*, XVIII:290, 18/11/2013 (2013), available at https://letralia.com/290/articulo06.htm [last accessed 4 September 2024].
González del Pozo, Jorge. 'Cine rural: representación cinematográfica del campo hasta la España vacía de hoy', *Arizona Journal of Hispanic Cultural Studies*, 25:1 (2021): 124–34.
González-Ruibal, Alfredo. 'Returning to Where We Have Never Been', in *Ruin Memories: Materialities, Aesthetics and the Archaeology of the Recent Past* (2014), available at https://digital.csic.es/bitstream/10261/95916/1/Gonzalez-Ruibal_Returning%20to%20where%20we%20have%20never%20been.pdf [last accessed 24 November 2023].
Gopegui, Belén. *El padre de Blancanieves* (Barcelona: Anagrama, 2007).
——. *Un pistoletazo en medio de un concierto. Acerca de escribir de política en una novela* (Madrid: Editorial Complutense, 2008).
——. *El comité de la noche* (Barcelona: Penguin Random House, 2014).
——. *Existiríamos el mar* (Barcelona: Literatura Random House, 2021).
Gramsci, Antonio, ed. and trans. Quintin Hoare and Geoffrey Nowell Smith. *Selections from the Prison Notebooks* (London: Lawrence and Wishart, 1971).
Greenberg, Clement. 'Avant-garde and Kitsch (1939)', in Charles Harrison and Paul Wood (eds), *Art in Theory 1900–2000* (Oxford: Blackwell Publishing, 2003), 539–49.
Gutiérrez, Pablo. *Democracia* (Barcelona: Seix-Barral, 2012).
——. 'Literatura social en España. La crisis perpetua', in J. Mecke et al. (eds), *Discursos de la crisis: respuestas de la cultura española ante nuevos desafíos* (Madrid: Vervuert, 2017), 187–98.
——. *El adjetivo mata* [blog], eladjetivomata.blogspot.com [last accessed 26 June 2023].
Guzmán Ramírez, Aura and Martha Quiroga Riviere. 'La crisis económica y el movimiento independentista catalán', *Oasis*, 18 (2013): 55–71.
Han, Byung-Chul, trans. Erik Butler. *The Burnout Society* (Stanford: Stranford University Press, 2015).
——, trans. Daniel Steuer. *Capitalism and the Death Drive* (Cambridge: Polity Press, 2021).
Haraway, Donna. 'Staying with the Trouble for Multispecies Environmental Justice', *Dialogues in Human Geography*, 8:1 (2018): 102–5.
Haro Tecglen, Eduardo. 'La generación bífida', *El País*, 26/11/1988 (1988), available at https://elpais.com/diario/1988/11/27/opinion/596588409_850215.html [last accessed 27 November 2023].

Harvey, David. *Spaces of Hope* (Edinburgh: Edinburgh University Press, 2000).
——. *The New Imperialism* (Oxford: Oxford University Press, 2003).
——. *Rebel Cities: From the Right to the City to the Urban Revolution* (London: Verso, 2012).
Hermoso, Borja. 'Fuego real en el "crematorio" de Chirbes', *El País*, 07/03/2011 (2011), available at https://elpais.com/diario/2011/03/07/cultura/1299452402_850215.html [last accessed 27 November 2023].
Hernández, Esteban. *El fin de la clase media* (Madrid: Editorial Clave Intelectual, 2014).
Hernández Herrero, Roberto. 'Transgresión del discurso hegemónico y poesía para enfrentar la crisis en la novela *Democracia* de Pablo Gutiérrez', dissertion (Lund University, 2013), available at https://lup.lub.lu.se/luur/download?func=downloadFile&recordOId=3811194&fileOId=3811195 [last accessed 26 June 2023].
Herrera, Elena and Victòria Oliveres. 'La mayoría de los españoles quiere un referéndum para decidir entre monarquía y república', *eldiario.es*, 26/11/2023 (2023), available at https://www.eldiario.es/politica/mayoria-espanoles-quiere-referendum-decidir-monarquia-republica_1_10713240.html [last accessed 18 December 2023].
Hessel, Stéphane, trans. Telmo Moreno Lanaspa. *¡Indignaos! (Indignez-vous!)* (Madrid: Destino, 2011).
Hochschild, Arlie Russell and Anne Machung. *The Second Shift: Working Parents and the Revolution at Home* (New York: Avon Books, 1989).
Huyssen, Andreas. 'Nostalgia for Ruins', *Grey Room*, 23 (Spring 2006): 6–21.
Ibáñez, Luis Enrique. 'Acerca de la novela *Democracia* de Pablo Gutiérrez', text used during the novel's presentation in November 2012 (2012), available at Pablo Gutiérrez's blog *El adjetivo mata*: http://dueloliterae.blogspot.com/2012/11/acerca-de-la-novela-democracia-de-pablo.html [last accessed 26 June 2023].
Ibarretxe Diego, Arkaitz and Luisa Elena Delgado. 'Comunidades inimaginables: narrativas sobre la España vaciada', in Christian Claesson (ed.), *España comparada. Literatura, lengua y política en la cultura contemporánea* (Granada: Comares, 2022), 101–22.
Jameson, Fredric. 'Future City', *New Left Review*, 21 (May/June 2003), available at https://newleftreview.org/issues/ii21/articles/fredric-jameson-future-city [last accessed 19 August 2024].
Jenkins, William. *New Topographics: Photographs of a Man-altered Landscape* (Rochester, New York: International Museum of Photography, 1975).
Jiménez, Carmen. 'Pablo Gutiérrez: "Para mí la literatura es una forma de resistencia"', *El mono lector* (blog) (2013), available at http://elmonolector.blogspot.com/2013/01/pablo-gutierrez-para-mi-la-novela-es.html [last accessed 26 June 2023].
Jiménez, Jesús. 'Aquí vivió, la lucha contra los desahucios llega al cómic', *El cómic en RTVE* [blog] (2016), available at https://www.rtve.es/noticias/20160316/aqui-vivio-lucha-contra-desahucios-llega-comic/1318901.shtml [last accessed 4 September 2024].
Jiménez, Mauro. 'Rafael Chirbes o cómo pinchar la burbuja', *Quimera*, 394 (September 2016): 20–23.
Korcheck, Kathy. 'Speculative Ruins: Photographic Interrogations of the Spanish Economic Crisis', *Arizona Journal of Hispanic Cultural Studies*, 19 (2015): 91–110.

Labrador Méndez, Germán. 'Las vidas "subprime": la circulación de "historias de vida" como tecnología de imaginación política en la crisis española (2007–2012)', *Hispanic Review* (2012): 557–81.

——. 'El precio del espacio: los desarrollos últimos del giro espacial en los estudios peninsulares y la producción de espacio en la España actual', *Revista Hispánica Moderna*, 66:2 (2013): 221–34.

——. 'The Cannibal Wave: The Cultural Logic of Spain's Temporality of Crisis (Revolution, Biopolitics, Hunger and Memory)', *Journal of Spanish Cultural Studies*, 15:1–2 (2014): 241–71.

——. *La marea caníbal. La lógica cultural de la temporalidad de crisis en España, entre revolución, biopolítica, hambre y memoria* (Archivo de la Fontera, 2015), available at http://www.archivodelafrontera.com/wp-content/uploads/2015/01/Germ%C3%A1n_LAbrador-La_marea_can%C3%ADbal_.pdf [last accessed 24 November 2023].

——. 'Lo que en España no ha habido: la lógica normalizadora de la cultura postfranquista en la actual crisis', *Revista Hispánica Moderna*, 69:2 (2016): 165–92.

——. *Culpables por la literatura: imaginación política y contracultura en la transición española (1968–1986)* (Madrid: Ediciones Akal, 2017).

Larraz, Fernando. 'Rafael Chirbes, Paris-Austerlitz', *Revista Caracol*, 11 (2016): 328–35.

Laxe, Óliver. *O que arde* (2019).

Lefebvre, Henri, trans. Donald Nicholson. *The Production of Space* (Oxford: Blackwell, 1991).

——, trans. Robert Bononno. *The Urban Revolution* (Minneapolis: University of Minnesota Press, 2003).

León Vegas, Carolina. 'En busca del espacio perdido. La crisis y el espacio urbano en *La habitación oscura* de Isaac Rosa y *Animales domésticos* de Marta Sanz', *Revista de Literatura*, LXXXI:162 (2019): 549–72.

Lichfield, John. 'Let Them See Kitsch', *Independent*, 10/09/2008 (2008), 24–25.

Lizarte Fernández, Mónica. *Estudio de la obra narrativa de Belén Gopegui*, PhD thesis (UNED, 2022), available at http://e-spacio.uned.es/fez/eserv/tesisuned:ED-Pg-Filologia-Mlizarte/LIZARTE_FERNANDEZ__Monica_Tesis.pdf [last accessed 26 June 2023].

Llamas Martínez, Jacobo. '*La Celestina* como modelo de Rafael Chirbes en *Crematorio*', *Celestinesca*, 44 (2021): 163–90.

López Bernasocchi, Augusta and José Manuel López de Abiada (eds). *La constancia de un testigo. Ensayos sobre Rafael Chirbes* (Madrid: Editorial Verbum, 2011).

Lorente Ferrer, José. 'La mayoría de los españoles respalda la Monarquía Parlamentaria', *La Razón*, 05/11/2023 (2023), available at https://www.larazon.es/opinion/mayoria-espanoles-respalda-monarquia-parlamentaria_2023110556546d4e9f6ca7200014ca61c.html [last accessed 18 December 2023].

Lorenzo, Santiago. *Los asquerosos* (Madrid: Blackie Books, 2018).

Lorey, Isabell. 'Becoming Common: Precarization as Political Constituting', *e-flux*, 17, June 2010 (2010), available at https://www.e-flux.com/journal/17/67385/becoming-common-precarization-as-political-constituting/ [last accessed 26 June 2023].

——, trans. Aileen Derieg. *State of Insecurity: Government of the Precarious* (London and New York: Verso, 2015).

Luján, Carlos. *Desahucios. Los escenarios del horror*, first published in *XL Semanal*, 31/03/2013 (2013), available at http://nophoto.org/desahucios [last accessed 19 August 2024].

Maltby, Paul. 'Kinkade, Koons, Kitsch', *Journal for Cultural and Religious Theory*, 12:1 (2012): 53–81.

Marchena, Domingo. 'Dos mercados agónicos reflejan la evolución de "Villa Desahucio"', *La Vanguardia*, 16/01/2018 (2018), available at https://www.lavanguardia.com/local/barcelona/20180116/4449466158/ciutat-meridiana-mercado.html [last accessed 4 September 2024].

Martín-Cabrera, Luis. 'Contra la suspensión de la mirada crítica: reflexiones sobre la persistencia del conflicto capital/trabajo en la cultura contemporánea española', *Arizona Journal of Hispanic Cultural Studies*, 14 (2010): 117–38.

Martín-Estudillo, Luis. 'Pornoprecariedad: crisis biopolítica, trabajo y régimen visual en *Hermosa juventud* (Jaime Rosales, 2014)', *Romance Quarterly*, 64:4 (2017): 196–205.

Martínez, Guillem, et al. *CT o la Cultura de la Transición. Crítica a 35 años de cultura española* (Madrid: Debolsillo, 2012).

Martínez Fernández, Ángela. 'Marta Sanz: *Clavícula (mi clavícula y otros inmensos desajustes)*', *Diablotexto Digital*, 2 (2017): 236–41, available at https://roderic.uv.es/bitstream/handle/10550/65529/124424.pdf?sequence=1 [last accessed 27 June 2023].

Martínez Rubio, José. 'Precariedad, subjetividad y trauma en la novela de la crisis. Desorden psíquico y enfermedad social en *La trabajadora* de Elvira Navarro', *Rassegna iberistica*, 106 (2016): 289–306.

Matos-Martín, Eduardo. 'Narrating Spain's Economic Crisis: Unemployment, Precarity and Subjectivity in Pablo Gutiérrez's *Democracia*', *Hispanic Research Journal*, 18:6 (2017): 520–37.

Mbembé, Achille, trans. Libby Meintjes. 'Necropolitics', *Public Culture*, 15:1 (2003): 11–40.

Mecke, J., et al. *Discursos de la crisis: respuestas de la cultura española ante nuevos desafíos* (Madrid: Vervuert, 2017).

Medina, Alberto. 'De flujos, lugares y peceras: Mutaciones y permutaciones del "cualquiera" en el 15M', *Journal of Spanish Cultural Studies*, 16:3 (2015): 293–316.

Méndez, Begoña. *Lodo* (Madrid: Lengua de trapo, 2023).

Mesa, Sara. *Silencio administrativo. La pobreza en el laberinto burocrático* (Barcelona: Anagrama, 2019).

——. *Un amor* (Barcelona: Anagrama, 2020).

Miguélez-Carballeira, Helena. 'Cinema e novos consensos estatais na Transição ecológica: "As bestas" (2022) e os significados políticos da discapacidade', *Anuário: textos completos do Caseto… em claracorbelhe. gal*, 2 (2024): 207–14.

Miguélez-Carballeira, Helena and Maite Usoz de la Fuente. 'Cultural Engagements with the Rural in Contemporary Spain: Manifestations and Critical Tensions', *Journal of Spanish Cultural Studies*, 25:4 (2024): 465–75.

Molino, Sergio del. *La España vacía. Viaje por un país que nunca fue* (Madrid: Turner, 2016).

Monedero, Juan Carlos. '15M and Indignant Democracy: Legitimation Problems Within Neoliberal Capitalism', in Óscar Pereira-Zazo and Steven L. Torres (eds), *Spain after the Indignados/15M Movement: The 99% Speaks Out* (Basingstoke and New York: Palgrave Macmillan, 2019), 21–63.

Montano, Bruno. 'Trabalibros entrevista a Isaac Rosa, autor de "Lugar seguro" (Premio Biblioteca Breve 2022)', *Trabalibros*, 31/03/2022 (2022), available at https://trabalibros.com/noticias/lugar-seguro-isaac-rosa [last accessed 9 September 2025].

Montero, Rosa. *La buena suerte* (Barcelona: Alfaguara, 2020).

Mora, Vicente Luis. 'La construcción del realismo fuerte en algunos libros de narrativa hispánica actual', *Diario de lecturas* [blog] (2014), available at http://vicenteluismora.blogspot.com/2014/05/la-construccion-del-realismo-fuerte-en.html [last accessed 26 June 2023].

Morales, Cristina. *Lectura fácil* (Barcelona: Anagrama, 2018).

Morán, Gregorio. *El precio de la transición* (Barcelona: Planeta, 1991).

Moreno-Caballud, Luis, trans. Linda Grabner. *Cultures of Anyone: Studies on Cultural Democratization in the Spanish Neoliberal Crisis* (Liverpool: Liverpool University Press, 2015a).

——. 'La otra transición: Culturas rurales, Estado e intelectuales en la encrucijada de la "modernización" franquista (1957–1973)', *Arizona Journal of Hispanic Cultural Studies*, 19 (2015b): 111–28.

Naficy, Hamid (ed.). *Home, Exile, Homeland: Film, Media and the Politics of Place* (New York and London: Routledge, 1999).

Navarro, Elvira. *La trabajadora* (Barcelona: Penguin Random House, 2014).

Navarro, Jose María. '"Nada queda a salvo de los efectos demoledores de la historia". Entrevista con Rafael Chirbes', *Iberoamericana*, 32 (2008): 155 58.

Nichols, William J. 'Sifting through the Ashes: An Interview with Rafael Chirbes', *Arizona Journal of Hispanic Cultural Studies*, 12 (2008): 219–35.

Nin, María Cristina and Stella Maris Shmite. 'Manifestaciones sociales en ciudades españolas. El 15M y la resignificación del paisaje urbano', *Geograficando*, 11:2 (2015), available at https://www.geograficando.fahce.unlp.edu.ar/article/view/Geov11n02a04/7084 [last accessed 24 November 2023].

Nixon, Rob. *Slow Violence and the Environmentalism of the Poor* (Cambridge and London: Harvard University Press, 2011).

NoPhoto Collective. *This Is Spain: An Incomplete Travel Guide* (Madrid: PHREE, 2015).

O'Dwyer, Manus. 'Reading Rafael Chirbes's *Crematorio* as a World-Ecological Text', *Bulletin of Contemporary Hispanic Studies*, 4:2 (2022): 151–67.

Ortiz Heras, Manuel. 'Nuevos y viejos discursos de la transición. La nostalgia del consenso', *Historia contemporánea*, 44 (2012): 337–70.

Otero-García, Laura, et al. 'Austerity Measures and Underfunding of the Spanish Health System during the COVID-19 Pandemic: Perception of Healthcare Staff in Spain', *International Journal of Environmental Research and Public Health*, 20:3 (2023): 2594.

Palley, Thomas. 'Europe's Crisis without End: The Consequences of Neoliberalism', *Contributions to Political Economy*, 32:1 (2013): 29–50.

Pavlović, Tatjana. *The Mobile Nation: España cambia de piel (1954–1964)* (Chicago and Bristol: Intellect, 2011).

Pensky, Max. 'Three Kinds of Ruins: Heidegger, Benjamin, Sebald', *Poligrafi*, 16:61/62 (2011): 65–89.

Peris Blanes, Jaume. 'Cultura, literatura e imaginación política. La verosimilitud va a cambiar de bando', in Jaume Peris Blanes (ed.), *Cultura, literatura e imaginación política* (México/París: RILMA 2/ADEHL, 2018), 1–24.

Plataforma de Afectados por la Hipoteca (PAH) (website): https://afectadosporlahipoteca.com/ [last accessed 4 September 2024].

Portela, Edurne. *Mejor la ausencia* (Barcelona: Galaxia Gutenberg, 2016).

——. '*Clavícula*, de Marta Sanz: una poética de la fragilidad', *La Marea*, 22/03/2017 (2017), available at https://www.lamarea.com/2017/03/22/clavicula-marta-sanz-una-poetica-la-fragilidad/ [last accessed 28 June 2023].

——. *Formas de estar lejos* (Barcelona: Galaxia Gutenberg, 2019).

Portillo, Juande. '¿Cuántas familias perdieron su casa por la "leyenda urbana" de los desahucios?', *Cinco Días*, 31/01/2018 (2018), available at https://cincodias.elpais.com/cincodias/2018/01/30/midinero/1517339842_922977.html [last accessed 4 September 2024].

Potok, Magda. 'Mujer y economía. La "narrativa de la crisis" desde la perspectiva de género', *Studia Romanica Posnaniensia*, 47:1 (2020): 93–105.

Prádanos, Luis Iñaki. *Postgrowth Imaginaries: New Ecologies and Counterhegemonic Culture in Post-2008 Spain* (Liverpool: Liverpool University Press, 2018).

Precarias a la deriva. A la deriva por los circuitos de precariedad femenina (Madrid: Traficantes de sueños, 2004), available at https://www.traficantes.net/sites/default/files/pdfs/A%20la%20deriva-TdS.pdf [last accessed 26 June 2023].

Prieto, Carlos. 'Miedo y asco en Marina d'Or', *El Confidencial*, 30/04/2015 (2015), available at https://www.elconfidencial.com/cultura/2015-04-30/miedo-y-asco-en-marina-d-or_763662/ [last accessed 27 November 2023].

Queralt, Raquel. 'Un padre de familia a punto de ser desahuciado se ahorca en plena calle', *La Vanguardia*, 11/11/2010 (2010), available at https://www.lavanguardia.com/sucesos/20101111/54067710058/un-padre-de-familia-a-punto-de-ser-desahuciado-se-ahorca-en-plena-calle.html [last accessed 3 September 2024].

Rachman, Gideon. 'Spain, Italy and Identity Politics', *Financial Times*, 17/03/2008 (2008), available at https://www.ft.com/content/12dd0ea0-f443-11dc-aaad-0000779fd2ac [last accessed 19 April 2024].

Rancière, Jacques, trans. Steven Corcoran. *Dissensus: On Politics and Aesthetics* (London: Bloomsbury, 2010).

——, ed. and trans. Gabriel Rockhill. *The Politics of Aesthetics* (London: Bloomsbury, 2017).

Raventós, Sergi. 'No son suicidios, son asesinatos', *Ctxt*, 23/06/2024 (2024), available at https://ctxt.es/es/20210601/Firmas/36425/suicidios-desahucios-salud-mental-catalunya.htm [last accessed 4 September 2024].

Ribeiro de Menezes, Alison. 'Memory as Disruption: Entanglements of Memory and Crisis in Contemporary Spain', *Bulletin of Hispanic Studies*, 94:8 (2017): 883–901.

Ribera-Almandoz, Olatz and Monica Clua-Losada. 'Health movements in the age of austerity: rescaling resistance in Spain and the United Kingdom', *Critical Public Health*, 31:2 (2021): 182–92.

Robinson, William I. '"The Great Recession" of 2008 and the Continuing Crisis: A Global Capitalism Perspective', *International Review of Modern Sociology* (2012): 169–98.

Rodríguez López, Julio. '1997–2007: el auge inmobiliario más largo, gracias al euro', *Clm. economía: Revista económica de Castilla-La Mancha*, 11 (2007): 9–36.

Rodríguez Marcos, Javier. 'Belén Gopegui: "Hay mucha alta literatura muy cursi"', interview with Belén Gopegui published in *El País*, 07/01/2015 (2015), available at https://elpais.com/cultura/2014/12/30/babelia/1419945272_995715.html [last accessed 9 July 2024].

Rojo, Javier. 'España en la economía mundial', *Cinco Días*, 10/04/2007 (2007), available at https://cincodias.elpais.com/cincodias/2007/04/11/economia/1176404146_850215.html [last accessed 19 April 2024].

Romanos, Eduardo and Igor Sádaba. 'Evolución de la protesta en España (2000–2017): un análisis de sus ciclos y características', *Revista Española de Investigaciones Sociológicas*, 177 (2022): 89–110.

Rosa, Isaac and Cristina Bueno. *Aquí vivió. Historia de un desahucio* (Barcelona: Penguin Random House, 2016).

Rosenberg, Capri. 'Don't Shoot the Messenger: Jeff Koons and the Aesthetics of Frivolity', *International Journal of the Humanities*, 8:11 (2011): 105–10.

Rovecchio Antón, Laeticia. 'Marta Sanz: "Me interesa una autobiografía que desdiga el tópico de la vanidad" (I)', interview published in *Pliego Suelto. Revista de literatura y alrededores*, 11/11/2017 (2017), available at http://www.pliegosuelto.com/?p=24161 [last accessed 27 June 2023].

Royo, Sebastián. *Lessons from the Economic Crisis in Spain* (Basingstoke and New York: Palgrave Macmillan, 2013).

——. 'From Boom to Bust: The Economic Crisis in Spain 2008–2013', in *Why Banks Fail* (Basingstoke and New York: Palgrave Macmillan, 2020), 119–40.

Sainz Borgo, Karina. 'Doménico Chiappe: "Escribir este libro fue como si golpeara a un gigante en el hígado"', *Vozpópuli*, 01/11/2013 (2013), available at https://www.vozpopuli.com/altavoz/cultura/Culturas-Literatura-Novelas_0_638636173.html [last accessed 4 September 2024].

Sánchez-Cuenca, Ignacio. *La desfachatez intelectual: escritores e intelectuales ante la política* (Madrid: Catarata, 2016).

Sanz Pastor, Marta. 'Crematorio, Rafael Chirbes', *La tormenta en un vaso* [blog], 21/12/2007 (2007), available at http://latormentaenunvaso.blogspot.com/2007/12/crematorio-rafael-chirbes.html [last accessed 27 November 2023].

——. *No tan incendiario* (Cáceres: Periférica, 2014).

——. '*En la orilla*: notas de lectura', *Turia: Revista Cultural*, 112 (2015): 215–24.

——. *Clavícula* (Barcelona: Anagrama, 2017).

——. 'Razones para hablar del cuerpo – y su Clavícula –', Talk given by Marta Sanz in Elche on 21 April 2017, coordinated by Frutos del Tiempo (2017b), recording available at https://www.youtube.com/watch?v=_ui6un-Kox8 [last accessed 27 June 2023].

Sanz Pastor, Marta and Luis Landero. 'Ciclo Encadenados: Encuentro entre el escritor Luis Landero y la escritora Marta Sanz', held at Biblioteca Nacional Española (Madrid) on 7 March 2018 (2018), recording available at https://www.bne.es/es/agenda-eventos-actividades/cicloencadenados-encuentro2 [last accessed 27 June 2023].

Sanz Villanueva, Santos. 'Tiempo de encierro', *El Cultural*, 31/01/2014 (2014), available at https://elcultural.com/Tiempo-de-encierro [last accessed 4 September 2024].

——. 'La literatura de la crisis: algunas conjeturas', *Quimera. Revista de Literatura*, 394 (September 2016): 16–19.
Savall, Cristina. 'Ayudar a Villa Desahucio', *El Periódico*, 30/12/2012 (2012), available at https://www.elperiodico.com/es/barcelona/20121230/ayudar-a-villa-desahucio-3965495 [last accessed 4 September 2024].
Seguín, Bécquer. 'Environmental Apocalypse and the Spanish Crisis Novel', *Hispanic Issues Online*, 24 (2019): 272–88.
Sevilla Buitrago, Álvaro. 'Espacio público y protesta ciudadana: reflexiones sobre la espacialidad del 15M', in *Madrid, materia de debate* (Vv.Aa) (Madrid: Club de debates urbanos, 2014), 207–17.
——. 'Espacialidades indignadas: la producción del espacio público en la #spanishrevolution', *ACME: An International Journal for Critical Geographies*, 14:1 (2015): 90–103.
Simón, Ana Iris. *Feria* (Madrid: Círculo de tiza, 2020).
Simón, Carla. *Estiu 1993* (2017).
——. *Alcarràs* (2022).
Smith, Susan J. *International Encyclopedia of Housing and Home* (Jordan Hill: Elsevier Science & Technology, 2012).
Smuga, Łukasz. 'Entre la distopía y la heterotopía: espacios de la crisis en las novelas de Isaac Rosa', *Studia Romanica Posnaniensia*, 49:1 (2022): 67–82.
Sontag, Susan. *On Photography* (New York: Rosetta Books, 2005).
Sorogoyen, Rodrigo. *As bestas* (2022).
Standing, Guy. *The Precariat: The New Dangerous Class* (London: Bloomsbury, 2011).
Stiglitz, Joseph. *Freefall: Free Markets and the Sinking of the Global Economy* (London: Penguin, 2010).
Suárez García, Noelia. 'La desaparición del exterior en *La trabajadora* de Elvira Navarro', *LL Journal*, 11:1 (2016), available at https://lljournal.commons.gc.cuny.edu/2016-1-garcia/ [last accessed 27 June 2023].
Tedman, Gary. 'Origins of Kitsch', *Rethinking Marxism*, 22:1 (2010): 56–67.
Tejerina, Benjamín and Ignacia Perugorría. *Crisis and Social Mobilization in Contemporary Spain: The 15M Movement* (Abingdon and New York: Routledge, 2018).
Tomšič, Samo. *The Labour of Enjoyment: Towards a Critique of Libidinal Economy* (Berlin: August Verlag, 2020).
Tooze, Adam. *Crashed: How a Decade of Financial Crises Changed the World* (London: Penguin, 2018).
——. 'Welcome to the World of the Polycrisis', *Financial Times*, 28/10/2022 (2022), available at https://www.ft.com/content/498398e7-11b1-494b-9cd3-6d669dc3de33 [last accessed 20 December 2023].
Tsianos, Vassilis and Dimitris Papadopoulos. 'Precarity: A Savage Journey to the Heart of Embodied Capitalism', *Transversal*, October 2006 (2006), available at https://transversal.at/transversal/1106/tsianos-papadopoulos/en [last accessed 26 June 2023].
Tudela, Ana and Antonio Delgado. *Playa burbuja. Un viaje al reino de los señores del ladrillo* (Madrid: Datadista, 2018).
Usoz de la Fuente, Maite. 'Belén Gopegui's Literature in Crisis: Anticipating the Literatura de la Crisis?', *International Journal of Iberian Studies*, 33:1 (2020): 9–25.

Usoz de la Fuente, Maite, Carmina Gustrán Loscos and Leticia Blanco Muñoz. 'Interview with Belén Gopegui', *International Journal of Iberian Studies*, 33:1 (2020): 61–66.

——. 'Interview with Isaac Rosa', *International Journal of Iberian Studies*, 33:1 (2020b): 67–72.

Valdivia, Pablo. 'Narrando la crisis financiera de 2008 y sus repercusiones', *452F Revista de teoría de la literatura y literatura comparada*, 15 (2016): 18–36.

——. 'Literature, Crisis, and Spanish Rural Space in the Context of the 2008 Financial Recession', *Romance Quarterly*, 64:4 (2017): 163–71.

Valle Detry, Mélanie and Isaac Rosa. 'Entrevista a Isaac Rosa, por Mélanie Valle Detry', *Orillas. Rivista d'ispanistica*, 10 (2021): 171–75.

Vallés, Elena. 'Marta Sanz: "Las mujeres escritoras hemos de reivindicar nuestra mordacidad y dejar de ser comedidas"', *Diario de Mallorca*, 22/06/2018 (2018), available at https://www.diariodemallorca.es/cultura/2018/06/22/marta-sanz-mujeres-escritoras-hemos-3174139.html [last accessed 8 July 2024].

Van Tongeren, Carlos. 'Melancholia and Deceleration in the Spanish Crisis: A Reading of *Crematorio* and *En la orilla* by Rafael Chirbes', *eHumanista: Journal of Iberian Studies*, 53 (2022): 121–37.

Veld, Laurike in't. *The Representation of Genocide in Graphic Novels: Considering the Role of Kitsch* (London: Palgrave Macmillan, 2019).

Vidal Pérez, Aina. 'Falso esplendor en la ciudad turística: imaginario y panóptico en el skyline costero de *Crematorio*, de Rafael Chirbes', *imagonautas*, 11 (2018): 1–16.

——. 'La piscina global. El Mediterráneo de Rafael Chirbes desde el spatial turn y la ecocrítica', *452F*, 21 (2019): 73–91.

Villamía Vidal, Luis. 'La cólera de la memoria y la gravedad de los cuerpos: Arqueología de las novelas de la crisis de Chirbes', *MLN*, 132:2 (2017): 407–25.

Zafra, Remedios. *El entusiasmo: precariedad y trabajo creativo en la era digital* (Barcelona: Anagrama, 2017)

Zamarreño Méndez, Fabio. '*Democracia* de Pablo Gutiérrez', *Castilla. Estudios de Literatura*, 7 (2016): 86–89.

Ziarkowska, Justyna. '"Poderoso caballero es don dinero." Las metáforas del simulacro y desengaño en auxilio de los actuales discursos españoles de la crisis', *Itinerarios*, 27 (2018): 27–37.

Žižek, Slavoj (ed.). *Mapping Ideology* (London and New York: Verso, 2003).

——. 'Neighbors and Other Monsters: A Plea for Ethical Violence', in Slavoj Žižek, Eric L. Santner and Kenneth Reinhard, *The Neighbor: Three Inquiries in Political Theology* (Chicago and London: University of Chicago Press, 2005), 134–90.

——. *Violence: Six Sideways Reflections* (New York: Picador, 2008).

Index

Printed and bound by CPI Group (UK) Ltd, Croydon, CR0 4YY

13/09/2026

14961098-0003